AN UNKNOWN ROAD

AN UNKNOWN ROAD

A record of the faithfulness of God

I will lead them in paths they
have not known (Isaiah 42:16).

Show me Your ways, O Lord;
teach me Your paths.
Lead me in Your truth and teach me
(Psalm 25:4-5).

Douglas TL & Marjorie Howell

JOHN RITCHIE LTD
CHRISTIAN PUBLICATIONS

40 Beansburn, Kilmarnock, Scotland

Dedicated to
Andrew, Ruth and Mark who,
with their spouses and children,
have enriched our lives.

ISBN 0 904064 03 5

Nov 2004.

Typeset by John Ritchie Ltd., Kilmarnock
Printed by Bell & Bain Ltd., Glasgow

Contents

Foreword

These memoirs had their origin in an impelling twofold desire. Firstly we wished to testify to the reality of a loving God who, ever faithful to His promises, can be implicitly trusted at all times. Secondly we wanted to leave with our children a record of our Heavenly Father's gracious provision, protection and guidance along a road spanning many years. As the road unwound before us and the evidence of God's overruling increased, so did the urge to commence this record. When our eldest son, speaking of his ignorance of our lives before his age of understanding, asked, 'Why don't you write about these things?' we knew we had to start.

Eventually the record reached its climax. It may well have ended there if some of our friends had not encouraged us to make it available to a wider public. We happily acknowledge our indebtedness to them, especially to Ron and Len Davies and Jean Cooke for their most helpful comments and also their united criticism.

The story written was lengthy, spanning a period of over eighty years. For this publication it needed abbreviating. That important matter has been very effectively and sensitively dealt with by Dr. Bert Cargill and we gratefully acknowledge his freely giving of valuable time to achieve this. We are also deeply indebted to the publishers, John Ritchie Ltd., for the interest they have shown and their involvement in this effort to declare, for the glory of the Lord, the things that He has done. Our prayer continues to be that this record of our Heavenly Father's love and goodness will bring praise to His holy name.

Douglas & Marjorie Howell
Holt, Norfolk

October 2001

Prologue

As the overloaded liner battled its way through the storm-tossed Mediterranean, my spirits plumbed new depths. The pitch black night, the rolling white-capped waves foaming over the heaving bow, and the mournful sough of wind through the rigging, did nothing to raise them as I stood alone on the rain-swept deck. The tranquillity of Valetta's grand harbour had long been left behind and now as we headed for Port Said I felt desperately lonely, disturbed and, gripped by momentary panic, afraid. Up to that point I had been confident and assured, free from doubt, worry and undue care, even exhilarated by the prospect of the new life ahead. England and the comforting security of warm family relationships had been surrendered in the belief that we were obeying the will of God, but on that dark, dismal, lonely night anxiety struck.

My anxiety was intensified by news from the ship's hospital that my wife's pregnancy had terminated in a miscarriage and the uncertainty of the future obtruded forcibly upon me. Standing there, barely conscious of the violent motions of the ship or of being buffeted by the wind and dampened by flying spray, questions pounded through my mind: "How was Marjorie coping with her grievous disappointment?" "Who were we to think we could be instrumental in doing God's will?" "Why were we enduring this wintry journey to Egypt?" "Where would our final destination be?" "When would we arrive?" "What would we do then?" "How would we live if finances failed?" My thoughts, almost as confused as the sea through which we sailed, ran on and on, and the sense of being adrift in a whirl of uncertainty increased.

They were more confused the following day when, having collected our luggage in preparation for disembarking, I happened to look over the side of the ship. To my dismay I saw Marjorie being carried on a stretcher to a waiting launch which almost immediately sped off. "What had happened?" "Where had they taken her?" "How could I, a complete stranger in Port Said, locate her?" "What should I do next?" If ever there was a time to pray for enlightenment this was it.

How were those vital questions of who, what, why, when and where resolved? The answers to some could already be told, the rest would, in the main, be revealed in the experiences of the yet unfolded years as an unknown road opened before us.

CHAPTER 1

The Road Commences

He knoweth the way that I take (Job 23:10).

On 22nd June 1916 the home of James Thomas and Elizabeth Martha Howell was graced with - and possibly disturbed by - my arrival, the final member of the family. Whether there was disappointment or joy at the arrival of another boy I do not know, but at least the family was now balanced with three of each sex. At this time, British forces in France, at war with Germany for almost two years, had been placed under the command of Field Marshall Douglas Haig. His initial popularity resulted in many children being named after him, and my parents followed the general trend.

Shortly after my third birthday the family moved from London to a small village on the outskirts of Nottingham and for the next eleven years Gedling became our home. My earliest memories stem from the day we moved; leaving the bustle of a London terminus, waking in the dim light of a new day, walking through almost deserted streets between stations in Nottingham to catch the first train to Gedling, watching its huge green engine belching out a cloud of steam as we turned into the avenue which led to our new home.

My early impressions are of a very happy united family. Father had a good position and to young children our house with its five bedrooms seemed large and the garden intriguingly spacious. There was never an abundance of toys but that was no loss. Imagination created various games and, weather permitting, there was the seemingly great outside to explore. Father also had a car, a bull-nose *Morris Oxford* two-seater with a rear dicky seat, which in turn was superseded in the early 1920s by a Morris Oxford saloon. The dicky seat was where my sister, brother and I rode, suitably attired to cope with the vagaries of the British weather.

Quite early in life I learned there was someone called God who not only had a claim upon my parents' lives but was interested in children as well. My parents attended the Gospel Hall situated in the nearby village of Netherfield. There we went three times on Sundays. In the morning we attended what was, to me, an incomprehensible service during which, at some point, a broken loaf of bread followed by a cup of wine passed from hand to hand. It was to be a number of years before I realised the beautiful and meaningful symbolism of that broken bread and outpoured wine, poignant reminders of our Lord's death and resurrection. There was no musical instrument, and I took childish pride in the fact it was my Dad who, after giving a tap with a tuning fork, commenced the singing and everyone followed. Father did not believe in using the car on Sundays, so we children had a hasty walk back in the afternoon to Sunday School where I first learned of One named Jesus. The walk home dragged in the afternoon but Sunday teas gave renewed energy for still another walk to the evening Gospel meeting through which, in my very early days, I simply slept! Later my brother and I devised a means of avoiding the first part of that service; we simply stayed outside to hand out tracts to passers by! The motive was certainly not honourable, and when Mother cottoned-on to what we were up to, she promptly curtailed our freedom and ensured we were in our seats in time for the first hymn.

I had a dislike of school, but there was much to be enjoyed outside of it. But shortly after my tenth birthday, a shadow began to spread across our happy home. Father suffered a stroke, and, in spite of early signs of improvement, it proved to be the beginning of a long and painful period of ill health. Another stroke confined him first to hospital and then to being almost bedridden at home. Two years slipped by and then came the most traumatic moments of my young life. Being alone with father I suddenly saw him rise from his couch, heard him utter three times the name of Jesus, the One whom he had loved and served for many years, before collapsing under a final massive stroke. So, at the age of 12, I had my first close glimpse of suffering and death.

Father's homecall had a radical effect upon all our lives. My sister had to forego University and undertake the responsibility of becoming the main bread winner. My brother who had been enlisted in the army as a Cadet in the Royal Engineers came home and began searching for work. Any hopes I had of going to Secondary School were dashed and, shortly after my fourteenth birthday, I left school to share in providing for the family. I found a place at a firm of hosiery machine manufacturers where for the princely sum of eight shillings (forty pence) a week I began my working life. After a few weeks I advanced to operating a milling machine where for hours on end I endured the boredom of repetitive work. Also the bulk of my pay vanished on train fares and a midday snack! Before long I found a situation nearer home. The pay was less but the overheads more than halved!

Those days seemed hard at the time, but in them I began to learn what people meant when they spoke of trusting in God as their Heavenly Father. Our home environment, linked to regular attendance at Gospel meetings and Sunday School, had taught us that God was no fearful ogre but One who loved and cared for those who put their trust in Him. Furthermore, belief in a God who is holy and righteous was reinforced by Scripture lessons taught daily in our schools. There the Bible was a book to be revered and obeyed, and from early days children were made aware of the difference between right and wrong.

However, as far as I was concerned, this was only head knowledge until shortly before my thirteenth birthday I came to know God personally as my Father. One evening, while browsing through a book I was brought up short by the one word *death*. It struck me forcibly; this was something all had to face and I became disturbed by the thought of 'after death, what?'. The next few hours were ones of agony and distress. Sleep eluded me until part way through the night I rememberd the things I had been taught. The thought flashed into my mind that if Jesus died on the cross for sinners He had died there for me. Slipping out of bed I knelt down and thanked Him for dying for me and prayed He would make me one of His followers. A wonderful sense of peace and calm superseded the hours of distress. When I awoke there came the conviction I had now truly become a Christian, a follower of Jesus and a child of

God whom I could now in sincerity call my Father. I was staying with relatives at the time and, being challenged by one of them to openly confess my faith, I could think of no better way to do so than to write home. For years Mother cherished that letter and finally it found its way back to me.

With the conviction I could address God as Father, I was later able to thank Him for His provision, even though it was a meagerly paid job. At the same time I prayed for a situation which could provide more help to the family. Soon that prayer was answered and I commenced working in a stationery store in Nottingham, with prospects of a settled job and a possibly a career. But the recession of the 1930s hit the firm hard, redundancies became inevitable, and for the third time I began the hunt for work. Shortly after being made redundant I met a mature Christian who, after asking how I was faring, referred me to Job 23:10, *'But He knows the way that I take: when He has tried me, I shall come forth as gold'*. Ever since then that verse has been a comfort and strength to me. After a brief period in a grocery store, I commenced working in the office of the British School of Motoring. This, my most enjoyable situation, came to an abrupt end at the commencement of the Second World War.

Throughout these various changes I was stabilised by two factors, the first my faith in God, and the second the fellowship of a vibrant Christian community. For a number of years I had attended a Christian assembly in Nottingham known to many simply as Clumber Hall. There a lively young people's work made excellent provision for spiritual instruction, provided opportunities for recreational activities with people of like mind, and gave ample scope for being occupied in evangelism. Many are the memories of outings and hikes, usually on a Bank Holiday or Saturday afternoon, to the villages of Nottinghamshire or the hills and dales of Derbyshire. The assembly had a vigorous open air mission work and many of us found pleasure, and gained experience, in sharing in this. The young people's meetings, not surprisingly, resulted in the founding of some very happy marriages and, in a measure, played a part in my own romance which began in 1934 when a certain young lady was received into the fellowship at Clumber Hall. Friendship with Marjorie Undy deepened during the next few years and in September 1938 we were engaged. By the beginning of 1939 we were talking of marriage. Then in September 1939 life took a dramatic change when Britain with her ally France became embroiled in war with Germany.

CHAPTER 2

Two Lives Meet

(1933-39)

I will instruct you in the way you should go (Psalm 32:8).

Marjorie was born on the 8th September, 1917. With her father absent in France, the whole care of the baby fell to the inexperienced new mother and an aunt, with the result Marjorie soon learned how to receive their almost undivided attention. That phase had an abrupt end when her father returned home from the war. Being by nature a disciplinarian and in rank a Serjeant, he had no intention of letting an infant rule the home!

The land 'fit for heroes to live in' hardly came up to expectations, and times were desperately hard, especially for those whose previous place of employment no longer existed. Marjorie's father had no option but to take a poorly paid job in his father's engineering firm. As soon as Marjorie was old enough to take care of her brother and sister, their mother, who never revelled in housework, took up daily employment in one of Nottingham's many clothing factories. With both parents at work, more responsibility began to fall on Marjorie who, as the eldest daughter, was expected to take a share in the household tasks as well as keeping a sisterly eye on her siblings. At times, these childhood days may have seemed hard, but throughout the year there were many enjoyable occasions. Nearby were wide open stretches of countryside interspersed with woodland where children could roam at will, and the time spent there helped to compensate for many hours confined to home.

As the years slipped by, Marjorie grew up a rather studious girl. Her success at school did not make for a wide circle of friendships and thus she learned to be somewhat self contained. By her fifteenth birthday she stood on the threshhold of a wider experience of the world. She could have obtained a scholarship for higher education but her father had other ideas; he thought it best for a girl to become a wage earner. So on leaving school in 1932 Marjorie obtained a position with the pharmaceutical firm *Boots*. But shortly before this she reached the first main crisis in her life. Like many young people she developed a love for the cinema and desired to participate more fully in the activities of her contemporaries. With keen anticipation she was looking forward to the Christmas period when she hoped to attend her first dance.

However this was not to be. There was another side to life for the Undy children, fostered through their parents' insistence that they regularly attend Sunday School at a nearby Baptist Church. Each Sunday saw them trooping off there, sometimes unwillingly on the part of Marjorie who was beginning to feel such activities were incompatible with the aspirations of a young lady on the verge of stepping out into the world. But the day came when the situation changed. Marjorie describes it in her own words.

"The last Sunday in October 1932 dawned cold, gray and wet. The morning had been spent helping my mother prepare Sunday lunch - roast beef and Yorkshire pudding, followed by fruit pie. When all was cleared away and the kitchen tidy I slipped upstairs, got the book I wanted to finish and ensconced myself on a low stool by the glowing fire in the sitting room. Normally I would have gone with Joan and Joe to Sunday School, but why should I? I was fifteen and growing into adulthood and could make up my own mind about such matters. Besides, it was such a wretched day outside and so warm and cosy in.

"As I sat in that warm sitting room, getting deeper and deeper into my book, my father came in, obviously angry seeing me there. Throughout all my childhood he had insisted on my regular attendance at Sunday School. This was my first real attempt at rebellion and it didn't work! My father would listen to no excuses and insisted I got ready and go to Sunday School as usual. I had always feared his displeasure and obeyed his commands so on that day too I went out into the cold wet afternoon - obedient but seething with resentment. What thoughts raced through my mind as I took the short walk to the church school room and took my place with the assembled company. Soon I would be really grown up and he wouldn't be able to order me about then! If he became too dictatorial I would leave home and live by myself so that I could do just as I liked!

"Our teacher that afternoon, Mrs. Cook (we had two who took alternate weeks) was the one I liked least, and this fact did nothing to help. The little group of us, about ten, sat around and Mrs. Cook gave us the lesson. I have forgotten completely what this was, but towards the end of her talk she told us a story. A godly widow had one child, a lovely girl of eighteen. Her mother spoke often to her about the love of the Lord Jesus Christ, His death on the Cross for her sin, His resurrection and ascension, and the need for each individual to come to Him in repentance and faith. She would laugh at the earnestness of her mother and say, "When I have tasted the pleasures of the world then I will think seriously about spiritual things." (Was that me talking?) A great ball was to be held in the town and the girl determined to go despite her mother's pleadings. Go she did, but the heat and excitement of the ballroom followed by the journey home in the bitterly cold night air brought on a severe chill. Despite all the doctor's efforts and the mother's care within a few days the girl died, passing from time into eternity without Christ.

"At that precise moment, around 3.25 pm that Sunday afternoon, I distinctly heard a clear firm voice behind me say, "I have come," repeated three times. The voice was audible, authoritative, yet kind. I heard it clearly, though no-one else seemed to. It shook me to my core and I knew that the Lord Himself had spoken to me. As the others filed out of the room to retake their places in the main body of the school I went to Mrs. Cook, and with tears streaming down my face, told her what had happened and that I knew I was saved and now belonged to the Lord Jesus Christ. The closing hymn that afternoon was, *I heard the voice of Jesus say, 'Come unto Me and rest'.* How meaningfully I was able for the first time to sing that hymn. What a change had taken place within me during that brief hour; remaining with me as I have sought to follow Him."

This spiritual experience resulted in a new outlook on life as Marjorie realised that a disciple of Jesus Christ should by her daily conduct be a constant witness to His lordship. The injunction 'whatever you do, do all to the glory of God' was a command which she would seek to obey henceforth. Her new found faith led her to fellowship with other young Christians while her desire to serve resulted in being involved in the Sunday School. Also, in her business life at *Boots*, there was a determination to maintain a faithful witness for the Lord. Before long she met another keen Christian girl who, in addition to becoming a lifelong friend, was destined to be a link with the next milestone in her life.

As 1934 sped on its way Marjorie did not know her holiday that summer would be a link in the chain which would lead to her future life's work. While visiting her former friend from *Boots,* now living in the London area, she attended a worship service at a brethren assembly and was deeply impressed by its deep devotional atmosphere. On her return home she was happy to continue in the church she knew so well and enjoyed being active in the Sunday School. Therefore it was surprising, and disturbing, when she experienced a growing conviction that God was calling her to leave the Baptist fellowship and join a brethren assembly in the centre of Nottingham. For two weeks she firmly resisted this conviction, not least because she did not know anyone there. Finally, she prayed that she might move to another assembly where she was friendly with a few young people. But even that degree of willingness failed to provide peace of heart. The words, "You should join the fellowship at Clumber Hall," continued to ring in her mind.

As many of us learn through experience, there can be no true peace for the Christian without full surrender to the will of the Lord. He was telling Marjorie to move to a certain place and only when submitting to that call did peace reign. Once the decision was taken, opposition came from different quarters. Friends in the Baptist Church, who valued her work amongst young people, sought to persuade her to alter her mind. Her father objected. He had already refused permission for her to be baptised by immersion and he could well have thought that Marjorie was seeking to make a move to assert her independence. He strongly objected to people using public transport on Sundays and cause others to work for their convenience. As attendance at the assembly in town involved transport, he made this his prime objection. Being convinced she knew what the Lord desired her to do Marjorie could only pray for

His overruling. More weeks slipped by before the desired permission was granted for her to go to Clumber Hall, and the next Sunday she attended the morning service. The elders were very strict on the subject of believer's baptism and, usually, one was only received into fellowship after this open confession of their faith. On that Sunday morning Marjorie may have felt unwelcome as she sat aside with those who were not 'in fellowship'. That situation soon changed. Her father withdrew his objection to baptism, and within two weeks she gave this public witness to her faith in Christ as Saviour and her submission to Him as Lord.

Within a short time she formed new friendships amongst the younger members of the fellowship and enjoyed sharing in their activities. A midweek meeting provided spiritual stimulus and it was there that, for her, a slight interest in someone of the opposite sex began to stir. Christmas of 1934 saw the beginning of a courtship which culminated in a supremely happy marriage and a lifetime partnership in the service of the Lord. Five years were to elapse before the wedding and, like many others, we discovered the course of true love does not always run smoothly. Our characters were very different so there were bound to be ups and downs and adjustments on both sides. Occasionally 'downs' became troughs - though thankfully never chasms - but we were convinced our relationship was ordained by the Lord. The 'downs', which could have been disastrous, eventually led to a deepening of mutual love. In those days we began to learn more fully the power of prayer, and the meaning of an active faith which places its trust in the guidance and provision of the Lord Jesus. We were receiving excellent training for an unknown road ahead.

CHAPTER 3

Two Lives Merge

(1939-41)

Can two walk together unless they are agreed? (Amos 3:3).

The possibility of war with Germany had loomed large for a number of years as Hitler's expansionist policies threatened one European country after another. In addition, Germany's horrific treatment of the Jews concerned many people and it became obvious that, unless steps were taken by other nations, the Jews in Germany could be completely exterminated. Thus when Britain went to war I felt a duty to enlist. As the conflict involved the future of the Jews, I believed Christians, who loved them as God's chosen people, had a responsibility to assist in their defence. The decision to enlist was not undertaken lightly nor without prayer. My horror of war was enough to make me pray that the Lord would block my path if the envisaged step was wrong. Recruits had to pass a thorough medical examination and I hoped if I was doing wrong I would fail the medical. I saw six doctors, all passed me A1, and within days I was on my way to Portsmouth bound for the Royal Army Ordnance Corps.

The stay in the Portsmouth area proved to be short. Within a few days any who had clerical experience were ordered to report to the Serjeant. About fifty of us who did, soon found ourselves being issued with rifles which hardly seemed to fit in with the concept that the pen is mightier than the sword. The majority of our group had never held a rifle before and its mysteries were many including the way it ought be carried. Should it be muzzle up or muzzle down, on the shoulder sloped or straight by the side and, in any case, how did you put the things in that came out of the business end? More importantly, how did you prevent the weapon going off and making a hole in your best friend? Fortunately a first world war veteran proffered invaluable advice on our first march.

Within days we joined another draft and were transferred to the Royal Army Service Corps at Aldershot. This was a bewildering maze of barracks and parade grounds and we wondered if the authorities were also bewildered for they seemed to have no idea what to do with us. It was a relief to all our group when orders were given to move. A few of us were dispatched, complete with kit bags and the still unmanageable rifle, to London's Kensington Barracks and the company of regular soldiers. This was where one found Army life in the raw. Here was where a definite stand, morally and spiritually, had to be taken. I well remember the coarse oaths, the comment, "In a week we will make you like us", and the necessity of holding fast to the promises of God. Then came a move to Hounslow Barracks and regular work in the Headquarters of Eastern Command.

It was the time of the so called phoney war. The Germans lay entrenched behind their Siegfried line; the Allies relaxed in the shelter of the Maginot line. People in Britain expected the war would be over in less than six months. Those few comparatively calm months gave Britain a much needed breathing space to increase her military potential. It also enabled me to have some weekends of leave when I would either dash up to Nottingham for a few happy hours with Marjorie or she would travel down to meet me at my sister's home in North London.

Obtaining leave at peak holiday times was never easy so it was not surprising I failed to get home for Christmas 1939. The best we could do was for Marjorie, who was still occupying a secretarial position at *Boots* in Nottingham, to join me for a brief break in London. In spite of the optimism of some, we were convinced that the war was likely to drag on for some time and the great decision facing us was whether we should postpone our marriage or have a war time wedding. We were young, enthusiastic, hated being apart and perhaps not very wise, but saw no reason why we should let Hitler run our lives. We prayed about it but could not claim there was any blinding light from heaven to give guidance. We just felt it was the right thing to do even though it would mean financial stringency. My Army pay was still only seven shillings a week. If we were married there would be a weekly marriage allowance of another seven shillings, to which would be added a living-out allowance, whilst Marjorie could earn a reasonable salary in secretarial work. Having viewed the situation from every angle we planned for an Easter wedding in Nottingham and I immediately applied for leave. Seven days commencing on the 21st March were granted and we began making preparations for the 23rd. In fact Marjorie did most of the arranging, even paying for the marriage licence which, I am reminded, I never paid back!

The wedding in Nottingham was very much a family affair followed by a brief honeymoon in Derbyshire. Then the harsh world soon re-imposed itself and we were on our way back to Nottingham and the first of many separations in our married life. Within another twenty four hours I was back in the Headquarters in Hounslow and Marjorie living in her old family home.

By now, drastic events on the field of battle had left Britain devoid of Allies, facing the might of a seemingly invincible Germany. In the spring of 1940, Germany had struck, not at the Maginot line as anticipated, but moved north into a defenceless and unsuspecting Holland and Belgium, then southwest into France. The British forces were hopelessly outnumbered and out maneuvered. At that time I was working in a section of Headquarters which dealt with Operations and well remember the concern with which, hour by hour, maps of northern France were being amended. The line of demarcation moved inexorably westward until the British troops were penned in along the coast and it seemed inevitable that the decimated and war-weary army would be wiped out.

Then came one of the most stirring episodes of the war. Royal Navy vessels, merchant ships, ferry boats, fishing smacks and launches of various shapes and sizes ploughed back and forth across the Channel day and night evacuating the battered forces. In spite of appalling losses in ships and men, thousands were rescued, and the major part of the original expeditionary force was brought safely home, weary, bedraggled and devoid of its military hardware.

That weekend I was due for leave and Marjorie was coming down from Nottingham. We would be staying at an address unknown to her and so we agreed to meet at the terminus. Not surprisingly, leave was cancelled at short notice and, there being no way of letting Marjorie know, I worried how she would cope. I need not have worried; shortly after 10pm. the door bell rang and there she was, bright and cheerful! The weekend culminated in our finding and renting two furnished rooms in the pleasant area of Isleworth.

Within a few days of moving to Isleworth, Marjorie obtained a position at *Minimax,* a firm specialising in fire-fighting equipment. For a few delightful months we shared the austerities of war together and found much pleasure in the simple things of life. We also had the joy of opening our home to other, often lonely, servicemen. We trusted our times of prayer and worship would result in an atmosphere of peace and contentment which in turn would enable us to speak of the Lord Jesus and encourage others to put their trust in Him.

The situation changed when Germany decided the quickest way to win the war was to bomb London into submission. For many months there was hardly a night when enemy planes were not overhead. During the first two weeks we retreated to the air raid shelter in the garden but, as this meant a drastic loss of sleep, we decided, bombs or no, to sleep in the house and trust ourselves to the Lord for safety. After placing a mattress in a corner of our downstairs room, as far as possible from the window, we began sleeping indoors. For the first night or two we found it difficult but gradually adjusted to the situation and many a night were oblivious to a raid. Only one evening did our home suffer a near miss. We were sitting chatting when suddenly Marjorie jumped up and disappeared round the back of the settee, so I followed suit. Her more sensitive hearing had caught the whine of bombs coming our way and, within a few moments, there came a tremendous crash. The place shook, I saw the curtains fly up to the ceiling and the door burst open as the blast swept through the house but, to my surprise, there was no sound of shattering glass. Further explosions resounded as the stick of bombs completed their trail of devastation and then all was eerily quiet. The bombs had landed further down the street demolishing two houses and damaging many others. Ours must have been on the edge of the blast, resulting in negligible damage. Only our nerves received something of a jolt.

Since moving to Isleworth both our brothers had been conscripted. Marjorie's brother Joe had joined the Royal Navy early in 1940 and was a Chief Petty Officer in the submarine service. The harsh realities of the war were brought home to us early in February 1941 when Joe's submarine, the *Snapper*, was sunk - possibly in the Bay of Biscay - with the loss of all the crew. My brother, another Joe, had been posted to a Royal Signals Unit. Shortly after initial training his unit came under orders to move firstly to Singapore then Hong Kong where he was killed during the Japanese bombardment. Our parents found it very difficult to come to terms with their losses.

For us life continued a fairly normal pattern until early 1941. I was moved to Reigate in Surrey and Marjorie went to live with friends in Feltham. I had been promoted to serjeant and was fortunate to be billeted with a delightful elderly couple. They had a lovely spacious home and when this uniformed and heavily booted fellow, laden with kit bag and other equipment, turned up at the front door their servant's look was anything but welcoming. The couple gave me a cautious but very polite welcome, showed me to my room, and left me to my own devices. But on the following day I found a very different atmosphere, with a smile and an invitation to join them in the lounge to listen to the evening news. The change arose because of my Bible at my bedside, from which they assumed that one who daily read the Scriptures could not be altogether bad. I could not have wished for more comfortable accommodation.

As 1941 progressed Germany maintained a relentless bombing of many of Britain's vital industrial towns and ports, but despite tremendous material damage and loss of life, the will of the nation appeared to be undaunted. At South Eastern Command we were, surprisingly, spared any air raids. Night by night bombers droned overhead aiming for London and the Thames shipping lanes, but our only danger was from bombs jettisoned by planes fleeing from the RAF or heavy anti-aircraft fire.

Whilst the work in this particular section had some interest, I became increasingly restive with being nothing more than a civilian in uniform. I began to feel I should be making a greater contribution to the war effort. We were discussing the situation during one of our rare weekends together when, to my surprise, Marjorie suggested I apply for a commission. Within a few days I presented a request to my colonel for application papers and, with a faint feeling of excitement, awaited the outcome. In due course a form arrived and, though simple to complete as far as personal details were concerned, it presented a major problem. I had thought to apply for a commission in my present Corps, the RASC, but the form required the applicant to state, in order of preference, three branches of the Army he would desire to join. I noted there was no guarantee one would be posted to any of them! Believing our lives should be guided by the Lord, we prayed about this and came to a conclusion: if the step envisaged was wrong then the Lord would not allow the application to succeed. I put as my first choice the Royal Army Service Corps. For the second, possibly influenced by the fact we had been at the receiving end of air raids and never been able to hit back, I chose the Anti Aircraft division of the Royal Artillery. I appreciate this hardly seems a Christian attitude but we were supposed to be defending the country! It was compulsory that one of the choices be an Infantry Regiment and I cannot recall which I chose, mainly because it played no part in subsequent events. The form, bearing the colonel's comments and signature, moved on to higher authority and in due course returned with its signature of approval. In September I received orders to proceed to a camp in the vicinity of Aldershot for a few weeks of fairly intensive training.

Another decision had now to be made. Should Marjorie continue to work at *Minimax* or move back to Nottingham? In the event those with whom Marjorie was staying needed to rent out their home, and so she had to move. She soon found another secretarial position, this time in the Health Department of the Nottingham County Council. So commenced another part of the unknown road to face a challenge which significantly affected the whole of our future, influenced the lives of many others and, not least, those of our own children.

CHAPTER 4

To Other Lands

(1942-43)

You alone, O Lord, make me dwell in safety (Psalm 4:8).

My application for a commission resulted in being accepted for the Royal Artillery, Light Anti-Aircraft division, subject to a satisfactory initial training period. After a period of drilling, interspersed with basic instruction in the mystery of Anti-Aircraft weapons, we were shunted off to a firing camp in Wales. After four months I was back to Shrivenham for the final months of fairly intensive training, culminating in a passing-out parade when, commissioned as a Second Lieutenant in the RA, I had a week's leave before travelling to my first posting.

This was to a Light AA unit on the outskirts of Warrington but, within a few weeks, we were moved hastily to the vicinity of Brighton. Germany's sporadic hit and run raids on the south coast called for the strengthening of air defences in that area. Then, in typical Army fashion, some of us who had trained on Light AA were transferred to Heavies and I moved to a Heavy AA Unit near Newhaven. I felt at home in that Unit, enjoyed the company of fellow officers and, though living under canvas with primitive washing, toilet and catering facilities, life in general was quite pleasant. From Newhaven we were moved to Foulness Island near Southend where the powers that be reckoned we would be on the line of flight for bombers heading for London and the Midlands. If that were the case the enemy must have taken fright for we never had sight or sound of him!

November came and with it an order for me to report to Headquarters. There I was informed, actually for the second time, that an overseas posting was in the offing. Within a few days I was on my way to Nottingham for two week's embarkation leave. It was a delightful break though overshadowed with the thought it would be the last for many a long day. By now, we were accustomed to farewells but on this occasion a certain sadness prevailed as we appreciated the dangers which might well lie ahead. My immediate destination was Woolwich, the assembly point for Royal Artillery personnel due for overseas service. No one had a firm idea of where we were bound though the issue of certain equipment gave the impression it would be eastward. However, there were stories of troops being kitted out for the East and landing somewhere in the Arctic circle! A few weeks dragged by and then, unexpectedly, we were given another forty eight hours leave which gave me time to spend two precious days with Marjorie.

A few days later we were confined to barracks still waiting. Then, suddenly, the order came to move and within a few hours hundreds of us, officers and other ranks, entrained. In typical troop train manner it crawled and jolted its way across the country en route for Liverpool. Late in the evening the train screeched its way over numerous points before coming to a final jerking halt by the side of one of the port's huge dockside sheds. There we joined a milling mass of humanity and, with kit bags as our only means of comfort, sat waiting for the order to embark.

As the hours wore on, the cold of a January night began to penetrate even our heavy greatcoats. The dimmed mist-shrouded lights threw parts of the huge customs' shed into shadow which gradually took on some form and movement as further trains disgorged their complement of troops. The cold, the darkness, the sheer dreariness of the place tended to depress one's spirits and the very shadows seemed to symbolize the uncertainties of the way ahead. Where were we all heading? What difficulties, problems and even battles would have to be faced? How many out of that great throng would return to home and loved ones? Then, through an open door was a glimpse of the huge bulk of the liner which was soon to be our home, and the pattern of thought changed to embrace the dangers of a war time voyage

At length troops heavily laden with kit bags and sundry equipment, filed on board the *Dominion Monarch,* a graceful liner of some 32,000 tons. In peacetime she would have been fitted out with every luxury but her war time role demanded maximum space for troops and cargo. Two berth cabins now contained six bunks and no doubt others had more. Wardrobe space was virtually nil, bags and equipment being stowed under bunks and in any available corner. One luxury remained, the wash basin with a constant supply of hot water! There was only one problem, it was sea water and one soon discovered the value of a special kind of soap. This liner was now our floating home for the next ten weeks. As we settled down for our first night I asked for an encouraging word from the Lord and He gave it. My daily reading was in the Psalms and I have never forgotten the sense of peace, which literally flooded through me as I read Psalms 3 and 4. *'I laid me down and slept; I awaked; for the Lord sustained me'* and, *'I will both lay me down in peace, and sleep: for thou, Lord, only makest me dwell in safety'*. I took those words as a definite promise from the Lord. For me it meant, come what may, there was no need to fear and so I continued to claim them for the whole of the voyage.

During the night the ship sailed and by morning we were entering the Clyde to anchor near Gourock. As we embarked it was announced the Defence Ministry had decreed that every ship should carry an increased number of personnel; a decision resulting in considerable overcrowding. The lower decks were partitioned to create large areas in which troops ate, slept and generally lived. Long tables and benches crisscrossed the rooms whilst above hung numerous hooks for the slinging of hammocks. 'Thick' is about the only word to describe the air, and those who voyaged for weeks under such disagreeable circumstances had every reason to complain. Officers' quarters were quite superior, however! I am convinced that conditions on troop ships turned many a man into a socialist if not a downright communist.

The reasons for overcrowding were clear. The tide of war in North Africa had turned and the famous Desert Rats were hard on the heels of Rommel, but Germany and her Italian Allies still maintained control over most of the Mediterranean. The islands of Malta and Cyprus were still under British control but the former was constantly under fierce aerial attacks and supply convoys, attempting to break the enemy's blockade, suffered considerable losses. Thus the only viable route for reinforcing the Middle East, Egypt and the North African desert continued to be the long haul round South Africa, then along its eastern coast to either the Red Sea and Aqaba in Jordan, or the Arabian Gulf and the Iraqi port of Basra. The war in the east was also intensifying and it was a matter of utmost urgency to provide men and supplies to help stem the rising tide of Japanese aggression through Burma into India.

For two days we lay at anchor in the Clyde and during that time I became increasingly aware of being off colour. I shrugged it off as symptoms of a slight cold but finally decided to visit the clinic. As a result I found myself incarcerated in the ship's sick bay being dosed with one of the newer sulpha remedies and feeling horribly nauseated. Then about midnight the purr of engines and a slight sense of movement indicated we were, at last, on our way. Leaving calm waters the convoy headed straight into an Atlantic storm and we landlubbers had our first taste of the extent to which huge vessels could be tossed around like toys.

By now the convoy was well out into the Atlantic and, as all my companions had found their sea legs, I thought it time for me to find mine. To make lurching progress up a companionway and onto the open deck was a feat of endurance but well worth while. I stepped out into a maelstrom of howling wind and on to a deck lashed by teeming rain. First impressions were mixed. As the bow of the ship buried itself in tons of water it looked as if it would never rise again and the heaving masses swirling round the ship were bound to engulf it. But slowly the bow rose, with streams of water pouring from its scuppers, as the next huge wave rolled obliquely towards the liner to sweep it high on its foaming crest. For what seemed an age, the *Dominion Monarch* would be poised above a huge gulf before it descended sickeningly into the trough of troubled water only to be swept skywards again. During those brief elevated moments the size and extent of the convoy became apparent. Ships of all sizes, from small scruffy looking freighters to luxury liners, and a huge aircraft carrier, were scattered as far as the eye could see. The convoy was now travelling through U-boat infested waters, with a zigzag course to provide a more difficult target for the enemy. It included a few small cargo vessels of very ancient vintage which were, of necessity, slow and as the speed of the whole group had to be governed by the slowest, this increased the danger to all.

We sailed west for a long time before turning south. After about a week the seas calmed and the weather continued to improve, much to the relief and joy of us all who were taking a compulsory cruise at His Majesty's expense. The days slipped by with little to relieve the monotony of our slow zigzagging progress. Possibly a skeptic would say this was why on our first Sunday every Church service was packed to capacity. I believe the reason went much deeper. God becomes a reality in times of distress and the war drove many to their knees. In times of peace the statement, *'God was not at all in their thoughts'*, has often proved true, but, with their backs to the wall, men hardly know where else to turn. The dangers at sea certainly focused many men's thoughts on their need of divine protection and most expected the Padres to have the key to its provision. There were five ordained churchmen on the *Dominion Monarch* and the services continued to be well attended on the Lord's Day. Two weeknight Bible studies led by the Methodist Padre also drew a good crowd.

At these services friends of like mind were found, and before long a few of us decided it would be spiritually beneficial and would develop our bonds of friendship if we met daily for prayer. A pre-breakfast time of fellowship in one of the cabins was arranged and continued for the rest of the voyage. By the first Sunday, the fact the ship's Captain was a keen Christian had become generally known, and no doubt many were relieved to find that the responsibility for the safety of the ship rested with a man of prayer. The ship's complement included a detachment of the Queen Alexandria's Nursing Sisters one of whom I had met while in the ship's hospital. Our paths crossed occasionally and, though the lady never realised it, she became a link in the chain which resulted in Andrew, our eldest son, going to Boarding School. This Nurse possessed a copy of the Officers' Christian Union's hospitality list and, not knowing where I might finally land, I made a note of addresses both in India and the Middle East. The benefits resulting from those addresses, and their influence upon our future, will become apparent later.

A month passed by and the sea grew calmer, or else our sea

legs meant we never noticed the ship's slow roll. We continued slowly southwards through days of clear blue skies and star-lit nights. To stand on the top deck beneath the vast expanse of a sky, studded with myriads of glittering points of light, or bathed in the soft glow of a waxing moon, was an unforgettable experience. At such a time the Psalmist's words, *'the heavens declare the glory of God'*, took on a deeper meaning. Time tended to pass slowly and tediously.

One bright morning, the sea began to change colour, losing its lovely blue before turning to a dirty grey and later a light shade of brown. Land lay just over the horizon and, as the convoy turned in a more easterly direction, speculation increased as to what African port lay ahead. Dawn revealed the entrance to an almost landlocked harbour and, in the distance, outlines of low lying dwellings. Our landfall was Freetown in Sierra Leone. The ships were reprovisioned and the convoy sheltered, and sweltered, safe within its vast lagoon. It was hard to realise after so many days of travel we were barely half way to the south of Africa. Eventually the convoy reached Capetown where half of the ships docked, and the rest of us continued round the Cape to the calm waters of Durban Bay,

The weekend in Durban gave brief opportunities for Christian fellowship and sightseeing. Shortly after sunrise on Monday, ships slipped slowly out of the harbour into deeper water where the convoy gathered in formation under the eyes of a guardian destroyer of the Royal Australian Navy. The last long leg of our voyage had begun. During the day the sun beat down pitilessly but nights under the star spangled sky were fairly cool, a factor which, coupled with the prospect of the journey nearing its end, helped to maintain the morale of the troops. Then came the great day when land showed as a fine line on the horizon; gradually to take on depth and height as the vast city of Bombay came into view. This then was to be our destination, India, the jewel in the Empire's crown, but now under threat from the might of a seemingly invincible Japan.

The *Dominion Monarch* moved slowly and majestically towards her berth. As the quay drew nearer berthing ropes struck the muddy water with a resounding splash, boatmen rapidly conveyed them to dockers and in a few minutes the huge liner was linked to land.

Engine bells sounded, propellers churned, filthy looking water swirled round the stern, and the ship moved gently to rest snugly against the quay, dwarfing warehouses, cranes and people. Then there was an unusual quietness - the throb of the engines had stilled, and at last, for most, the journey was over.

But for some of us it was not. We watched others disembarking and as heavily laden units of various regiments marched smartly off, we wondered what the future held for them as well as us. For some it would be the North of India and the jungles of Burma; for our contingent it was the Arabian gulf, gateway to Iraq, Syria, Palestine, Egypt and the battlefields of North Africa.

We transshipped to a small liner which in her prime must have been luxurious, but now bore evidences of having come down in the world. Daily the heat became more oppressive and debilitating and we were increasingly thankful that a remnant of the old luxury remained, a small fan over each bunk. The days drifted by without incident though the nights introduced us to some of the creepy-crawlies of the Middle East - especially a large specimen of cockroach which lurked in many a dark corner. Within a week we reached the calm of the Arabian Gulf and, finally, the Shatt Al Arab where the slow moving Tigris, after its one thousand mile journey from Turkey through Iraq, mingles its waters with the much longer Euphrates. Our elderly liner took on new proportions in the narrow confines of the Shatt and dwarfed the profusion of small craft gliding in all directions. As it made its way, the decks were lined with men who feasted their eyes on the dense groves of luxuriant date palms lining the banks, and thought they had arrived in a lush and fruitful land. Only later did the truth reveal itself. Beyond the face of beauty lay the harsh arid deserts of Iraq and Iran.

Gradually approaching the port of Basra we could see on the eastern bank the oil town of Abadan, and discovered the source of a most unpleasant smell which had assailed us for a couple of days - the smell of an oil refinery which later would become too familiar to be noticed. Docking at Basra in the early morning chill it soon became obvious that, like the palm trees, the cool was misleading. Within an hour the temperature rose dramatically making any spot of shade truly welcome as we waited for the order to disembark. Eventually we piled into tarpaulin covered lorries and skirting the thronged streets and bazaars of the old Arab town, trundled on far from any semblance of civilisation to arrive at a sprawling tented camp pitched on a desert waste. In the distance the mud walls of a small Arab town appeared to be floating in the haze, apart from that it was desert as far as the eyes could see. This was Shaiba, the main transit camp in southern Iraq, well known but not enjoyed by thousands of military and RAF personnel. For many it has remained in the memory as the place where they were introduced to heat, flies, dust, disease, and the skillful methods adopted by some natives to take possession of one's kit.

We had left Britain in early January in the midst of cold and storm. Now it was early April and the days scorchingly hot as the sun shone from a clear blue sky. Wind and rain had given place to desert breezes and sand - sand in your hair, ears, eyes, clothing, meals and bed, especially when an increasing breeze lifted gritty particles on rising air currents to whip them into huge spiralling columns whirling across the desert. But there were calm days and then it was the flies. They bred by the million. It is doubtful if anyone in transit through Shaiba ever forgot the first sight of the mess tents with fly traps of varying types spilling over with crawling captives, and the dozens more ready to share the food. Sand, dust and flies abounded - and were detested - but it was strange how soon they came to be accepted as part of life. Nevertheless it was a relief to hear of a new insecticide called DDT which helped to control the fly pest.

Our original contingent of officers and troops began to disperse. The majority entrained for the north and spent a few days in a transit camp within a few miles of the ruins of Babylon. From there most of them went on to the Middle East to reinforce troops in Palestine and Egypt. Others joined Montgomery's forces in North Africa and eventually participated in the invasion of Italy. In the inscrutable wisdom of the military the rest of us made the long dusty trip back to Shaiba. Our train had rumbled well on into the night before it slowly came to rest. Curiosity caused me to draw back the blind and, to my surprise, a few feet away was a signboard announcing 'Ur Junction'. To this day I have not been able to ascertain if there really existed a junction at Ur, but the name certainly evoked thoughts of Abram who, so many centuries ago, lived in that ancient city. The word 'Junction' spoke of the parting of ways and I thought of the day when Abram left his home in Ur in obedience to the call of God. It evoked the question; would my wife and I be prepared likewise to step out in faith in response to a call from God?

Our small group, now back in fly-ridden Shaiba could be forgiven for wondering how much longer this purposeless shuttle from place to place would continue. Another week had to elapse before two of us knew. Our final destination was Abadan. There we would join an AA Regiment of the Indian Army encamped near the Anglo-Iranian oil terminal and refinery. So once more I faced a change of scene and with it, one of the most important developments in my life.

CHAPTER 5

Iranian Call

(Abadan 1943)

I have called you by your name; you are Mine (Isaiah 43:1).

Life took on a completely new complexion with the move to Abadan. It was only a short journey from Shaiba by ferry across the Shatt Al Arab, but it was the beginning of a host of new sights and experiences. The waterway was alive with a bewildering variety of shipping - freighters swung at anchor, dhows drifted with the current, fragile skiffs steered by yellow turbaned Arabs. Halfway across the Shatt, the ferry entered Persian territory, passed under the towering bows of empty tankers waiting to take on oil, then slipped into the bustling, noisy, terminal. From here an Army truck deposited us at different gun sites a mile or two out of the town and its awful smelling refinery.

The regiment was located in the area for two reasons. The Abadan refinery was vital to the British war effort, its port a significant link in the forwarding of military supplies pouring in mainly from the United States to support the hard pressed Russian forces from the south east. The supply line ran from southern Iran to Tehran then on north to the Black Sea and beyond. Consequently the port's importance to Britain, and the line's strategic value to Russia, made both a potential target for German air strikes. Therefore sound military sense dictated provision of anti-aircraft cover along the line and around the refinery. The second reason for the regiment's presence was the need to train Indian troops to participate in the war against Japan.

The daily routine revolved around training and more training and it was no wonder the British NCOs were disgruntled. The task of trying to bring to the peak of efficiency men who had only a rudimentary knowledge of English, and whose background ill-fitted them for coping with modern equipment, called for the patience of saints - a virtue not usually found in serjeants! Living conditions were also tough, mainly due to the heat which made life under canvas almost unbearable. Insects, especially the minute sandfly, were a constant irritant whilst the ubiquitous fly conveyed dysentery and other diseases. Sunstroke and heat exhaustion were ever present problems and one soon realised the value of the daily dose of salt.

I received a warm welcome, but a certain amount of reserve existed until we were more familiar with each other's temperaments and idiosyncrasies, mine being what they would term 'somewhat religious'. On the long voyage there had been constant Christian fellowship but now out on a gun site, one was isolated and considered by some an oddity. The Army in those days was very much a man's world - drinking, smoking, enjoying a smutty joke and, if needs be swearing profusely, were considered to be marks of a man. For the Christian who desired to honour the Lord it was a matter of seeking to be consistent in behaviour and proving he could hold his own in the real world. Thus, attitudes which may have bordered on contempt often changed to grudging admiration if one stood fast by his principles, showed loyalty to his associates, displayed reasonable efficiency in his duties, participated intelligently in discussions, and proved his worth in some form of physical activity. There were occasions when I fell far short of the ideal and can only thank the Lord that in times of somewhat severe temptation, He proved that, *with the temptation He will make a way of escape.*

With no possibility of Christian fellowship on site I was thankful for the addresses of certain missions and individuals in the Middle East obtained on the boat. Through them I was soon in contact with a young chemical engineer working with the Anglo Iranian Oil Company. Colin Williamson not only gave me a warm welcome but introduced me to a small company of expatriate believers who met in a similar way to my assembly at home. Colin's own home became a spiritual lifeline and a welcome change from the atmosphere in camp. I was also fortunate in being able to attend a very special event. About two months after my arrival a notice appeared in daily orders mentioning a Conference to be held in Hillah, near Babylon, under the auspices of the OCU and SASRA (Soldier's and Airmen's Scripture Readers Association). Men who wished to attend were to be granted leave and travel permits and I was not slow in applying. It was a memorable occasion as some 500 men, and a few nursing sisters, attended the three days of Conference. The atmosphere was lively, the singing uplifting, the fellowship stimulating and the Bible addresses deeply spiritual, informative and challenging. Listening to one Squadron Leader ministering I had no idea he would later become a friend on the Mission field, nor did I know that the British Consul who shared in organising the meetings would in later years be offering us hospitality in his home in Jerusalem. The Christian world is indeed, very small.

Back in Abadan, training, supplemented by various duties, continued with no end in sight. One duty I did not appreciate was the patrolling of Abadan's red light area, a section of the town out of bounds to British and American forces. Inevitably this meant that periodically one had to spend most of the night along with four or five men, visiting shady premises mostly in the poorer part of the town. The object of arresting any straying personnel and returning them to ship or camp could, usually, be accomplished without any serious trouble.

These occasional patrols were always unpleasant but one of them had a very significant impact on our lives. Midnight had long passed but there was still one more visit to make. The corporal who knew the area well turned down a dark, filthy lane, bordered on both sides with high mud walls broken here and there with rough wooden doors. Banging on one he unceremoniously pushed it open to reveal a courtyard where all that could be seen were outlines of a few patches of rough earth embellished with straggly shrubs. At the far end was the verandah of a flat roofed, mud brick house where two or three long robed women reclined, one of whom languidly indicated the place was open for inspection. As I lingered outside, with the flickering glimmer of oil lamps dimly lighting up the scene, my glance was drawn upwards to the velvety blue-blackness of the night sky garnished with myriads of twinkling stars. It spoke of beauty and purity whilst, all around me I could only see squalor, degradation and evil. Suddenly I felt overwhelmed with it all; the nauseating smell of the place made me long to get out of the area into the comparatively fresh air of the wider streets. But then came the mental query, 'Do people have to live like this; is there no better way?' No doubt influenced by my Christian heritage I thought, 'Wouldn't it be wonderful if these people could hear of the Lord Jesus Christ and know of His love for them?' Then in a flash, and with almost devastating clarity, the challenge was printed on my mind, *'How shall they hear without a preacher?'* It was as if God Himself had read my thoughts and clearly said, 'Well, what are you going to do about it?' Returning to camp through the early morning hours I felt strangely disturbed.

What does God want me to do? That became the recurring and burning question during the ensuing days as I struggled with the implications of the words, *'How shall they hear?'* At no time had I considered the possibility of engaging in missionary service. My ambition was to get into the commercial world as soon as the war was over and carve for myself a profitable career. Missionary service with all its potential problems and possible sacrifice had no part in my plans. In any case, I had promised Marjorie to do my best to give her a secure future; could I possibly let that ambition go? Thus I found myself entering into a dialogue with God - or was it really a monologue seeing as I did all the talking!? In reality I wanted to find a way of escape from the challenge and sought to do so by raising a number of apparently reasonable questions. Surely, I thought, I had a right to query if God was really calling me or whether my feelings were merely an emotional reaction to a sordid situation. The questions multiplied. How could I know? Would Marjorie be prepared to go with me? If not, had I the courage to go alone? Was it right to embark on an overseas mission and leave my sister as the sole supporter of mother? Had I the faith necessary to turn my back on the provision of regular, well paid employment and launch out into the unknown in complete dependence upon the Lord? Would the church which met at Clumber Hall, Nottingham, be prepared to commend us to full time service? If most of these were answered in the negative my dilemma would be solved. But heaven was silent, no answer came.

The Spirit of God would not let me rest. To all my questionings there seemed to be but one response, *'How shall they hear?'* For three months I resisted those haunting words but finally the crisis point arrived. One night, alone in the officers' mess, my reverie was suddenly disturbed by a voice distinctly asking, *'How shall they hear without a preacher?'* Startled, I looked around and seeing no one, relaxed, but the voice continued, 'Tonight is the last time I am going to speak to you, *how shall they hear?'*, and I was shaken to the core. It may be said there could not have been a voice, it was merely an impression from my own mind but, whatever the medium through which it came, it was as clear as any human sound and, for me, it was the very voice of God. I realised a point of decision had been reached and from my response that night the future would be determined. In an agony of doubt I went to my room, knelt, prayed, and possibly argued, but at last grace was given to say, 'Lord, if you want me to go, even though it means leaving Marjorie behind, I will.' There was no sense of exaltation, just a great feeling of peace. The decision had been made, come what may I had committed myself to serving the Lord wherever He directed. My final thoughts centered around Marjorie; how could I share my decision with her, what would her reaction be?

The following day I penned a vital letter home. For the first time I revealed to Marjorie the spiritual struggles of the past weeks and related the events which forced me to the point of decision. I commented on the fact that my decision would obviously affect her and that I appreciated I had no right to commit her to such a way of life. I expressed my conviction that, even though it could mean my going alone, I must be prepared to serve the Lord in the place of His choosing. With the letter sent I had to bide in patience wondering what sort of reply would arrive. War conditions resulted in long delays in the mail service and during the next few weeks there were anxious moments as I pondered on how Marjorie would respond to my letter. Then came the day when the letter arrived and I sensed the answer was in my hands. I cannot recall my feelings as I slit the envelope but remember I read the letter with increasing excitement, and a deep sense of gratitude to God.

Marjorie began with what for me were thrilling words:-

'Your letter was no surprise to me. For three months the Lord has

been calling me to yield my life to Him for full time service. My main stumbling block to responding to that call was in fact, you, for how was it possible for me to take the initiative in a decision which would so vitally affect both our lives?'

My initial reaction to this letter was to give thanks to the Lord, and then to marvel at His over-ruling. We were thousands of miles apart and, even though we corresponded regularly, neither of us had divulged anything which would indicate we were facing a vital, life changing, decision. Yet, during the same length of time, the Lord had been calling us to the same form of service, whilst both of us faced the same principal stumbling block, a deep concern for the future of each other. We could not help but feel this must be the Lord calling and directing but yet nagging doubts arose. Was this really the Lord speaking or a mere coincidence that our thoughts moved in the same direction? On my part, was it only emotional reaction after seeing the dire poverty and moral degradation facing certain people? For Marjorie, was it a natural zeal to serve the Lord she loved, stimulated by the stirring ministry of some erudite speaker? We shared our thoughts and covenanted to pray that God would graciously confirm the call by granting a definite seal. There was a Scriptural precedent for this in the story of Gideon and his fleece. At the same time we were aware from the account of Moses' reaction to his call to divine service that one must never trifle with God. We did not seek to specify, like Gideon, the way the seal should be given but, having prayed for confirmation, decided to wait until we were convinced God had answered 'yes' or 'no'.

CHAPTER 6

Palestinian Interlude

(1944)

I will never leave you nor forsake you (Hebrews 13:5).

In December 1943 I was made Battery Transport Officer, an imposing title which meant nothing more than overseeing the state of our meagre supply of transport. The position, however, brought a bonus; I was assigned to a training course to be held in Gaza - along with it an opportunity to see something of the land of Israel, so I applied for two weeks leave and shortly after Christmas was on my way to a host of new experiences.

These began with the journey from Baghdad to Damascus by road. The quickest route could take fifteen to twenty four hours, but this way sometimes posed a problem in winter. Torrential rains in the northern hills could result in it becoming water logged and this was the case the day I travelled. Consequently we had to make a lengthy detour following the Iraq Petroleum Company's oil pipe line as far as Mafraq in Jordan. There the road divided. To the south lay Amman, to the west Irbid and Galilee and a branch to the north brought one to Ramtha and Damascus.

For miles we had driven across an undulating dreary, barren land with the occasional interest of a poverty stricken looking village. But at last the bus breasted a small hill and there in the distance lay the beautiful sight of a city embowered in green. The contrast with its surroundings was almost a shock; Damascus was in truth an oasis in the desert. I have since heard it called 'a pearl in an emerald setting', but arriving there one saw the flaws in the pearl. At close quarters ancient Damascus was more yellow than white, a mixture of past and present. The old city presented a fascinating jumble of noisy crowded bazaars, narrow streets, dim mysterious alleyways, and the domes and minarets of numerous mosques. The new was composed of beautiful blocks of flats, wide tree-lined streets, gardens, fountains and the occasional park. Numerous areas still under construction and the gaunt spectre of half finished buildings extended the flaw. But for me it was a thrill to be in the oldest, continuously inhabited city in the world and know I was treading on ground closely connected with the spread of the gospel.

On reporting to Movement Control I discovered a few days would elapse before I could continue. Consulting my list of contacts I found an address in Damascus of the British Syrian Mission. Its work at this time rested in the capable hands of a number of very devoted ladies, many of whom could be described as intrepid. During my brief visits I met a number of the missionaries whose zeal and devotion to the Lord, in difficult and daunting circumstances aroused my admiration. The contacts made during those few days laid the foundation for lifelong friendships. It changed its designation to the Lebanon Evangelical Mission and then more recently, Middle East Christian Outreach.

Within three or four days my journey continued, this time by a train whose vintage and dusty first class carriages conveyed an atmosphere of departed glory; and its second class an aroma of crowded humanity. For a few miles the line ran through the verdant orchards of Damascus then, emerging into more open land, there was a glimpse of the majestic snow-crowned head of Mount Hermon. But soon we were crossing again the drab plain of Bashan where undulating barren acres held little to grip the interest. Signs of life were few even at the occasional isolated villages where our train paused, the only sounds being the subdued noise of talkative passengers against a background of a gentle hiss of steam. Then, suddenly, as the train slowed to another stop, everything seemed to come alive. Carriage doors swung open, hordes of men streamed out, faced almost due south, and began to bow and prostrate themselves till the faint murmur of a myriad voices drifted through the noontide air. It was my first experience, an unforgettable one, of the Muslim's zeal to maintain his right standing before Allah, and his awareness of the great Islamic brotherhood manifested by uniting to fulfil the obligatory prayers.

The prayer session ended, the worshippers drifted back, the train crew leisurely replenished the engine with water, the guard finally appeared, the engine blew off a vast quantity of steam and then with a sudden jerk, proceeded on its way to Deraa, a place linked with the name of Lawrence of Arabia. The train then turned westward to wend its way slowly down the sides of a steep valley to lovely Galilee. As we descended the valley, the surrounding hills retained the clouds, but high above the valley a long strip of blue sky marked the line of the ancient river Jordan. The closer we came to the lake the more the waters reflected that lovely strip of blue whilst all around early flowers created extensive areas of brilliant colour against a background of green. From a distance it was a breathtaking sight. Regretfully a lack of time prevented lingering amongst sights and sounds not so far removed from those experienced by the Lord Jesus Himself.

Three weeks at Gaza were followed by a brief visit to Tel Aviv and Haifa where I joined a crowded, noisy, jolting Arab bus to Jerusalem. There I made my way to a Guest House owned by The Mission to Mediterranean Garrisons, an organisation which has for many years carried on a fruitful spiritual ministry amongst men and women of the Armed Forces in the Middle East. The Home on Deir Abu Tor was under the efficient management of Mr. and Mrs. Cupples who gave of themselves unstintingly to make their guests welcome. Mr. Cupples' extensive knowledge of Palestine and the Scriptures ensured that his teaching and guided tours were an inspiration to any who had a love for the Bible. He had the gift of an evangelist and his powerful preaching was used to lead many to faith in Christ. He constantly challenged believers to commit their lives fully and without reserve to the service of Christ. No doubt this emphasis brought me to my next crisis.

Each evening ended with a short devotional period but on Sundays it became an extended time of fellowship. This consisted of lively singing, brief testimonies and a full length sermon from Mr. Cupples. On my second Sunday the Lord challenged me afresh concerning the matter of full time service. I recalled that special evening in the officers' mess when the Lord spoke so clearly and I had said, "If you want me to go I will." Now I realised something was wrong with that prayer and it bothered me. In a flash I saw that the little word 'if' was, in reality, a reservation on my part. God had spoken to me for three months; was not that long enough for the Lord to convince me He desired my life to be fully committed to His service? I left the meeting convinced the 'if' would have to be erased and, once again kneeling before the Lord, in all sincerity I yielded my future to Him simply saying, "Lord you can take away the 'if'; I will go."

The die was cast, the future would be devoted to His service wherever He would lead. At that moment who should walk into my room but Mr. Cupples and I could not refrain from telling him of my commitment. He did not boost my ego but solemnly said, "Douglas, remember Luke 9:62: No man having put his hand to the plough and looking back is fit for the kingdom of God." These challenging words remained with me through the years, having a salutary effect when difficulties, opposition, and the hardness of the way brought the temptation to think of giving up. Mr. Cupples stayed to pray and chat but as soon as he left I put pen to paper. I found it impossible to rest until I had shared with Marjorie what was, for me, a thrilling experience, and in so doing posed the question, 'Could this be the Lord's confirmation of our call to full time service?'

Some time elapsed before that query received a reply but when it came I knew without doubt the Lord had set His seal on our calling. Two nights after my decision in Jerusalem Marjorie also had an experience which convinced her the Lord had confirmed the call. That evening the preacher, Fred Elliot, a well known and gifted evangelist, stopped in the middle of his address, strode up and down the platform looking very puzzled, and then said, "I'm not sure why I am giving this message tonight. Travelling on the bus this evening I felt the Lord was saying to me, 'Forget your prepared message - speak on Luke 5:4. Someone who is afraid to launch out into the deep in full dependence upon me needs this message.' " Marjorie felt the words were for her. In spite of our having agreed to serve the Lord together a niggling thought had remained: could one really launch out into the deep of the unknown, fully dependent upon Him alone for all things? Quietly bowing her head she said, "Lord I will launch out at your bidding." Immediately came the conviction that the Lord had placed His seal upon her calling. So once again, before either of us could influence the other, and while we were still thousands of miles apart, the Lord had spoken to us both. Neither of us could further doubt that God had called us both individually and mutually. This fact has been a tremendous help over the years, especially for Marjorie. When facing difficulties, discouragements, sometimes danger and sorrow, she has been able to say, "I am here, not as a missionary's wife, but as a servant of the Lord. He is my guide, my strength, my comfort, and I am in His hands."

CHAPTER 7

Eastward Bound

(India and Ceylon, 1944-45)

In all thy ways acknowledge Him,
and He shall direct thy paths (Proverbs 3:6).

The day after my decision to cancel out the 'if' I set off towards Damascus and the East, this time by the desert route. As the shades of night fell and despite the bouncing and lurching of the coach over the desert track, I sank into unconsciousness. Sleep had been in short supply during the last few days and I hoped the night journey would provide an opportunity for the much needed rest. But a tremendous bang brought us all awake. The vehicle swerved, straightened again and finally stopped with a decided list. A tyre had succumbed to the strain of desert travel. The drivers acted as if it were a common occurrence! A little while later a second tyre went the way of the first! Eventually I arrived in Abadan without further incident and once again became involved in the Battery's uninspiring daily round.

The pleasant warmer days of spring slipped by and the prospect of living through another scorching summer loomed ahead. The seeming uselessness of our continual training frustrated the British troops and so there were mixed feelings when rumours spread that the regiment would move. Then came the definite orders; the regiment was destined for India.

Training now gave way to packing and, in due course, moving to the docks for embarkation to Bombay. There the regiment entrained and during the next few days endured the discomforts of an Indian troop train. It was a very roundabout journey, first to the north, then east before taking a southerly direction to Jubbalpur.

In its earlier stages it held much of interest - the contrasts with Iraq and Persia were almost startling. Here vast areas of cultivated land dotted with trees and shrubs, interlaced with numerous canals and the occasional slow moving river, stretched as far as the eye could see. Instead of the camel and the donkey, lumbering oxen drew heavily laden carts and broad-shouldered water buffalo wallowed in vast village ponds. In contrast to the heavily veiled, dark-robed Muslims, Indian women in bright saris presented a glimpse of colour against the background of mud huts, hovels and dusty streets as the train rattled by. The whole episode, with its varied sights and sounds, proved a good introduction to India, whilst the conditions under which we travelled made future journeys seem luxurious by comparison.

The hutted camp at Jubbalpur sited in open country proved to be a very dreary place from which troops would move to their final destination. However, the regiment being part of the Indian Army had come home and was due a month's leave. The Indian troops dispersed to their respective areas and the rest of us were left to decide how to spend the unexpected four weeks of leisure. I had a choice between going south to Bangalore to visit a mission station, or north to a Christian Guest House in Mussoorie bearing the name of 'The Deodars'. Both places had their attractions but the latter won, possibly because of the anticipation of leaving the torrid heat of the plains to relax in the cool of the hills.

Mussoorie, a beautiful hill station, stretches along a ridge from which are breathtaking views of the plains some three thousand feet below. 'The Deodars' lay to the west of the town - a lovely, old, colonial, house, sheltering in a grove of huge old trees and surrounded by pine needle strewn gardens. The whole place immediately impressed me as being ideal for a quiet restful holiday in the relaxed atmosphere of a Christian home; an impression enhanced by the cordiality of the hostess and other guests, most of whom had links with the Indian Civil Service, the Military or one of India's numerous Mission Societies.

The first week I enjoyed browsing round the town getting my fill of new sights and sounds, but towards the end I felt a sense of lassitude and loss of appetite. I woke in the middle of the night troubled by severe pains with every breath I drew. Eventually one of the guests, a Dr. Harper, diagnosed pneumonia and stressed the need for hospitalisation. Fortunately, an Army hospital existed in a small village in the hills behind Mussoorie, and Dr. Harper's medical status proved sufficient to get me admitted.

No motor road or cart track led from Mussourie to Landour. The only transport consisted of a rickshaw followed by a lift on the back of coolies! Swathed in blankets, in a rickshaw with my luggage piled on my knees, I was hauled, bumping and bouncing, through the centre of town, thankful for the hood which concealed me from the inquisitive gaze of the local population. Eventually we rendezvoused with the coolies waiting to carry us up the hill. They used a long narrow box, about eight inches deep, with a short headboard, and slung between two long poles. They bundled me together with my luggage into this contraption, and hoisted onto the shoulders of the bearers we were off up the steep and stony track. The carriers were sure footed but I felt vulnerable and helpless perched high above the ground and a rock strewn slope. After what appeared to be a long, long time we arrived at our destination and, with a tremendous feeling of relief, knew that medical attention lay to hand.

On my first night the nursing orderly appeared to forget my existence and in addition to breathing difficulties I had an appalling thirst. No amount of bell ringing brought any response, but the arrival of the Nursing Sister in the morning changed the situation. Then two days later one of the loudest, and most brilliant thunderstorms I have ever experienced rent the night air. Tremendous crashes shook the place and then a blinding light and a louder crack as lightning struck a corner of the room. There was no evident damage but the whole incident hardly calmed nerves already on edge. Those nerves might have been more on edge had I known the reputation of the hospital! On my way back to my unit I met an Army doctor on Delhi station (by a great coincidence the husband of Dr. Harpur) who wryly commented, "You were lucky to come out of there alive!" Well, obviously, I did and, after some ten days recuperating in the fresh, pure air of the hills felt fit enough to face the hair raising drive to Dehra Dun.

Shortly after returning to my unit I found myself being challenged about the possibility of living the life of faith which we envisaged.

I was discussing with a fellow officer the vital subject of what we intended doing after the war. The two of us sketched out our individual plans and my companion, interested in our thought of missionary service, asked which Society would we be joining. My answer, that we would go overseas trusting God to guide and provide through any channel He ordained, brought a barrage of protest. He declared it would be impossible to live overseas without a headquarters at home. This in turn led to a discussion on the reality of God and His personal interest in all His servants. I pointed out that we believed it would be possible to follow the New Testament pattern whereby a missionary commended by his local church, looked to the Lord for guidance, protection and provision. The officer forcibly stated if we desired to live in poverty that was our affair but we had no right to impose this on our children. They would, he declared, grow up undernourished, poorly educated and unfitted for coping with adulthood. My answer was that we firmly believed if the Lord granted us children He would care for them as abundantly as He would for us, adding that I believed they would have just as good an education, and be as capable of holding good positions, as they would if I were in business at home. Marjorie and I are deeply grateful that over the years the Lord honoured that declaration of faith.

The regiment's next move was to Ceylon, destination Trincomalee, an extensive naval station on the eastern side of the country, where my unit camped a few miles out of town waiting for the final posting to a gun-site overlooking the harbour. This camp had one great drawback. Though beautiful to look upon, the area attracted the most bloodthirsty of mosquitoes, as well as other insects, some of which possessed a vicious bite. One of these creatures, or a combination of them, landed me in hospital yet again. After a week or so I became conscious of a painful itch. Antiseptic lotion and ointment failed to ease it, and swellings occurred, so I decided a visit to the doctor would be advisable. On seeing the infected places, he almost exploded with anger, asking why I had not come to see him before. He said there was a real danger of septicaemia. A few hours later it would have been too late to prevent my whole system being infected. Thus before the day ended I was in bed, and the following morning the swellings were lanced and drained. Back in the ward I awoke feeling decidedly sick, a normal result in such circumstances. But the contents to which my stomach objected were certainly not normal for, to my surprise, they included a long, fat round worm! How long it had been feeding on me I did not know, but I did know great relief at being rid of it and hoped fervently it had left behind none of its relatives. The nursing staff were fascinated, pickled it and brought it for me to keep as a memento. I flatly refused!

By the time I returned to my unit it had moved to a gun site in the forested area north of Trincomalee Bay. The guns were to provide protection for the shipping frequenting Trincomalee Bay and its adjacent creeks. Now, with the tide of war turning against Japan and the conflict ever moving eastward, there was little likelihood of aerial attack, so again we were back to a routine of training and maintenance. Such a routine inevitably produced a state of dissatisfaction among some British personnel who had been overseas for a very long time. The long separation from wives and families, and the inability of some couples to maintain effective communication by mail, brought strain and, for a few, the tragedy of marital breakdown.

While I had been changing locations under orders, Marjorie had also been on the move but, in her case, quite voluntarily. It had been suggested that she would profit from a two year course at one of the Bible Colleges but, being in a reserved occupation, this seemed to be an unlikely prospect. Nothing daunted she applied for release from her health department post and simultaneously forwarded an application to the Bible Training Institute in Glasgow. Both requests were granted and she was enrolled at the BTI for the September 1944 term. Thus, not long after I entered Ceylon, Marjorie travelled to Glasgow. Her Bible College training has been a tremendous help over many years. Her periods of intensive and extensive reading supplied me with study material, and valuable lessons from her studies and personal experience were passed on to me.

Whilst Marjorie discovered new areas of Christian fellowship in Britain I also enjoyed them in Trincomalee. A Forces Canteen not far from the Camp, held church services each Sunday and more informal meetings during the week. This canteen operated under the supervision of an intrepid elderly lady, Miss Kate Kaane, who for many years had worked in Ceylon with the Bible Churchmen's Missionary Society. Her concern for the spiritual welfare of British troops reached back to the first world war when she had opened canteens around the Suez Canal. On the outbreak of the second world war she decided, despite her advancing years, to repeat that activity in the same area. However Japan's entry into the war made travelling impossible and, realising troops would now be coming to Ceylon she opened this canteen at Trincomalee. Kate was small in stature, bent in frame and partially lame. Her hearing and eyesight were impaired and this, coupled with her age, meant that she hardly seemed to be one who would attract the confidence of young men. But Kate had been blessed with a gracious motherly spirit and many a downcast, homesick man found strength and comfort in her wise counsel. She was an ardent evangelist and, when counselling a young man, would sometimes discover him to be the son of someone she had led to faith in Christ years ago in the Canal zone. In her canteen I found constant Christian fellowship and there met a lovely couple who have had a warm place in our affections throughout the years.

One morning our leisurely programme received a jolt when I was deputed to take charge of a camp being erected to receive Japanese prisoners of war. Though these were due in a few hours I found the camp was still not fully prepared for occupation. Tents had been pitched and cookhouse facilities prepared, the perimeter wire and guard towers were almost complete but electricity had still to be connected. A diesel engine was on site to provide emergency lighting but we needed a more powerful and consistent supply to be installed by army electricians.

Eventually our guests arrived, some sixty or so miserable looking men whose demeanour spoke of a resigned submission to whatever fate might have in store. One wondered what thoughts really lay behind those submissive looks and I considered it would be wise for us to be on our guard. The men had just been fed and allocated to their tents when a senior officer arrived. He examined the area and, to my surprise, quizzed me on the comforts provided for the prisoners. I appreciated that in spite of the way the Japanese had treated their prisoners, and my own emotional involvement due to my brother having died a violent death at their hands, conventions required these men be treated humanely and provided with the necessities of life. However, I did feel the Brigadier was going over the top concerning their comfort. I nearly choked when he asked if they had all had their due rations of cigarettes!

After darkness fell I had hardly got my head on the pillow when the lights failed and we were enveloped in the darkness of a moonless night. I shot out of bed, imagining all sorts of things in my half dreamy state, made for the generator and called to the Ceylonese officer to look alive and get it started. Immediately it became apparent he hadn't the foggiest notion of what to do. I was grateful for my brief experience with generators in Iran. After a few seconds it coughed, a faint flicker of light went round the Camp and I gave a sigh of relief.

The day brought new orders. I had to oversee the movement of the prisoners to a security section near Colombo. Shortly before midday four trucks arrived. The men looked so dejected and spiritless it seemed unlikely any would try to vanish during the journey but as a precaution, a British guard was allocated to each truck. In due course the little convoy set off for one of the most hair raising rides I have ever experienced. For sheer fast, reckless, and seemingly unskilled driving I doubt if these Ceylonese soldiers could be bettered.

We arrived at the detention centre with no more damage to our truck than a bent canopy frame. With a feeling of satisfaction that the main part of my duties had been accomplished, but with a certain amount of concern about the return journey, I moved to mount the truck only to be obstructed by a Ceylonese private. He smiled and gave a very unmilitary greeting. For a moment I was taken aback but then recognised him. Sometime before I had been a member of a panel of judges at a court martial where the presiding judge was known for his severity; also that he expected others meekly to agree with his verdicts. I had felt strongly that certain evidence for the defence did not receive fair consideration, and said so. My comments were brushed aside and the judge wanted to bring in a guilty verdict. I stuck to my point and, though he expressed his annoyance, he did pronounce not-guilty. The smiling soldier now before me was the convicted man and he just wanted to say thank you. It certainly helped to make my day. The return journey to Trincomalee was fast, scary but uneventful and I thankfully returned to the familiar routine of my own unit.

With the military situation improving, the British Government introduced a scheme whereby personnel serving overseas could be granted a month's home leave. My Commanding Officer suggested I should apply on health grounds and early in April I received confirmation leave had been granted. As I was told the journey would be by air I anticipated being home in just over a week but this proved to be overly optimistic. However one great event cheered up those weary waiting weeks. News of Germany's capitulation came on the day I caught the train for the first stage home.

From the Royal Air Force base at Poona we took off on DC3s piloted by young Air Force personnel, bound for Karachi. The following day the journey westward really began, but five days were to elapse before landing on English soil. Bahrain became our first refuelling stop and then Habbaniyah in Iraq. Here the crew reported a fault in one of the engines and warned us there would be a delay of some hours. 'Some hours' became 'many' and another dawn arrived before we boarded the plane again. In the brightness of a cloudless day one thoroughly enjoyed the scene unfolding below until, without warning, the view took on a new aspect as one engine cut out and the plane, banking steeply, began to dive. Then the engine came to life again and, with the dive checked, the plane resumed a level course. A moment later a head popped round the door and a cheery voice sang out, "It's all right fellows, we often do that!"

The next two or three hours brought us to Lydda in Palestine then we were off through the night only to land again at a remote desert strip in North Africa. There we were told there would only be one more stop in Sardinia before completing the journey home. But before we had completed two thirds of this leg of the trip, it became clear we were heading into a violent storm. One minute a flash would reveal the awesome sight of densely banked clouds, a few moments later torrential rain pounded on the windows blocking all from view. One of the crew took the trouble to assure us all was well, a comment which would have been more comforting if the plane had kept on an even keel. In the cabin we were only conscious of the plane twisting and turning, climbing and falling, leaving us completely disorientated and with no idea whether we were just above the waves or nearer the stars. At long last calm returned and, from the tone of the engines, we knew we were coming down to land. Dawn began to break and we looked eagerly for our first glimpse of Europe but, as the wheels dropped and land flashed before our eyes, we could see only sand, sand and more sand. Then an apologetic voice over the intercom informed us we were landing in North Africa! The crew had done their best to get round, above or below the storm but found no way through and, with fuel running low, had to turn back. As morning progressed the wind eased, the clouds dispersed and by lunch time we were airborne again with a request to keep a sharp look out for wreckage and survivors of an American plane which had gone missing in the night. We saw nothing and, without more excitement, arrived in Sardinia. Then came the final hop to an air force base in Somerset. Clouds covered most of France but the weather cleared as we crossed the Channel. The sunlit fields of Britain seemed to radiate a welcome home. Within a few minutes of landing I phoned Glasgow only to discover that the next day Marjorie had to sit the term-end examinations. The knowledge of my arrival hardly improved her ability to concentrate; however she coped and topped the list.

With the term ended we commenced a busy round of visits, one of which had an important bearing on our missionary service. The elders of our local church in Nottingham, wishing to assure themselves of the reality of our call to full time missionary service, asked us to meet with them. Understandably they could not recommend the assembly to support us until they themselves were fully convinced we were in the line of the Lord's will. We had known most of them from our early teens and held them in awe and great respect, so it was something of an ordeal to face them. But they soon put us at our ease as we shared with them the details of our call to full time service. The assembly already supported a missionary couple in Brazil and, though being keenly interested in our call, the elders could not make a definite promise that the assembly could support us as well. Then, just as we were preparing to leave, someone said, "By the way, you haven't told us where you are going." We hadn't for the reason we had not yet come to any decision!

From the time we were convinced of our call to serve overseas the vital question of 'where' had been before us. My experiences in the Middle East did not necessarily mean we were to serve there; in any case Marjorie had no personal knowledge of the area and needed to be assured from the Lord where He would have her be. We had prayed constantly for guidance. Our prayers began to be answered through a doctor informing Marjorie she would never be able to stand the heat of the tropics which, of course, ruled out a vast area. No matter how much we thought of countries other than the Middle East we had no peace of mind concerning any of them, and now we were faced with the crunch. How could the elders commend us if we had no answer to their most obvious question? Now, as soon as the question was asked, Palestine flashed into my mind and I answered, "Palestine of course." From that moment we had a firm conviction Palestine, which for us meant Arabs, would be our destination.

Two days before my leave expired a letter informed me it had been extended for another week, and then another gave a later date still. Marjorie was due to spend the summer vacation helping in a Forces Canteen in Liverpool and my final notice to report to London coincided with her departure for that city. I reported to the Reception Centre expecting to be soon flying east, but instead I was informed the journey would be by boat from Liverpool. On arrival at the docks I discovered we were not due to sail until the following day and, with that welcome news, set off to locate Marjorie's address. An unexpected few hours together helped to soften the pain of separation. The next day the liner cast off her moorings and, heavily laden with returning troops and equipment, headed out to the Irish Sea enroute to India.

This voyage was vastly different from 1943. No U-boats lurked beneath the waves and the threat of air attack no longer existed. Blackout regulations were cancelled and night-time saw the ship ablaze with light. With the Suez Canal open the journey could be accomplished in three weeks instead of ten. For many of us the trip proved pleasant and intensely interesting as we had our first glimpses of the bustling town of Port Said, experienced the passage through Lesseps Canal, and smelt the heavy air as we lingered near Suez. In the Indian Ocean tension mounted slightly, for Britain was still at war with Japan and no one could be sure the seas were clear of Japanese craft. The anti-aircraft guns were manned and I had some happy hours with the gunners on the bridge. The nightly vigil continued until news came that a devastating bomb had been dropped on a major Japanese city and the war was virtually over. Hiroshima had been destroyed by an atomic bomb on 6th August, followed by a similar attack on Nagasaki. On 14th August, Japan surrendered to the Allies and before we sailed into Bombay harbour, the second great war had ended.

With the war finally over, the British Government faced the problem of demobilising its Forces in an equitable manner while maintaining enough troops to keep the peace in what remained of the British Empire. They solved it by demobilising men in numbered groups and my length of service meant I could anticipate being demobilised about the end of 1945. However a further pronouncement stated that officers would be delayed for a further few weeks and our unit would return to India to join the rest of the regiment. Realising that for those of us seconded to the Indian Army this could mean an indefinite delay I immediately applied for a transfer to stay in Ceylon, and within a few days I was posted to a Coastal Unit whose captain was due to leave for Britain. This meant I received promotion even though it came rather late in the day. By the end of December my group had received orders to leave and, early in January, my journey from Colombo commenced.

This journey differed considerably from that on the *Dominion Monarch*. There was definitely a shortage of cabins, at least for males and officers of junior rank, the majority of whom were allotted hammocks between decks. Some, claiming their rank entitled them to better accommodation, grumbled fiercely, but shipping was in short supply and one either accepted the situation or stayed behind. At least it was a new experience and, within a few hours, most of us were adept at slinging and occupying hammocks. The second vast difference from the previous voyages soon became apparent. Then there had been daily prayer meetings, and regular Bible studies; now the voyage home was marked by a complete absence of any religious service. Even Sunday passed without any arrangements for a church service. In the times of daily danger, men were anxious for God's protection; now it seemed He was no longer in their thoughts.

The cruise across the Indian Ocean, and through the Suez Canal into the Mediterranean was pleasant, but conditions deteriorated rapidly after we passed Gibraltar. The Bay of Biscay seemed to be pounding us with its worst, with wind, rain, waves and a wild sea. Next morning the ship's movement subsided to a gentle roll, and the news that we would dock in thirty six hours spread like wildfire from group to group. Seeing the Liverpool skyline and experiencing the joy of tying up to a bit of England, to the strains of a welcoming military band, speedily dispelled all thoughts of Biscay Bay. From Liverpool docks a train took us to Edinburgh, where, tired and dishevelled, hungry and badly needing a shave, we ended the journey at a busy demobilisation centre. A few hours later, still wearing uniform but having been officially demobbed and kitted out with the regulation civilian suit, shirt, hat etc, I made my way to the station for the last leg of the journey home. All I remember next is walking up the familiar steps of Victoria station and there, in the vastness of the booking hall amongst the milling crowds, seeing the one I longed to meet. Marjorie had come to welcome me.

There was no need to talk on the bus travelling home. The war had ended, I was once more a civilian, even though still on the reserve for a while. The days of separation were past, a new life had just begun, the thrill of the future lay before us. We could now begin to plan, under God's direction, for whatever service He desired us to do.

CHAPTER 8

Into Palestine

(1946)

Behold, I send an Angel before you to keep you in the way (Exodus 23.20).

The war with Germany ended on the 8th May, 1945. On July 26th a new Labour Government was elected, with an overwhelming majority under the premiership of Clement Attlee, and could contemplate pushing through any legislation it desired. Thus the Left had the opportunity for which it had waited, to test its theory of creating a socialist Utopia. The evils of capitalism would be swept away, major industries and utilities would be nationalised, and a Welfare State created which would ease the people's lot from the cradle to the grave. All families were to receive allowances for children, there would be free health and dental services for everyone, unemployment benefit and disability allowance would cover the whole range of eventualities. The new scheme was widely hailed as the plan which would ensure contentment for all. Unfortunately it failed to take into account a number of vital factors including the cost of its administration, and abuse of the system. However, there is no doubt the Welfare State raised living standards and improved the health of the majority of people and we also, as a family, benefitted from its provisions. But in 1946 as Britain began to depend on the security and provision of the State, Marjorie and I were turning our thoughts to a new and different way of life, one in which the Lord of heaven and earth, and not the State, became our trust.

We began planning for our move to the Middle East. Contact had already been made with missionaries in Jerusalem who assured us of a warm welcome, though they warned there could be delay in obtaining entry visas. This did not concern us unduly for we could not travel before Marjorie had completed her course at BTI and surely, if the Lord wanted us in Palestine a little thing like visas would not be allowed to hinder! At that time we were completely ignorant of the workings of immigration laws, and the hurdles facing civilians wanting to travel in a world so recently torn by war. In the meantime we had plenty to do before Marjorie returned to Glasgow. Acting on the advice of the elders of our local church we arranged an interview with the editors of *Echoes of Service,* a missionary magazine which also issued a prayer list of missionaries associated with brethren assemblies. We were a little hazy about their role but were assured they were not a missionary society, sending out and directing workers, but were what could be termed a service agency. They received news from missionaries from all round the world and, through the magazine, conveyed it to many individuals and assemblies; also communicating with the missionaries and forwarding gifts received on their behalf. We enjoyed our brief visit to Bath and deeply appreciated meeting the three editors who, sensing our nervousness, did their best to make us feel at ease. After hearing our testimonies, and knowing we would have the full commendation of our assembly, they confirmed that once we were overseas, our names would be included in the prayer list. At the same time they made it clear that if one went overseas trusting the Lord for all things that is exactly what one did!

Before Marjorie returned to Glasgow, the question of how I should occupy myself became important. On demobilisation I heard my Army Commission could be considered as qualification for entrance to a university and I found the prospect of studying for a degree extremely tempting. It might help me to achieve those dreams I had shared with Marjorie before the war, dreams of status, an affluent home and a high position in society. As we prayed concerning this, both of us felt the call to overseas service must take priority unless the Lord definitely closed the door.

In Palestine, the strife arising from the conflicting claims of Jew and Arab placed a great strain on the Government forces as they sought to maintain order. The authorities were compelled to place further restrictions on immigration and we wondered if we would ever obtain visas to enter that troubled land. In fact, a letter from the Knowles in Jerusalem mentioned that a recent Government decision would prevent the issue of any new entry permits. However, though we did not know it, the Lord was working on our behalf and, a few days later, a telegram arrived with the cryptic message 'visas granted'.

Early in the year our assembly elders, wanting to ensure a well attended valedictory meeting, had asked if we could tell them the approximate date of our departure. In answer, though not quite knowing why, we suggested October would be the appropriate month and, as time rolled by, it became clear they had taken this as a definite date. Therefore by July we were under pressure to confirm travel arrangements, and that was far from easy. We approached a London travel agent and, on stating our reasons for travelling and proposed date of departure, discovered it would not be possible to get a passage direct to Palestine, but we could travel to Egypt and then by train to Jerusalem. Nothing was said about any problems concerning shipping, nor having to book through a certain Agency. We were simply told that the exact date of departure would be sent in due course. Naively, assuming the approximate date had been fixed, we set about making the requisite preparations and patiently waited for news from the travel agents.

The first step of obtaining passports, duly stamped with those important visas, presented no problem, nor did I have any difficulty in obtaining permission to leave the country. The procuring of clothing and equipment turned out to be somewhat more difficult. We were moving to an area where long hot summers were followed by brief but very cold winters, and we would need both lightweight and warm clothing. Clothing for a semi-tropical climate presented a double problem; first its scarcity, and then the fact it could only be obtained from a few specialist sources with a somewhat higher price tag. The shipping agents were helpful. They put us in touch with the specialist sources and this proved a boon as far as ration coupons were concerned - clothing for export escaped rationing providing it went straight to the ship. This unexpected arrangement taught us that the Lord had His own way of meeting a need.

Then we had a frustrating period of waiting. By the end of July there was still no news from the Travel Agents, and phone calls only elicited the comment a date would be given in due course. We called again and discovered the main reason for the delay. The end of the war had put tremendous pressure on ocean transport facilities. Ships were needed to bring home thousands of service personnel and to return civilians and troops to India and the Far East. Accommodation on ships had to be allocated on a basis of priority and the Government and Armed Forces had first claim. Only then did we learn that missionaries of recognised Societies returning to their field of service had a degree of priority over others. However no one mentioned that in order to take advantage of this priority one had to apply to an Agency which dealt with missionary allocations.

By now August had almost expired with still no news of when we could sail. More telephone calls told us that, due to the overwhelming demand for passages to countries east of Suez, no berths were being allocated for the Middle East. By early September we were more than a little concerned, especially as the elders had advertised the date for our farewell meeting. We had visions of a well attended, and deeply moving, valedictory - and then the embarrassment of turning up at Clumber Hall weeks later. We had believed October would be the right time to travel because Mr. and Mrs. Knowles of Jerusalem were planning to return to New Zealand some time that month, and they had graciously offered us the use of their home during their absence. We saw in this another evidence of the Lord's ability to provide for our needs, and were keen to meet them and be introduced to their work prior to their leaving.

Finally I went to London to see the Travel Agents personally. They were apologetic about the delay and went on about ships being full and no berths available. Only then did they mention what they could have told us months before. The responsibility for our allocation lay with the Agency handling missionary passages. Immediately I asked for the Agency's address and set out to find it. To my surprise as I walked into their office the receptionist asked, "Are you Mr. Howell?" She further surprised me by asking how soon could we travel! It transpired that due to the back-log of people waiting to go to Egypt and Palestine, a special boat destined for Port Said had been detailed to sail late in October. There were just two berths left and would we take them? There could only be one answer! It was a delight to return home with this tremendous news. The way was open for us to travel in the month we had suggested and all arrangements could now be finalised. We always said the Lord had laid on a special boat for us!.

The next few weeks were frantically busy with visits to relatives, meetings, dispatching luggage and that long expected valedictory meeting. The most difficult thing was saying good-bye to our parents. We could not be unaware of their heartache. Loved sons had been lost in both families during the war and now they were being denied the help and fellowship of other children. People talk about missionaries making sacrifices but little is said concerning the cost to those left behind. Neither our parents, nor my sister or any of our relatives, said or did anything to hinder our following the call of the Lord. We have always been deeply grateful for such co-operation even though at times it must have been at great emotional cost.

The day after the valedictory meeting, which drew believers from many assemblies, we were on our way to Liverpool and our ship, the *Ascania*. It is impossible to recapture how we felt as it gathered speed and gradually the coast of England slipped from sight. We were sailing into the unknown. It would have been a tremendous help if we could have had a quiet time to ourselves to cope with the emotional experience involved. We needed to be able to talk and pray together and share each others thoughts as we embarked on this new venture for God. But that intimate sharing failed to materialise for the *Ascania* had not yet been converted from a troop ship, and had only dormitory accommodation. I had a berth along with a group of men, somewhere in the bowels of the boat whilst Marjorie shared a cabin with five other women. Privacy became virtually impossible and in a crowded boat, finding a quiet spot anywhere on deck proved impossible. Fortunately the sea was relatively calm as far as Gibraltar and it was possible to stroll, talk and share both our hopes and concerns.

Those concerns now included more than the very important matters of where we would live and what we would do. Shortly before leaving home the signs had been confirmed that Marjorie was pregnant, but it was far too late for plans to be altered. Believing there was no option but to go forward, we would trust the Lord to overrule. Naturally we realised an addition to the family would result in greater responsibility but the Lord granted us peace of heart as we committed the matter to Him. That peace soon faced trial. As the ship headed through the Straits of Gibraltar the winds increased, storm clouds gathered, the sea began to heave and rage and our calm progress gave way to violent tossing and rolling which rapidly brought many to their beds. Not surprisingly Marjorie succumbed fairly quickly, and being confined to an all female cabin, I could not visit. The next two days seemed endless as we ploughed through the storm but relief appeared to be at hand when, gleaming through the evening murk, the lights of Malta's Valletta harbour finally hove into sight. But the storm prevented the ship docking and the prospect of resting on an even keel vanished. Instead, the ship spent the night heaving and rolling round the island until, at dawn, we entered peaceful waters. It was not long before the majority of passengers took advantage of the privilege of getting their feet onto solid land. With Marjorie feeling considerably better we thoroughly enjoyed strolling through the unfamiliar, fascinating streets. But the hours sped all too quickly for our liking and, shortly after re-embarking, we headed once more into the swirling waters of a storm tossed Mediterranean sea.

On towards Port Said the storm continued unabated, and Marjorie's sickness returned. For both of us, and especially for Marjorie confined as she was to her cabin, these few days were lonely. With time on my hands I would walk round the rain swept decks pondering on the immediate past and wondering about the future. One night, clutching the ship's rail to steady myself against its violent tossing, I suddenly felt enveloped by the dark, beset by a strange fear and besieged by questions for which I had no answer. How was Marjorie coping with her lonely situation? What would we do when we arrived in Palestine? How did one begin to develop a spiritual ministry amongst complete strangers? These and many more coursed through my head as I wondered if we had made a terrible mistake. No doubt it was one of Satan's attacks only overcome by the sustaining grace of the Lord.

Shortly after this experience I received a terse message asking me to go to Marjorie in the ship's hospital. Her sickness had contributed to a miscarriage. This was the first I knew of such a possibility and whilst it hit me hard it must have been traumatic and a great disappointment for Marjorie. It certainly cast us both on the Lord for His comfort and strength. The following day we were due in Port Said and it was obvious Marjorie would be in no condition to walk off the boat. The authorities assured us they would arrange for her to be transferred to a hospital and, after that, we would be on our own to cope as best we could. I could not help but wonder during the night what facilities would be provided for getting Marjorie to hospital and how I would cope with all the rush and bustle of landing in a foreign port. In the morning, as the liner inched slowly towards the quay, I saw the answer to my first concern. Happening to glance over the side of the boat I caught a glimpse of Marjorie, strapped to a stretcher, being carried down the ship's narrow steps. At the bottom a small launch bobbed in the slight swell and, at a convenient moment, when steps and launch coincided, the stretcher slid across and the craft sped off. My first thoughts were, Where to? and my second, How do I find her? A few minutes later the boat berthed and, as the gangway clattered down onto the quay, my concern for Marjorie was temporarily superseded by another as a hoard of porters swarmed onto the deck.

With hand luggage in two different parts of the ship, and freight in the hold, I had a problem. How could I gather my possessions, hire a porter whose language I would not understand, bargain in a currency of unknown value, get through Customs where, according to repute, backhanders smoothed the way, find a hotel, and then discover the whereabouts of my wife? As I endeavoured to fend off half a dozen porters, most of whom were yelling loudly, "Me good, me good!" a smiling youth pushed through the throng and, holding out a note, enquired, "Mr. Howell, yes?" The Christian grapevine had been at work and here was wonderful evidence of the Lord's providing. The note, from Mr. Etjamian, director of the Bible Society, introduced me to one of his employees who would be responsible for seeing me off the boat and to a hotel. Whatever unspoken prayer I had been offering a few moments before had been speedily and abundantly answered. My anxiety concerning Marjorie was somewhat alleviated when I learned she had arrived safely at the British Hospital. Concerns too about accommodation proved needless for, shortly after guiding me through Customs and Immigration, my guide deposited me at the House of the Palms, a pleasant Christian Guest House. When Marjorie came out of hospital, we relaxed there while she regained strength for the onward journey.

The unanticipated hospitalisation and delay in Port Said provided us with practical evidence of the Scripture, 'before they call I will answer'. The expenses incurred in both hospital and Guest House placed an extra burden on our resources but we could see clearly how our God had ensured we had enough in hand. The night of our farewell meeting the elders of Clumber Hall passed on to us a parting gift of £40 and now we knew why this provision had been made. It covered all the expenses in Port Said, and we moved on to our next stage with slightly more in hand than anticipated. The Lord was endeavouring to teach us that He knows what needs you have; yes, even before you ask Him.

Due to the delay in Port Said we had to rearrange our schedule and some time elapsed before the necessary reservations for the train journey to Jerusalem could be made. At last we managed to get on our way, loaded with two heavy tin trunks, numerous pieces of baggage, and charged with renewed enthusiasm we anticipated journey's end. Late in the night the Egyptian railway network deposited us at Al Kantara and we crossed the Canal to transfer to the Palestinian system. Sleep eluded us as we rattled and rocked over the plain of Sinai and it was a relief when, as dawn broke, we could take our first look at the land over which the Israelites had wandered so many centuries ago. At last we rumbled into Lydda where, feeling rather the worse for wear, we had to offload our numerous pieces of luggage and transfer to another very ancient looking train for the final leg of the journey. It was a superb ride, first through the abundant orange groves, then with magnificent views interspersed with tunnels and bare rock walls, as twisting back and forth the train slowly climbed the tortuous track, till at last the engine grew silent as we slid into Jerusalem's station.

The uncertainty of our stay in Port Said had made it virtually impossible to send advance notice to anyone in Jerusalem. In any case we had only the Knowles' address and, in Port Said, we learned they sailed for Tasmania the night before we arrived. However, we felt as the Lord had so graciously overruled in our movements thus far, we could trust Him to see us safely through to our new address. We were certainly not disappointed. We had hardly placed foot on the platform when we were accosted with the words, "Are you the Howells?" and, on acknowledging the fact, were treated to a brief lecture. Apparently Mr. Cooper had been meeting the train each day for a week! Our hurried explanation soothed the situation but we could not help but think we had got off to a bad start. He also viewed our numerous items of baggage with some dismay and wondered how they would all fit into a local taxi, but the Lord had the answer to that. As we stood outside the station Mr. Cupples of Todd Osborne House, who had been a link in the chain which brought us to Jerusalem, drove by in his van. Within a few minutes we and our baggage were on our way to Upper Bakka where we anticipated residing for the next two years.

CHAPTER 9

Early Days in Jerusalem

(1946-47)

The Lord... knows those who trust in Him (Nahum 1:7).

Within minutes of being deposited in our new home we saw that the Knowles, having piled most of their furniture into one room, had thoughtfully left enough for all our needs. The stone built house consisted of two storeys and our front door opened off a short balcony approached by a steep outside staircase. This vantage point provided an extensive view across partially cultivated land, dotted with small red roofed homes and vestiges of ancient olive groves, sloping away in the distance to merge with the sky as the western edge of the Judean hills dropped to lower levels. Our first few days were spent in finding our way around the fascinating maze of streets and alleys lying within Jerusalem's ancient walls. The unfamiliar sights, sounds and smells held a charm which even time failed to dispel, and the fact of being in the city once graced by the holy Son of God, stirred emotions varying from joy to grief. There was joy at the thought of His redemptive work but grief at seeing the City over which He wept, harbouring a Judaism which failed to recognise Him, a corrupted Christianity, boasting in shrines and holy relics rather than the Cross, and an Arabian religion flaunting the crescent where, centuries before, a magnificent temple had witnessed to the power and glory of the one true God, maker of heaven and earth. But our business in Jerusalem was not tourism, fascinating though that might be, but preparing for the ministry for which we had come, and that involved attending a language school as soon as possible.

Within a few days we heard of the Bishop's School, a language centre specially geared to the needs of those undertaking Christian work amongst Arabic speaking people. A couple of weeks later we were attending our first classes and taking very hesitant steps in acquiring the basics of a new and strange sounding language. The school occupied a large house in the Street of the Prophets and the daily journey involved a ten minute bus ride followed by a short walk from Damascus gate. The bus route skirted the walls of the old City and passed well within rifle range of a militant Jewish area from which, on the odd occasion, someone would take a pot shot at an Arab vehicle. The school week was Monday to Friday with lessons commencing at 8 am, a short break for devotions usually taken by one of the students, followed by coffee, and then lessons until 12.30. The school anticipated students would spend the afternoon in study; those with household duties had to squeeze their chores into the evening hours. Such a programme called for a great amount of self discipline and, I am sure, we were not the only ones who failed at times to fulfill the afternoon stint. Apart from the director, all the teachers were Palestinian Arabs, possessed it seemed with an unlimited fund of patience. They certainly needed it as we struggled with basic grammar and the pronunciation of a language which, they cheerfully informed us, no foreigner could ever really learn!!

In addition to contacts made at language school we had the benefit of Christian friends linked with the English speaking brethren assembly. The majority of members were expatriate British or local Armenians, there were three or four converts from Judaism, but Arabs appeared to be non-existent. We found the majority in the assembly were pro-Jewish and only later heard of a small group of Arab believers who met elsewhere. The British were mainly business men or civil servants; among the Armenians were a delightful couple, Mr. and Mrs. Touryan, whose main work lay amongst those of their own race. The fairly large group of business men included Mr. Clark, the brother who had helped to facilitate the granting of our visas, managing director of Barclays Bank (DCO). He and his wife were a very gracious couple and their home often became the venue for prayer and Bible study, whilst the pool in the garden frequently took on the role of baptistry. Among the Government officials were another couple, Will and

Zoe Foster who, some time later, would play a significant part in our lives.

The brethren had always laid great stress on the centrality of the Jewish people in the purposes of God, firmly believing the Jewish nation would one day be established in its ancestral home. From the Scriptures they believed that the nation would pass through a time of great tribulation culminating in the return of Jesus to earth when the Jews, recognising Him at last as their true Messiah, would be restored to favour and share in a millennial reign of peace. Also, before the commencement of the great tribulation, there would be the rapture of the Church when, suddenly, all true believers would be caught up to meet the Lord in the air. The long awaited Jewish home seemed now to be almost a reality and this led many Christians to believe the promises concerning the coming of the Lord Jesus for His church would soon be fulfilled. The main opposition to the creation of the new Israel came from the Arabs who thus, in the eyes of many Christians, were thwarting His purposes. Thus to be friends with the Arabs placed one in the category of being antagonistic to God, His chosen people and His divine plans! Some of our brethren, especially those engaged in full time work amongst Jews and Armenians, could not understand our leanings towards the Arabs.

Settled into a definite routine, we discovered life in the ancient City to be full of interest. The daily trip to school usually involved a frantic rush, but the midday walk back to the bus, sometimes through parts of the crowded bazaars of the old City, was much more relaxed. The sights, sounds and smells of the Arab markets continued to fascinate, also the jangling bells of various churches, the strident calls from minarets echoing back and forth across the city, the cries of porters as they hustled laden donkeys along the narrow lanes, or carried immense loads on their own backs. We often thought of the Lord as we threaded the City's streets and, especially when walking the 'Via Dolorosa', that way of suffering leading to the Cross.

The receipt of news from home became of prime importance and our daily return from school included a detour to the Post Office. We used Mr. Knowles' post box and, with great anticipation, would slip the key into the little door. On the first few occasions excitement rose as we saw the cavity half full of letters, but gradually died as the pile diminished with none addressed to the Howells! But the day came when a couple of letters from our parents brought joy, a deeply appreciated thread of communication traversing the thousands of miles from home, and gradually correspondence increased as friends and relatives got busy with their pens.

November had nearly run its course and, with the end of the early rains, the morning and evening temperatures took a nose dive. The chilly start to the day called for some form of extra heating, so prayers for a stove became rather urgent. The Lord undoubtedly heard for a cheque soon arrived sufficient to cover the cost of a simple oil stove! This had been sent by someone in Nottinghamshire who could not have had any idea of our particular need. Our praises that day were offered in the aura of a warm glow from a brand new paraffin burner, one which did sterling service for many winters to come. A few days later praise again accompanied prayer as a cheque arrived from Echoes of Service and our immediate needs were met. This ministry proved invaluable when we lived in countries where transfer of sterling had been banned, other than through authorised channels.

Soon we were anticipating our first Christmas overseas, trusting it would be a time of peace and goodwill, but sadly, both were scarce in Palestine towards the end of 1946. The Jews and Arabs were, to put it mildly, snarling at each other and only the presence of the British Armed Forces and the Palestine Police, ensured an uneasy peace. Britain held the Mandate over Palestine from 1920 and had a commitment to fulfill the League of Nations' resolution that 'a National Home for the Jews would be established in that land'. The same resolution declared, 'this must be without any detriment to the interests of the present inhabitants'. It hardly takes a brilliant mind to see the impossibility of fulfilling those two conditions simultaneously. Britain endeavoured to find and enforce a solution but the demands of the Jews for a State, not merely a homeland, and the refusal of the Arabs to surrender large areas of a land they believed to be theirs by the right of centuries of occupation, precluded a peaceful solution. Both sides were convinced that if only the British were out of the way they could solve the problem - forcibly - in no time. So, whilst the authorities sought to maintain law and order they themselves were the target of the animosity of both Jew and Arab. On the Arab side it was, at this stage, mainly vitriolic verbiage on the part of ardent Nationalists, but the Jews made their presence felt through the activities of two well organised terrorist groups.

In spite of the unsettled situation Christmas proved to be a happy and memorable one. For many years a carol service had been held in the area known as Shepherd's Fields some little distance from Bethlehem and we decided to go on foot. We set out under a cloudless, star-studded sky, with a nip of frost in the air. Gradually the flickering lights of Bethlehem came into view but before reaching the town, we turned down a steep track into a valley and, suddenly, born faintly on the night breeze, heard the sound of many voices raised in a familiar carol. It was an emotional moment to see a vast throng, silhouetted against the flames of a huge bonfire, calling to mind that momentous night when angels sang 'Glory to God, peace on earth, goodwill to men'. The carol drew to a close and all was very still and quiet apart from a faint rustle of a gentle breeze. The sky glowed with stars and away in the distance, crowning the blackness of the hill on which it stood, the faint outline of Bethlehem lay etched against the sky. It seemed to beckon the waiting and adoring throng to draw near and worship. Gradually the crowd began to move and, where once shepherds had sped on their way to see the marvellous thing which had come to pass, we followed, until, standing within the shadow of an ancient church, we listened to the joyful pealing of bells and thought of the millions world wide who would be sharing in the wonder of that moment.

In January 1947, increasing terrorist activity forced the Government to take drastic steps for the protection of British subjects, especially those in the Civil Service and others whose activities were essential to the economy. All essential personnel were required to live in zones which could be reasonably well protected, and all other British subjects to be evacuated. Possibly for security reasons those affected received very little notice, and along with many others, we were given only forty eight hours in which to pack and report to an evacuation centre. This was devastating news, presenting us with some very searching questions. Our time in Palestine had been so brief, could it possibly be that, after all the apparent leading and provision, the Lord did not want us there after all? What would the reaction be at home when these young and enthusiastic missionaries arrived back after six months? At first we declared we couldn't possibly leave but both Mr. Cooper and Mr. Clark assured us that even if I got permission to stay, in no way would Marjorie be allowed to do so.

This crisis drove us to our knees but the effort appeared devoid of any contact with the Lord. We knew a vital decision had to be made: should I stay and Marjorie go? If so would she be able to return? If not, then for how long would I have to remain on my own? We reviewed the events of the past three years and, being impressed by the fact our calling had been mutual in every detail, could see no reason why our paths should separate now. Therefore if Marjorie could not stay neither could I and, failing any orders to the contrary, we would join the forthcoming evacuation. We packed our cases, filled our trunks and boxes with the remainder of our goods hoping that somehow they could eventually be collected. This chore had hardly been completed when the Fosters called to ask if we could help them. His official situation meant he had to stay, but his wife could not unless someone could take their eight year old son to Britain - please could we escort Hugh home? For us this seemed like a glimmer of light in the whole situation; at least some good would come out of it if Will and Zoe could stay together. Readily we agreed, with the result when we queued for transport to the evacuation centre, our family had increased to three.

The RAF station near the old Biblical town of Lydda had been chosen as the evacuation centre, and dusk fell shortly after we arrived. We were comfortably housed for the night in huts but sleep eluded me. Whirring round my mind went the questions, Why am I leaving? Am I running away from where the Lord would have me be? Am I making my love for Marjorie an excuse for going? Am I being tested by the Lord to see if I really love Him more than wife, family and friends - is He really having first place in my life? Have I read into our former leading more than the Lord intends and is now the time for mutual sacrifice of personal interests? By dawn I had convinced myself that I should stay and Marjorie go on with

Hugh. We discussed the situation and, with a deep desire to be in the centre of the Lord's will, Marjorie agreed that after breakfast I should go to the Commandant of the Camp and have my name removed from the list of evacuees. Breakfast over I set out for the office but within a few yards was stopped by a message over the tannoy. It announced the names of the first to be evacuated and, possibly because of having a child with us, ours headed the list! The decision to stay had been made too late, the matter had been taken out of our hands. Within half an hour, for good or ill, we were on our way.

We had been given little information, other than the immediate destination would be Egypt and from there, transport by rail to Port Said where a boat bound for Britain would be available. The hot and stuffy flight terminated at Maadi Camp set in dreary sandy wastes lying some miles outside Cairo. The dusty bleakness of the site did nothing to raise spirits already depressed by disappointed hopes, fears of misunderstanding the Lord's will, apprehension concerning the future, and sheer physical tiredness. A brief siesta helped and as later in the day the Camp began to fill and friends arrived, life took on a rosier hue. These included Mrs. Ivy Knowles with her young son who, unknown to us, were to play a significant part in developments later in the day. Some visitors came out from Cairo, among them a small group from the assembly which met in Heliopolis who commented it was a pity we could not stay in Egypt and help the assemblies scattered throughout their country. Shortly after they left someone tuned in to the BBC Overseas Service just as the commentator made reference to the Palestinian situation. The item which gripped our attention concerned a question asked in Parliament that afternoon. A member, querying the reason for the evacuation, had asked if it were true that missionaries were among those being compelled to leave. To this the Government had given an unequivocal 'No'. This was shattering news for if it was correct we were where we had no reason to be. For us this news altered the situation completely and we could not help but think we had missed, or misunderstood, the Lord's guidance. At the same time we couldn't understand why I had been prevented from getting my name taken off the list, nor why the Lord had allowed us to be responsible for seeing little Hugh home to Britain.

We felt we were caught up in a situation beyond our control and the only action we could take was to pray.

We had no assurance that Egypt should be our final destination and the conviction grew that, if we had made a mistake, we would need to get back to where we had deviated from the Lord's path. Only then would He show us the next step ahead. Reaching that conclusion was easy but, how to get Hugh safely home, arrange for ourselves to stay temporarily in Egypt, and then obtain permission to return to Palestine proved a problem beyond our solving. But the Lord had His plans in hand. Ivy Knowles, saying Hugh would be a companion for Royston, offered to take him. A telephone call to Jerusalem secured the Fosters' agreement to this plan. Now we faced the problem of convincing the authorities we had been wrongly advised and had no intention of going any further. We were scheduled to go, visas to stay in Egypt were difficult to obtain - these required a definite address and we did not have one. Furthermore, we could not go back to Palestine without an address within a secure zone, and that would be an impossibility.

We stuck to the main point and set about demolishing the difficulties. Surely our places on the boat could easily be filled, no doubt the Consulate could help in obtaining visas, and the Cairo friends could supply an address. A phone call confirmed this, together with the assurance that accommodation would be available. With regard to returning to Jerusalem, this could be safely left in abeyance. Within a few days the requisite documentation had been completed. Provided with temporary visas we happily left the dusty Maadi Camp for the slightly less dusty streets of a Cairo suburb. We were also relieved when we heard of Hugh's safe arrival after what had been a very enjoyable voyage.

CHAPTER 10

Unexpected Odyssey

(Egypt - Palestine, 1947)

You will keep him in perfect peace,
whose mind is stayed on You (Isaiah 26:3).

The unplanned stay in Egypt brought us a new circle of friends who did their utmost to help us feel at home. The assembly premises in Heliopolis consisted of a ground floor flat in a three storey building and we were offered the use of one of its rooms which, for the next seven months, became sitting, dining, bed and store room. A Swiss missionary lady occupied another room and we amicably shared the kitchen and other facilities. The Wald family also opened their home to us and we were deeply indebted to them for their hospitality and wise counsel. Others gave us much assistance especially the Constantines. Their daughters gave freely of their time to assist us with Arabic grammar and reading. It was encouraging to meet people like this who urged us to apply ourselves to language study. So our first task had to be finding an efficient teacher or a school.

The American University in Cairo had been strongly recommended. The fees were considerably higher than the school in Jerusalem, but the Lord had made provision accordingly. One morning we were opening the mail when I suddenly exclaimed, "Here is an unusual letter. This person says he has met you and is now happy to send you a gift, but nothing is enclosed. Can you remember who he is?" Quickly scanning the letter Marjorie first of all shook her head, then recalled meeting someone on a train to Scotland who had expressed great interest in the account of our call and proposed missionary service. He had asked the usual question, "Which Society would we be joining?" and appeared to be somewhat bewildered by the reply. Apparently he had never heard of anyone approach missionary service simply looking directly to the Lord for guidance and provision and may have been a little dubious about the result. Just as the train arrived at his destination he asked for our address saying he might write to us and then, with a friendly good-bye, left and disappeared into the crowd. Marjorie appreciated the time of fellowship with another Christian but the memory of that encounter soon faded. Now came this letter and it became apparent his interest remained, though the absence of the mentioned gift had an air of mystery.

We assumed our benefactor must be absent minded and I casually commented, "Well, that is one letter we don't have to answer." My more courteous wife replied, "Indeed we do! We can at least thank him for his thoughtfulness." So, a letter of thanks was written and, to our astonishment, a reply came almost by return of post. In it was a gift which translated into today's figures would be around £9,000 and to say we were overwhelmed is an understatement. For us it came as a sign from the Lord that we were to make language study one of our priorities.

Therefore we were able to enroll for two parallel courses, one devoted entirely to reading and the other to classical grammar. Literary Arabic is known from Morocco to the Sudan, though dialects vary from country to country, usually getting closer to the classical form the nearer one gets to Saudi Arabia. As we had no intention of remaining in Egypt there seemed little point in learning the colloquial, on the other hand a good grasp of literary grammar would provide us with a good basis for any land in the Middle East. On considering the Middle East one had tended to assume that, where the same language and religion prevailed, the various countries would be similar in culture. However, it soon became clear that in Egypt we were encountering a different culture from Palestine. Fortunately we learnt this useful lesson in our early days and it prepared us for the differences we were to encounter later in Jordan, Syria and Lebanon. There were many other lessons for us to learn and our months in Egypt became a time of first experiences, enjoyable, amusing, annoying - but all invaluable.

Cairo remains vividly in our minds, partially due to its extreme contrasts. Large hotels and lovely buildings, some on tree lined roads and surrounded by delightful gardens, were less than a stone's throw from narrow lanes and meagre dwellings. Wide streets where shops, full of luxury goods and the latest fashions from east and west, were adjacent to local bazaars and stalls with fruit, vegetables, meat and sundry groceries all open to the sky and subject to the predatory attentions of a huge population of flies and their friends. Traffic always seemed to be in unmitigated confusion with limousines and rusty old bangers, overcrowded taxis and mule drawn carts, all competing for every inch of space amongst an uproar of blaring horns, cries of vendors, shouts of mule drivers and the frantic whistles of police trying to sort out seeming chaos. Pedestrian traffic had its drawback and, one soon learnt meekness did not have to combine with weakness when competing for a place on the pavement, or among a crowd waiting for a tram. Queuing systems simply did not exist - the one with the heaviest push got there first! Swarthy Egyptians, descendants of ancient Pharaohs, pale Europeans, black Sudanese and others of every shade between, thronged the streets in a variety of garb almost beyond description, whilst the air hummed with the murmur of a multitude of voices, talking, shouting, arguing in languages from around the world. Arriving at the haven of peace at the University became one of the day's pleasures.

Of the many hundreds of students attending the University we were the only ones enrolled for basic Arabic studies. We missed the friendship and challenge of other students but it guaranteed the undivided attention of our instructors. The reading sessions were conducted by a venerable, elderly Muslim sheikh who was the very epitome of graciousness. Never once did he show any signs of impatience and his attitude to Marjorie did not coincide with the traditional conception of a Muslim's towards women. He proposed the Gospel of Matthew as our text book and that our sessions consist of his reading a verse and our endeavouring to repeat it. He would then correct our pronunciation and diction, until a reasonable standard had been attained. By the end of the term Matthew's Gospel had been completed and the Sheikh's patient teaching, plus the valued help of the Constantines, resulted in our making good progress in reading. I happily admit Marjorie's pronunciation was better than mine, and this remained the case in years to come. The lessons in grammar were different and not quite so pleasant, partially because the tutor differed significantly from the calm and friendly Sheikh. A Coptic Christian, of rather rotund proportions, he oozed a certain amount of bombast. As he viewed our text books, he told us quite cheerfully he had never taught this subject before but, not to worry, he knew the subject well. He soon gave the impression of being unable to understand the text books, and he was certainly ignorant of the method of teaching Arabic to foreigners. The first day with him was one of those not easily forgotten. By the time he had endeavoured to explain in a variety of ways that a certain word was not a verb, even though it acted like a verb and, also, it had various sisters which acted in like fashion; and then added, 'do not worry it will all come clear some day', we were thoroughly confused. However matters settled down after a while and light began to dawn.

Lessons were followed by the long trek home and, as summer progressed, we became conscious of the weariness of the flesh as well as the mind. Tiredness from travel, study and heat during the day increased because getting a good night's sleep was so difficult. Our little room required the balcony door and window be left open if we were to get even a stirring of air. For security's sake the slatted shutters had to be fastened and the amount of air finding its way through on almost windless nights was minimal. Enough space remained though for midges and mosquitoes. The high pitched hum of a mosquito's wings, followed by the gentle feel of its presence on face or arm, is always enough to disturb anyone's dreams, whilst bites from unseen and unheard sand flies, can cause a maddening itch. Egypt, however, has another speciality guaranteed to disturb slumber. The dogs of Egypt are renowned for their howl. They are proficient in the hours of darkness and excel in the light of a silvery moon. The meeting place for our neighbours' dogs to perform their nocturnal programme always seemed to be a few yards from our room. Occasionally a well placed stone disturbed them but then, just as one began to drift into well deserved sleep, the chorus would resume. Rising heavy eyed in the morning one or the other would murmur, "I never slept a wink," but in fact, sheer weariness must have ensured a few hours of unconsciousness.

At this stage our contribution to active missionary effort could only be described as meagre. I had opportunities to participate in the English speaking assembly and made an occasional visit to an Arabic speaking one in town. My first visit to an Egyptian meeting was an eye opener, highlighting the vast difference between the ordered, quietly reverent, and sometimes staid, character of one bearing a British imprint, and the informality of a wholly Egyptian gathering. I arrived before the announced starting time and only then became aware this was more of a suggestion than a fixture. People wandered in as if time had no place in their reckoning, or in anyone else's for that matter. Even after the delayed start of an opening hymn and prayer, others arrived and sought a place on the already crowded benches. The opening exercise in itself proved to be a lesson in impromptu singing. There was no musical instrument and, after the opening line of a hymn had been read, someone commenced on whatever note he, or sometimes she, thought right and others followed to the best of their ability. Unfortunately, the opening note suggested various tunes to different people, resulting in the ensuing lines being sung in a variety of keys and with differing melodies in mind. Add to this the fact that many were illiterate and singing from memory, that volume, rather than harmony, appeared to be the aim, and you have all the ingredients for making the uninitiated foreigner wonder if he has strayed into bedlam by mistake. But there was no doubting the zeal, sincerity and joy of the believers nor could it be doubted they knew the content of the hymn. The fervour of their singing and the smiles on their faces indicated that the hardship, poverty, toil and day's problems had faded into insignificance as they felt drawn into the presence of the Lord.

Prayers were offered just as fervently and, though their contents were a mystery to me, there was no denying they prayed as those who knew their God. Then came the time for me to speak; not against a background of a quiet hush (or is it sometimes a spirit of resignation?) which pervades a gathering at home. The shuffling feet of latecomers, the women enjoying a brief chat, babies being nursed, young children strolling up the aisle, all continued unabated as, painfully conscious of my inexperience, I launched into my opening remarks. The interpreter's voice pierced the room, all eyes focussed on the front, a comparative silence prevailed and, feeling more confident, I spoke for a few minutes, but then disaster struck. The interpreter hesitated, gulped out some comment and, looking ghastly pale, staggered to a chair. Then a few moments later, groaning, "I am ill," he got up and left the building. Fortunately for me all was not lost. Another interpreter took over and the meeting ran its normal, somewhat chaotic, course with many a hearty amen at the end. On my future visits I came to appreciate, and enjoy, the uninhibited atmosphere and freedom of worship amongst men and women whose Christian testimony was a light, feeble though it might seem to be, amongst the darkness of Islam.

Marjorie had her own introduction to the problems, and joys, of seeking to reach under-privileged women with the Gospel when Jeanne Constantine invited her to join in a visit to a shanty town on the outskirts of the city. A normal tram ride into town was followed by a short walk to a wide irrigation canal where her new experiences began. The only means of crossing was a ferry consisting merely of a large wooden platform devoid of guard rails, or any signs of safety devices, immediately besieged by an uncontrolled crowd, all of whom are determined not to be left behind. Jeanne and Marjorie managed to get somewhere near the centre of the primitive craft which tilted precariously as more and more crowded on. Finally, when even the most optimistic could find no place on which to rest a foot, the craft pushed off and slowly pulled its way across. Arriving safely, a short walk along a dirt track brought the ladies to the outskirts of the town. Marjorie had experienced nothing like what faced her now. The shanty town was a vast huddle of hovels created from any sort of material which could be induced to stand up or lie flat - petrol tins, wooden crates, sheets of cardboard, rusty sheets of corrugated iron or lengths of ancient plastic. Narrow unpaved alleyways intersected the whole town, and the feet of donkeys, mules and men stirred clouds of dust which, caught up on a breeze, coated the traveller and filtered through unsealed doors and windows depositing a film on all within.

Stepping carefully to avoid the accumulation of filth in the central gutters, they finally arrived at their destination. The double warmth of their welcome could not be doubted. The warmth of the women's greeting left nothing to be desired but the oppressive heat of the room and unaccustomed odours almost suffocated the senses. The heat increased as neighbours crowded in to meet the guests, and the customary chat which would precede the main spiritual object of the visit, got under way. From outside came the usual village noises, children playing, animals giving voice, men talking - then suddenly, commotion and a noise of heavy thuds on hovel doors. A few moments later the door swung open and to Marjorie's surprise a number of uniformed men carrying equipment for spraying an insecticide appeared. Egypt is, or was, often plagued with hordes of disease-bearing insects and fly borne ailments were a common feature of the summer months. The health department sought to minimise the possibility of plague with sudden forays into certain areas to disinfect both place and people, and this day happened to coincide with one of these unexpected visits. So, whether the inhabitants of the place liked it or not they, their belongings, and their guests were smothered in powder. In spite of the discomfort, with temperature nearing 100 F, the ladies managed to fulfill the purpose of their visit. Then, thankfully, they commenced the long journey home, there to the luxury of a cooling shower.

This period in Egypt also gave us our first experience of the fast of Ramadan. It began about the end of July and coincided with longish days, as well as the hottest, most stifling, period of the year. As soon as the feeble daylight enabled one to discern the difference between a white and black thread, the day of fasting began and, from dozens of mosques, the cries echoed out calling the faithful to rise, pray and fast. Then from the cooler hours of dawn, through the fierce heat of the sunlit day and into the haze-tinged evening, every Muslim over twelve, bound by the tenets of Islam, refrained from all food and drink. Except for the lengthy midday siesta, business and life in general carried on but before the end of the twenty eight days of fast, emotional strains took their toll. One soon understood why a vast shout re-echoed across the city when the boom of the evening gun signalled sunset. Then the the evening meal could be enjoyed and a night of fellowship with family and friends begun, only to be followed by a few hours of sleep and again the cry, rise and pray. The fervour with which Muslims kept the fast impressed us but, at the same time, we began to appreciate why this period is a danger for the Muslim converted to faith in Christ Jesus. Many a Muslim who has yielded his life to the Lordship of Christ has been tolerated until the time of Ramadan. Then, if he broke the fast, he came into conflict with Islamic law and, therefore, could be declared an apostate. As such he faced being ostracised by all, and even considered a rightful target for the assassin.

These experiences were an excellent introduction to missionary life in Egypt, especially amongst the fellaheen. We knew the assemblies would appreciate help, and there existed a vital need for workers amongst both Muslims and Copts, but we felt no urge from the Lord to remain in the country. This caused misunderstanding amongst some of our friends. Senior missionaries, who often spent part of the winter months visiting among the assemblies, were at this time on furlough and they wrote seeking to impress upon us the golden opportunity we had to stay in Egypt. God, they believed, had miraculously opened the door for us to enter, then why not stay? Friends in Cairo made similar comments and, whilst emphasising the great need of the small assemblies in the regions of Upper Egypt, pointed out that the worsening situation in Palestine seemed to preclude any possibility of returning there. All this drove us to pray the Lord would make our pathway clear. During these weeks of language study we periodically visited the British Consulate to seek permission to return to Palestine. These visits were stimulated by news from the Fosters that accommodation was available in one of the compounds, but each one brought the same negative response.

The reasons for the unrest in Palestine in 1947 are not generally known. The British Government, finding it impossible to harmonise the promises made to both the Arabs and the Zionists, declared its intention of handing the Palestinian mandate back to the United Nations, the successor to the League of Nations. They in turn proposed partitioning the land between Arab and Jew with an enclave around Jerusalem being kept under United Nations control. A resolution, passed by a majority vote, stated the scheme should be put into effect the day Britain relinquished the Mandate during the early part of 1948. Neither the Arabs nor the Zionists were happy at having any arrangement forced upon them, and two Jewish terror groups, the Haganah and the Stern gang, stepped up their activities against the British hoping this would force them to increase the scale of Jewish immigration and so ensure the Jews had a greater claim upon the land. The Arabs were bitterly opposed to that idea and, believing the British were favouring the Jews, eagerly waited for the time when they could take the situation into their own hands and, in so doing, circumvent Zionist aspirations. In spite of this deteriorating situation, the conviction we should return remained, though we were beginning to appreciate a coming conflict would determine where we could locate.

About this time, for some inexplicable reason, our thoughts began to turn to the country beyond the river Jordan. We knew little about the land other than it was reputed to be rather barren, inhospitable, backward, sparsely populated, and the home of fierce Bedouin tribes. George Wald of the Nile Mission Press, had made colporteur visits there in the 1930s but for us to go would be a plunge into the unknown. With Transjordan figuring largely in our thoughts we earnestly prayed for guidance. How could we be sure the thoughts were from the Lord and not the result of a desire to avoid being involved in the Palestinian conflict? The answer was not long in coming. A letter arrived from a Mr. Robson who, many months before, had sternly warned us of the necessity of being guided by the Lord and not by emotions. No way could he have known our thoughts concerning Transjordan but, with surprise and awe we read his comments: "If you are unable to stay in Jerusalem, why not consider moving to Amman where there is already a small company of Arab believers?" He then mentioned the name of one of them and assured us that it would be easy to locate him seeing he occupied the position of chief clerk to General Glubb Pasha, the Commander of the renowned Arab Legion. We took this as a sign from the Lord indicating we would, at some time, be involved in His work in that land.

Shortly after receiving Mr. Robson's letter, we had the first intimation it could soon be a reality. The Fosters confirmed we could stay with them and, armed with this permission to reside in one of the compounds, we presented ourselves at the British Consulate. Within a few days we were requested to collect our Palestinian visas, and at last we thought we were on our way. Tin trunks, by now battered and splitting at the seams, were mended and filled, letters sent flying to Britain and Jerusalem announcing the date of our departure, a farewell round of visits began - and then, everything changed. First came a rumour that cases of cholera had been diagnosed, then confirmation of the disease spreading, followed by reports that a whole area had been affected and, later, the announcement of restrictions on movement between certain villages and the city. Fear of the disease spreading caused nearby countries to clamp down on cross border traffic. There could be no possibility now of travelling before being inoculated and, as this involved two injections at an interval of three or four weeks, we were compelled to wait. In the meantime the disease spread in spite of the determined efforts of the authorities to stem it. How the cholera began no one seemed to know, though finally its source was traced to a certain village. It transpired that a pilgrim returning from Mecca had been so keen for fellow villagers to share the water brought from the holy well of ZemZem, he poured the contents of his bottle into the local well, with disastrous results. No one suggested the possibility of the original water being infected, but blamed the bottle, saying it must have been previously contaminated. Five weeks later the situation improved but by that time our inoculations had been completed and we were at long last back in Jerusalem.

The Foster's home was situated in what had been, in pre-war days, the German colony. The area was now surrounded with barbed wire and official access points were few, though anyone bent on nefarious deeds found other ways both in and out. The language school on the Street of the Prophets still functioned and, within a few days, the daily routine of morning lessons resumed. The journey was now entirely on foot and sometimes with an increased element of danger. Jerusalem gradually divided itself into two distinct sections in which either Jew or Arab predominated. One part of our route lay in full view of a fanatical Jewish settlement and the other was overlooked by an area occupied mainly by Arabs. Occasionally firing would break out between the two, causing us to shelter behind an embankment as we carefully proceeded on our way. Then, having arrived in town, we turned away from the Old City to enter the more distinctively Jewish section. At first no obvious dividing line existed but gradually one came into being and, before long, a definite no man's land developed. The antagonism, from both sides, resulted in two unofficial barriers a few yards apart through which one passed under scrutiny of self appointed guards. We found it amusing to see such men holding one's passport very officiously, scrutinising it carefully with furrowed brow, and then handing it back with a gruff, "You can go!" without realising the document was being held upside down! Danger sometimes lurked even within the compound, a fact brought home to us one very dark night as shots rang out close by the house. How close only became clear when a visitor mentioned the pool of blood at our garden gate.

Like everyone else living in Palestine at that time, we were likely to find ourselves, quite unwittingly, in dangerous situations. Some friends of ours were responsible for the management of a Mission to Mediterranean Garrisons' canteen at a camp in Sarafand near Lydda and, occasionally, we had a restful weekend there. Normally we travelled by bus but, for one return trip, a Christian officer offered us a lift in an empty Army truck. There was no room for us in the cab, nor any seats in the rear, but we were quite comfortable squatting on the floor sheltered by the canopy from the burning sun. Being a time when vehicles were occasionally blown off the road by terrorist land mines, we were very pleased to reach the outskirts of Jerusalem without incident. Then the lorry halted and, judging by an animated discussion up front, the driver was seeking directions. A minute or two later we stopped again but, this time, a couple of well armed men came poking round the back and peered intently at us with anything but friendly looks. After a brief pause they commanded the driver to go on and, as the truck slowly proceeded, we were aware of an atmosphere of tension. Everywhere seemed to be unusually quiet, the normally busy road devoid of traffic, pedestrians stopped and turned round to stare, the pace of the truck indicated the driver had reason to be nervous and then, as the truck halted again, and more armed men came searching round the back, we wondered if we ought to begin to feel nervous as well! But we were commanded to move on and, as we did at snail's pace, a scene reminiscent of the bombing in London came into view. Down a side road was a scene of devastation where men scurried around in the rubble of a bombed building, no doubt seeking for survivors. Another barricade, manned this time by uniformed men, delayed us for a few moments and soon we were home, safe and well. That evening our officer friend phoned to explain he had been soundly reprimanded for passing along that particular road. The bombed building had been a Jewish Hotel and the perpetrators of the deed had been in apparently British uniforms. A Jewish paramilitary group, so incensed by the atrocity, had declared they would blow up any Army vehicle passing through that particular area. Later we learned that two vehicles previous to ours had suffered such attacks. Once again we were deeply grateful to the Lord for His protecting hand.

In spite of alarms and excursions we were very happy in Jerusalem and enjoyed the times spent at the language school. Unfortunately, they came to an end all too soon. The Jews made the Street of the Prophets out of bounds to our Arab teachers so, early in November 1947 all classes were suspended. Whilst the walk to and from school had its problems it also gave us much pleasure, especially the walk home when a detour enabled us to savour the atmosphere of the Old City. In time we became familiar with many sites which spoke of the Saviour, and never tired of the walk through the bustling Damascus Gate, onto and along the Via Dolarosa, into Christian Street and then, passing near David's tower, out at Jaffa Gate and then on home beneath the city's frowning walls. Occasionally we found time to turn aside into the Garden Tomb where, in the quietness of its precincts, one could feel in a special way the peace of the Lord. We came to love that Garden and one of our delights on a Sunday morning was to meditate amongst its beauty prior to attending the service of worship and remembrance. Across the Jordan Valley, the deep clefted, mysterious looking range of the mountains of Moab, came into view. Each season they looked different; from grandeur, slightly blurred in the haze of the summer sun, to grimness, as winter wreathed the craggy heights with ever darkening storm clouds. In each changing month the range from which Moses viewed the promised land, possessed a certain beauty but never more so than in the evening light of a clear December day. A veil, tinged with blue, would hang over the scene, only to fade as the sun dipped towards the west and its rays gilded the slopes until, finally, the lofty hills were transformed by a kaleidoscope of oranges, golds and reds culminating in a burst of purple.

CHAPTER 11

Transjordan Foray

(1947)

I will lead them in paths they have not known
(Isaiah 42:16).

Those mountains of Moab gripped our interest for beyond them lay the land towards which our thoughts were turning. Various accounts of the country painted a rather depressing and, as we discovered later, false picture of the land and the people - more uncultivated and undeveloped than Palestine, home to fierce, horse riding Bedouin tribes, herders of sheep and camels who followed ancient life styles, Muslims forming 95% of the population. That they were very resistant to the Gospel could also not be denied. But the existence of numerous settled villages, small Orthodox and Catholic Christian communities, and an Arab hospitality untainted by the corrupting effects of westernisation rarely had a mention. Eventually we decided the only way to discover if there could be an opening for missionary work would be to go and see for ourselves. Two friends, Dr. Graham Gillan, an eye surgeon working at St. John's Hospital, Jerusalem, and Noel Allen, serving with the Mission to Mediterranean Garrisons at Sarafand, expressed interest in Transjordan, or rather Jordan as it is now known, and agreed to join in an exploratory visit.

Both could spare only a week so we mapped out a route which would enable us to see as much of the country as possible in that time. Our first night stop would be in Jordan's capital, the ancient city of Rabbah Ammon where Uriah the Hittite had fought and died on behalf of David. From there, subject to public transport being available, we would go south to Ma'an and then retrace our steps northward through Amman, visit Irbid and return to Jerusalem via the region of Galilee. Service taxis taking six passengers plied frequently between Jerusalem and Amman so that part of the trip presented no problem. We found the journey fascinating, first down the winding road to Jericho then across the Jordan and up the long, steep, twisting climb to the town of Es Salt, sinister looking as it huddled in a side valley beneath the gloomy shadow of precipitous cliffs. A further snaking climb brought us to the edge of a plateau where the barren land, thirsting for the early rains, stretched away to the north east, unrelieved for miles by any sign of hedge, fence, hill, dale or village. The road now ran more or less straight and, with the driver putting on speed, barely half an hour passed before a straggling dun coloured village indicated the presence of a more inhabited area and, within a few minutes, the road dipped steeply and revealed a panoramic view of the capital, already spreading over its surrounding hills. Today Amman is a thriving city of over a million inhabitants, with wide, well made roads, heavy with traffic, threading their way across those same hills and far beyond. It is hard to recall the Amman of former days when the population, we were told, hardly exceeded twenty five thousand, and its main streets, lined with open shops and bustling with pedestrians, donkeys and the occasional camel, hardly allowed room for a car to nose through.

For accommodation, one of us knew of the Bishop's School, a missionary establishment founded by the Church Missionary Society. Our visit happened to coincide with a holiday and the school bore a deserted look, but the Principal was in residence and, though not being sure who we were and what we hoped to achieve by our visit, gave us a warm welcome. He kindly offered us a night's lodgings, if we did not mind sleeping on settees, and during breakfast gave good advice on how to get around the country. He also whetted our tourist appetite by mentioning the partially excavated site of Jerash; the Gerasa of the Bible. So, being assured the return trip could easily be done in a day, we decided to visit immediately, and, in so doing, quickly learned the vagaries of travel to villages outside the capital. Locating a bus and discovering its proposed time of departure was easy, but waiting for its actual departure proved a trial, especially to the patience of those influenced by western ideas of punctuality. We boarded a derelict looking vehicle, more people crowded in, then the overloaded vehicle seemed to groan as we pulled away, but almost immediately came to an abrupt halt as the cry of a belated traveller rent the air. Cluttered with baggage he was hauled aboard and at last, we were rattling our way out of town.

Some two hours later the entrance to ancient Gerasa hove into view. For most of the way the bus had bumped and swayed over an unsurfaced dry, dusty, and sometimes rock strewn, road which wound its tortuous way over barren hills and through seemingly waterless valleys. Here and there clusters of dwellings, sometimes shaded by clumps of stunted trees, gave evidence of underground streams whilst large, empty threshing floors spoke of past harvests and hopes centred on abundant early and latter rains. We travelled on, raising a cloud of dust which enveloped the vehicle. On three occasions, the engine gave up the struggle and died. At those times the driver and his friends appeared to have a slanging match before some tool or other, aided by wire and string came into operation, and then, with a crashing of gears, we would be off again. Whether the string fastened some hidden part or merely held down the bonnet remained a mystery. We were in the area of the Decapolis, that large territory occupied centuries ago by the Greeks and the Romans, where a sophisticated civilisation had flourished. Abraham moved across these hills with his flocks and herds, as he slowly journeyed from Haran to Canaan. His grandson Jacob wrestled throughout the night with the Angel of God on the banks of this selfsame Jabbok.

It did not take long to discover that very few tourists arrived in Jerash by local transport. Our westernised dress drew general attention, particularly from youngsters, many of whom clamoured to act as guides, and promptly attached themselves to us. However, deeply interested though we were in the extensive ruins of the ancient city there were other priorities. First we needed to slake our thirst and then check the time the bus returned to Amman. In both cases we were in for a surprise. Jerash boasted neither hotel nor eating place, and the bus would not return until the following day. Our informant had forgotten to warn us of the former and may have been ignorant of the latter. In Jordan the village buses stayed at home for the night then, very early in the day travelled to the city and returned at some vaguely appointed time after midday; and that was that. Fortunately the village store supplied bread, cheese and cola and, after some haggling, the owner of what may well have been the only car in the village, agreed to take us back to Amman.

Back in Amman we enquired about transport to Petra and, discovering there would be a train next day to Ma'an, due to return the day following, decided that would be our best mode of travel. Early next morning we were at the station, watching an engine far more ancient than the bus of the previous day, marshalling some trucks and a passenger coach seemingly more ancient still. By this time delays no longer surprised us and, in fact, thought we did well to get away within an hour of scheduled departure. For the first mile or so, speed seemed to be the order of the day but, gradually, the train slowed as the puffing engine hauled its load up the steep gradient out of Amman. Just as it seemed as if all movement must cease it breasted the slope, gave another blast on its whistle, and began to eat up the miles. The line now crossed a vast barren plateau in the region of the old Moabite town of Madaba. Apart from the Azrak oasis to the east, whatever villages and towns existed lay out of sight away to the west and, apart from an occasional group of hovels where the train took on water, life appeared to revolve around the black tented encampments of Bedouin.

During our wanderings in Petra we encountered a group of British soldiers and, as they were returning to Amman the following day, it was suggested that we might accompany them. When one of them mentioned their very dusty ride down to Petra, Dr. Gillan pointed out that another route which followed the crest of the mountains, might be better. This, the old road referred to in Numbers as the Kings' Highway, led through Edom into Moab and on to the land of the Ammorites. Moses and the children of Israel desired to travel that way to the land of Caanan, but the king of Edom would not allow them to enter his territory. After much discussion the officer agreed to take that road and shortly after dawn we commenced a memorable journey.

At some time, now long past, the road would have been well

kept and frequently traversed but, like many roads in the country, it had fallen into disrepair and, consequently, speed had to be severely restricted for our transport consisting of a truck and a jeep. There was a wild beauty as the road, twisting and turning, rising and falling, followed the contour of hills and valleys through sparsely inhabited land. But as the day wore on, our friends became anxious about reaching Amman before dark. All went well for a while but, as the light faded, the track became less and less distinct and a signless parting of the way helped to complicate the situation. By this time billowing clouds had obscured the stars and, as the officer now discovered he had an ineffective compass, progress became a matter of guess work. The driver of the jeep simply chose what he thought looked like a track and the truck lumbered on behind. Down hills and across dry stony river beds we rocked and jolted only to climb just as steeply again, with both jeep and truck leaning at such extreme angles it seemed they must finish on their sides. By midnight it became clear we were hopelessly lost and wisdom dictated bivouacking till sunrise. So making do as best we could with cushions and other items from the vehicles some of us sought sleep in the open and the rest sheltered in the truck, How Jacob endured a stone for a pillow I do not know; he must have been much tougher than us.

At dawn we reconnoitered for landmarks. Only then, as we surveyed the terrain around our resting place, did we know how closely we had courted disaster. Not a vestige of a road graced the side of the hills down which we must have come, the tracks nothing more than those made by sheep and goats! A few minutes walk from our resting place a string of telegraph poles was seen edged against the sky line. Within an hour the vehicles had been maneuvered from their inappropriate situation onto a definite track and were heading towards the safety of Amman.

Irbid in the north was our next objective, mainly to visit the village of El Husn. An intrepid missionary lady, Miss Coates, of the Church Missionary Society, maintained a lonely witness in that area. Quite graciously she sought to discourage us from any idea of moving into Jordan. Irbid, apparently, had the reputation of being a fanatical town, both politically and religiously, and the small Christian community, Catholic, Orthodox and Protestant, some five per cent in all, led a precarious existence. Next morning, sharing a taxi with three others, we descended from the hills of Gilead into the Jordan Valley and the region of Galilee. The only hitch of the day came at the Palestinian border post. My visa, obtained in Egypt to return to Palestine, did not permit permanent residence. Not realising this I had left without obtaining a return visa and this resulted in my re-entry being refused. At first the British official was, to say the least, unhelpful, but in due course entry was granted and we were on our way to Tiberias. There a visit to missionaries at the Scottish Mission hospital, provided us with more insight into missionary enterprise in Palestine. As we completed our return to Jerusalem along well paved roads, through extensively cultivated land and the modern town of Haifa, one realised afresh the need for clear guidance before facing life in the lands east of the Jordan.

Back in Jerusalem with the language school closed we found ourselves at a loose end. We endeavoured to make good use of our time by studying Arabic at home but were not sufficiently advanced to progress far without expert guidance. Our fellowship with the English speaking assembly continued. Whilst warmly welcoming all nationalities, it would always be a foreign group separated by language and culture from the national population. For a vibrant spiritual work to grow it must, even though commenced by a worker from another land, have its roots in, and be nourished by, those converted from amongst the indigenous population. Much zealous missionary work has been crippled by a layer of culture drawn from the missionary's own background, as if one's own culture is the only way in which Christianity can be expressed. The ideal missionaries are not only those who can, 'sit where they sit', but are humble enough to work themselves out of a job, and then co-operate with those they have been privileged to bring to the Lord.

When, in its wisdom, the Council of the United Nations decided to partition Palestine into Jewish and Arab States, it contemplated retaining Jerusalem and its environs under its own control as neutral territory. We were therefore, not surprised when a number of letters arrived from outside the country urging us to stay in Jerusalem on the assumption this would give freedom to visit both Arab and Jewish areas. People, certainly in England and America, failed to realise both the depth of the animosity between Zionism and the Palestinian Arabs and the tremendous significance of Jerusalem to both parties. This was crystal clear to anyone living in Jerusalem, and made the idea of either Jew or Arab permitting a neutral zone seem naive, almost laughable. As 1947 drew towards its close violence increased. Arab politicians, believing they would then be free to impede any Zionist plans to take over the country, wanted the British out of the way as soon as possible. With war in view, their leaders encouraged civilians to leave so as not to hinder the movement of any armies which would come to aid the Palestinians.

Not only nationals but many foreigners decided the time had come to leave, among them a lady who for many years managed the bookshop owned by the Nile Mission Press. The decision had been taken to close the shop, and Miss Davidson's need of assistance in checking, listing and packing stock provided us with a very interesting, though temporary, occupation, and helped develop our interest in the value of literature as a handmaid to many aspects of missionary endeavour. Unbeknown to us, the foundation was being laid for a literature ministry of far reaching proportions in years ahead. The shop closed and a vital form of service ceased, to be resurrected later in another Arab land.

So 1947 came to a stormy close. The Palestine Police Force, together with the British Military, managed to maintain a semblance of order but it was obvious to all a fierce conflict loomed on the horizon. Britain, having declared her intention of resigning the Mandate in Spring 1948, now had concern for only two things: how to leave a semblance of orderly Government in office and how to withdraw her troops with a minimum of casualties. The Zionists sought to increase the flow of Jews mainly from holding camps in Cyprus, into areas around Haifa and Tel Aviv. The Palestinians, supported by surrounding Arab states, declared their intention of driving the Jews into the sea as soon as the British removed their troops. Our conviction increased that if we were to serve the Lord amongst Arabic speaking people, then east of Jordan must be our home.

CHAPTER 12

Into Jordan

(1948)

Fear not, for I am with you; be not dismayed, for I am your God (Isaiah 41:10).

Cold winds swept the streets and the feel of snow was in the air as we hurried through the Old City and out of Damascus gate. A few minutes later, sharing a car with five others, we crossed the Kidron, passed Gethsemane, climbed the slope to Bethany and finally headed down the winding road to Jericho en-route to Amman. As we passed out of the gate on that bleak January morning the scars of Gordon's Calvary, looming large and grim before us, seemed to speak more of death than of the glorious hope demonstrated by the empty tomb resting at its feet. Sadly, for many, the New Year would usher in times of tribulation and distress. Fear had gripped many lives and scores of Arab families were on the move to the relative peace east of the Jordan whilst, in the predominantly Jewish areas, anxiety mounted as the prospect increased of facing the might of the united Arab armies. The Zionists, their numbers swollen by thousands who had survived the holocaust, were confident of sympathy and material help from the west. The Arabs had promises of support from Syria, Iraq, Transjordan and Egypt whose armies claimed to be ready for the fiercest of conflicts and whose commanders believed that they could not fail to sweep their Jewish opponents off the map.

To us it appeared to be sensible to move in the direction of the Arab lands, but how could we be sure we would be moving in line with the Lord's plan for our lives? On that January morning we were on our way to Amman trusting the answer would be revealed through a personal visit. Our specific prayer was, "Lord, if You want us in Transjordan please guide us to suitable housing at a reasonable price." If our visit drew a blank we would presume we were meant to stay in some town or village west of the Jordan. We hadn't a clue about finding and renting property in Amman. My only contact had been the director of the CMS Bishop's School and we had no right to impose our concerns upon him, but we had been advised to get in touch with Roy and Dora Whitman, independent missionaries who had served the Lord in Transjordan for many years.

The winding road plunged down into the Jordan valley and, leaving behind the delightful oasis of Jericho and the meandering Jordan, the car climbed the steep gorge leading upwards to the scattered town of Es Salt, darkly grey in the shadow of towering cliffs. Neither of us felt drawn to Es Salt and certainly had no inclination to reside there. For part of the journey we must have followed ways familiar to Jesus and His disciples, been within a stone's throw of sites familiar to prophets and kings of long ago, whilst the way now before us may well have echoed to the marching feet of David's armies, burning to avenge the insults of the King of Ammon against their sovereign. With excitement and trepidation as we faced another step in our missionary career, memories of Israel's ancient exploits and tragedies mingled with the expectation of serving the Lord amongst descendants of her previous enemies. Suddenly we saw the site of ancient Rabbah Amman spreading out before us. Deep in a valley through which the headwaters of the Jabbok threaded a silvery way, and surrounded by seven terraced hills dotted with dwellings, lay the expanding town of modern Amman. In the centre of narrow shop-lined streets rose the main mosque's dome and minaret and, almost within its shadow, our taxi came to rest. Stepping out we were bewildered by the milling crowd thronging the street, and partially deafened by the mingled noise of horns, engines, vendors and, above all, the sound of myriad voices in a strange tongue. Would we, could we, ever feel at home here?

The Whitmans lived out of town in the vicinity of the railway station so another taxi had to be hired. The driver assured us he knew the address but, having arrived in the region of the station, he had to ask for directions and then deposited us half way up a hill near a group of ramshackle buildings, a mixture of wood, corrugated iron and stone. Wondering where amongst the huddle of dwellings the Whitmans lived, we also had to ask for help and were directed up a narrow passage and a rough set of steps, where we found ourselves at the door of a one storey, flat roofed, wooden building. Our knock brought to the door a tall, broad shouldered gentleman, armed it seemed with a table lamp. Apparently the lamp had been giving trouble and our knock, possibly to his annoyance, interrupted an attempt to coax it back to life The announcement of our names brought a look of surprise; due to a breakdown in communications we had arrived on the wrong day! However, with true Arab courtesy, we were invited in and found ourselves in the company of two of God's choice servants. Inconvenient though the time of our visit might have been, they did their utmost to make us feel at home and willingly assisted in the locating of accommodation. We have always been conscious of owing them a debt of gratitude for their subsequent friendship, guidance and care.

Their small home was not overburdened with comforts and amenities. Roy had been in Jordan since 1926 and was joined by Dora shortly after their marriage ten years later. They were tremendous workers and the Lord had blessed their ministry abundantly, and continued to do so for many years to come. Skilled in language and culture and, loving the Arabs devotedly, they gave of their best for the Lord and delighted in encouraging others who had a similar burden. As far as we were concerned there could not have been better senior missionaries to guide us on our way. Being completely devoid of any links with a mission society they truly lived in dependence upon the Lord for all things, and their ability to continue in the work for so many years, was an outstanding testimony to God's faithfulness.

During the weekend Roy guided us all over Amman, uphill and downhill, from large stone built houses to sparse rooms in squalid back streets, but nowhere could we discover what we could call home. Two factors militated against us, the first being finance and the second increasing pressure on the housing stock. The flood of well heeled Palestinians moving home, decreased availability and pushed up rents, whilst the sight of foreigners automatically doubled the price! Late Saturday afternoon after nearly a week of searching we arrived back at the Whitmans' haven tired, somewhat perplexed, but still hopeful for positive results in the next twenty four hours. Sunday, both morning and afternoon, we met with Arab believers and thoroughly appreciated their times of worship, though we were completely lost as far as language was concerned. During the day Roy made further enquiries about accommodation but to no avail and, by evening, we were feeling God's answer to a proposed move to Amman would be a definite no.

Monday morning we packed our bag half convinced our journey had been futile, apart from the pleasure of meeting Roy and Dora and experiencing the warmth of the Arab fellowship. We found it difficult to accept we had misunderstood the Lord's leading, yet the sign we needed had not been granted. Our conversation tended towards the question, 'What next?' when Roy, who had been out making further enquiries, cut it short. Hurrying in, he excitedly said he had just seen a place which might be suitable, and then immediately threw cold water on his own idea by adding, "But I don't think you will want to live there." There could only be one answer to that statement - go and see, and so we did. A few minutes walk uphill, and along a short track, took us beyond the last house in the colony and there, many feet down a rough slope, stood an isolated and forlorn-looking shack. From the back it looked rather like a small barn with a corrugated iron roof, and a mixture of mud and straw plaster, wooden slats and flattened petrol tins for walls. One small barred window pierced the wall and at one end the pitched roof gave way to a lower one of metal, held down by large chunks of stone. Altogether it seemed a most unsuitable place but, on going round the side and passing through a door onto a small balcony we both immediately declared, "This is it." Maybe the open view across and down the valley influenced us but whatever it was, the place seemed to speak of home.

There were only three rooms, one with a tiled floor which sloped as if that area could at any time plunge down the hillside, but the two others, floored with solid looking concrete, seemed to give a sense of stability. The interior walls were mud and straw plaster, and ceilings made from sheets of hardboard concealed the corrugated iron roof. There was no sign of a kitchen, or a shower, or a toilet, but we were assured water was piped to the building and there would be no problem providing those amenities. The landlord would simply add an extension to make a kitchen and a toilet: the matter of a shower seemed to be forgotten. Once the promise had been given that within a month the additions would be made, we decided to go ahead and struck a deal. The rent, to be paid in advance, was fixed at £84 a year, at that time somewhat more than that of a decent three bedroom house in Britain. With the agreement made, we set off again for Jerusalem, pleased with the arrangements and keenly looking forward to occupying our own home in just over a month. Little did we know then that in the Arab's view of time, the promise of something being done in four weeks really meant there was no hurry to do anything at all! Only after some pressure from Roy were the promised additions commenced, and even then, tardy progress meant they were finished only a few hours before we and our furniture arrived.

Our first home in Amman

By February, the tension in Palestine became such that familie
were leaving in droves, either to Lebanon, Syria or Transjordar
and restrictions were placed on the movement of traffic and lorries
especially carrying household goods. An Arab brother agreed t
transport our goods, though he took a very negative prospect c
our getting through, and in any case, felt quite sure some of ou
goods would be looted in transit. In spite of this gloom
prognostication we loaded up. Marjorie travelled by service ca
and myself in the back of the uncovered lorry hoping to ensur
nothing disappeared into unauthorised hands. Our journeys wer
uneventful, Marjorie's quick and mine the reverse. Apart fron
delays in the crowded streets of Jericho and the inevitable dela
at custom posts, the lorry merely crawled, especially up the hill
until at last, we rattled slowly into Amman.

The centre of the town was chock a block with traffic forcing th
lorry to come to a standstill. The wheels had barely stopped turnin
before we were surrounded by a small group of shouting
gesticulating, rough looking men with coils of rope slung over thei
shoulders. Some climbed on the running board by the cab, other
clung to the side of the vehicle, whilst the driver seemed to pus
out his hand to fend off the invaders. The traffic moved and so di
we accompanied by the men, some of whom began to climb int
the back, whilst I got busy indicating I had no desire for thei
presence. Some vigorous comments, in very broken Arabic, plu
a few taps on hands clutching the sides of the lorry, got rid of mos
but, knowing help would be needed in unloading, I let one stay
Being ignorant of local custom I was unaware the driver woul
have no intention of doing anything so undignified as humpin
luggage, nor did I know that when he pushed out his hand, rathe
than trying to repel men he had been indicating he needed at leas
three! His dismay when we finally arrived and discovered only on
porter, was wonderful to behold! To give him his due, as soon a
Roy arrived to help unloading, he buckled in as well. He ha
tremendous respect for Roy, and no doubt felt his dignity woul
not suffer too much if he followed his example. Marjorie's valian
efforts before we arrived had ensured the floors were clean an
almost dry and, with the bulk of the furniture scattered around, th
shack looked more like a home. With no cooking facilitie

immediately available we appreciated the Whitman's hospitable offer of lunch. Then it was back to unpack and arrange as much as possible before darkness fell and we resorted to our first evening of living by lamplight.

Desperately tired and anticipating a night of refreshing sleep, we retired early but a multitude of thoughts, and the strangeness of our surroundings, kept us both awake. Finally drowsiness took over and a delightful relaxed feeling began to pervade - until I, and at the same time Marjorie, felt an uncomfortable crawly itch. The sense of something parading round my neck had me reaching for the torch while Marjorie sat bolt upright and, in a tone of almost awed wonder, said something like, "My word, look at that!!" I looked at the wall behind the bedhead and lo, down its whitish surface, crawled a great hoard of bed bugs out for a midnight feast. The ceiling must have been host to a nest of the little horrors and the thought of fresh blood must have given them immeasurable delight. We had been warned there could be a few bugs around (masterly understatement) and a few blasts of a spray had the foe on the run. Next morning we treated the wall again and, apart from an odd one or two, had no further trouble from that source. The experience confirmed we had been wise in accepting a gift of an old fashioned metal-framed bed which remained bug free.

Making the morning cup of tea highlighted the fact that living would be rather unsophisticated. All lighting and cooking depended upon paraffin or bottled gas and, as we couldn't afford the appliances for the latter, our illumination depended on oil lamps of varying sizes most of which emitted more black smoke than light. The one luxury was an Aladdin lamp which, with a mantle covering the wick, gave a much whiter light. But this could also give off smoke signals and, as the mantles were brittle, they disintegrated at the slightest touch. Later, when finance permitted, we upgraded to two pressure lamps and welcomed their more brilliant light even though accompanied by a constant hiss. Our original cooking equipment consisted of a medium sized primus stove and a rather old oven heated by two wick burners. These, if not adjusted to exactly the right height or in the slightest draught, would turn from a beautiful blue flame to a murky yellow and fill the whole contraption with oily soot. An anguished cry from the kitchen of,

"Oh no, not again!" became an indication of a ruined meal and another cleaning up operation. A huge pan or kettles heated on the primus supplied hot water for all purposes including baths. Kitchen furniture was non existent until we erected a few shelves. Our original larder consisted of a wooden cabinet constructed of slats from one of our crates, open on three sides and lined with mesh. The mesh gave protection from most insects, providing one remembered to latch the door, the one exception being marauding ants. The only solution to their attacks was to stand the legs of the rickety cabinet in tins of water and woe betide if these were allowed to dry out.

Life now took on a completely new routine. With the absence of a school geared to teaching foreigners Arabic, our studies became a matter of personal discipline and, with much to distract one's attention, concentrating on text books and dealing with a complicated grammar proved difficult. But we did have an inestimable source of help. We were worshipping with an Arab assembly and Roy, though he could be a hard task master where language was concerned, delighted to give us the benefit of his extensive knowledge. We were expected to attend all the meetings, Sunday and midweek, and the memory is still fresh of sitting, for what seemed hours, whilst Arabic poured out at a remarkable rate and reverberated in our ears. Occasionally a word or two made sense but, on the whole, prayers and sermons were incomprehensible. Hymns were slightly better as, being sung slowly, one had time to pick out a word here and there and, in any case, one could usually hum the tune! Sunday evenings often included a service in someone's home when the owner would seek to bring in as many neighbours as possible. Then, either the same night or next morning, we would have a visit from Roy with the inevitable question, "What new words have you learnt?" There were words of praise if voice could be given to new words and phrases, even if their meaning had to be queried.

Early in 1948 the Arab assembly numbered between fifty and sixty. Our inability to converse in Arabic was no hindrance to being involved in service. We were pressed into attending house meetings where an Arab brother would happily interpret, and we could attempt to hold a personal conversation. A few of the brethren were already making Saturday evening visits to a village some little distance away from Amman and after a few weeks we were invited to accompany them. Zerqa, a military area with a central camp, consisted of a small colony of roughly built homes approached along dusty, unpaved, streets. In one of the homes, a young Christian couple endeavoured to interest their neighbours in the Gospel, and it was not unusual, for the small, flat roofed, mud plastered house to be tightly packed. Living conditions were of the simplest and, in true village style, one sat or semi relaxed, on mattresses round the walls. As evening fell, the gloom would be partially dispersed by the flickering flame of the most primitive of oil lamps; usually just a wick fastened through the lid of a round cigarette tin filled with paraffin. The services were quite informal with people arriving, or maybe leaving, at irregular intervals. Singing, prayers, and a Scripture reading, plus sundry verbal asides, occupied a good portion of the time. Then, against a background of various noises, including children crying, adults coughing and dogs barking, an address would be given challenging the unconverted. They were precious times, especially when the Lord worked in the hearts of some, and the little company of believers grew to form the nucleus of a vital ongoing testimony.

Visitors to Amman and Zerka today will find them vastly changed from the town and village we knew, but will still experience the same, warm hearted fellowship amongst groups of Christians who truly know, love and honour their Saviour and Lord. The country has a deep religious divide. Transjordan, as we knew it, was principally Muslim with about 8% of the population being adherents of one of the ancient Christian communities, which must be admired for the way they have kept alive the truth concerning the person of Jesus Christ, despite the pressures of Islam, and still continue to faithfully celebrate His death and resurrection. However, sadly, the emphasis on personal salvation through repentance and faith in the Lord Jesus has been overshadowed or even lost, and replaced by church practices and dogma which teach a person becomes a Christian and a child of God through birth into a Christian family and infant baptism. As a result the vision of the Gospel being for all mankind has been lost, and the Christian community tends to hedge the good news to themselves, expressed in such statements

as, “Jesus is for us Christians, not the Muslim.” This attitude i
very difficult to understand or accept. The groups of Christian
with whom we were privileged to meet were often designated th
‘new born ones’, due to their emphasis on the familiar words spoke
to Nicodemus. Even some of these groups have in the past bee
chary of witnessing to Muslims and only occasionally did one fin
amongst them a convert from that faith. However, over the year
there has been a change and keen national Christians are bearin
a testimony for the Saviour amongst their Muslim friends.

Within a few weeks of being in Amman we realised how fortunat
we had been to secure even our simple abode. As the flow c
refugees continued, and living space became increasingly scarce
the vacant ground in the valley below our home gradually took o
the appearance of a shanty town. Inadequate housing, negligibl
heating, meagre water supplies and primitive hygiene; compounde
with piercing winds and bitter February cold, brought misery t
many hundreds. Many who recently had been living in th
comparative comfort of Jerusalem and its surrounding villages
struggled to exist in these horrendous conditions.

Winter storms gave way to April’s gentle breezes and milde
days brought physical benefits to those who were so inadequatel
housed, but the political situation brought them no joy. The Unite
Nations’ declaration that Palestine would be divided still stood, a
did Britain’s declaration her troops would be withdrawn. At midnigh
on 14th May the British Mandate for Palestine ended and the Jew
proclaimed the inauguration of the new State of Israel. Conflic
flared immediately with Egypt attacking from the south, Syria fron
the north east and Transjordan from the east. The first two wer
swiftly contained but the well disciplined, highly trained, Ara
Legion occupied the West Bank, including the old city of Jerusalem
and pressed on almost to within sight of the coast. If there ha
been no political interference by the super powers, particularl
America and Russia, they would have split the newly created Israe
in two. But in response to foreign pressure, they were pulled bac
towards Jerusalem and, by the time a cease fire was negotiated
the Arabs had lost control of much of the territory in the west. Thi
left dozens of villages at the mercy of the Jews, many of whom
having suffered indescribable horrors at the hands of the Nazis

were in no mood to show leniency to others. By force and various other means, they sought to intimidate the population and cause an exodus towards the north and east. This resulted in the development of a huge refugee camp in the vicinity of Jericho, whilst the one near our home overflowed.

About the same time as Britain laid down her responsibilities for Palestine, her Mandate over Transjordan ended, and the Hashemite Kingdom of Jordan came into being. Emir Abdullah became King and inherited a whole host of problems. His country was economically poor and backward, compared with Palestine, and his reign began with the State at war; a war which severed his only direct land route to a harbour in the west, and shut down the oil pipe lines from Iraq to the coast. The disruption of the pipe line meant a loss of important revenue, whilst the loss of a direct route to the west caused a steep rise in the price of imported goods. Only 25% of the land was suitable for agriculture and hardly any mineral resources existed at the time, so Jordan had to depend on imports to meet the demands of a rapidly increasing population. The sea outlet to the east through Aqaba and the Red Sea was of little help, with virtually no port facilities. King Abdullah, pragmatic in his outlook, knew his country's welfare depended upon a swift peace agreement with the newly formed State of Israel. This conviction in due course cost him his life. Thus the States of Israel and Jordan were virtually born at the same time, a situation which resulted in a renewal of an age-old conflict, one which from time to time had repercussions on our lives and influenced our missionary service.

CHAPTER 13

Reinforcements

(1948-49)

Rejoice in the Lord always. Again I will say, Rejoice!
(Philippians 4:4)

By the beginning of May we were feeling settled in our new home. A brush and a few pots of paint helped to brighten it both inside and out, Marjorie's efforts with curtain material added a touch of charm to bare window frames, and colourful platted mats transformed the bare, and cold, concrete floors. In spite of its barn-like appearance our home became a haven and not only for ourselves. Shortly after moving to the area we were in contact with men from the RAF base and, having known the benefits of hospitality during my time in the Forces, sought to extend it to them. Meeting them at a Sunday evening service in the RAF chapel gave opportunity to invite them home and, acting on the suggestion of one of the keener Christians, we commenced a weekly Bible study. I am sure we enjoyed the fellowship just as much as they and, whilst it did not assist our grasp of Arabic, the holding of extended conversations in our own language gave us pleasure. The fellowship and Bible studies were greatly appreciated and, in spite of the primitive cooking facilities, Marjorie managed to provide the homely touch by some very welcome baking, her apple pies being particularly popular.

The weeks and the months sped by and our roots slowly but surely took grip in the soil of our adopted land. Our sympathies were deeply stirred by the ongoing plight of the multitude of Palestinian refugees and we appreciated the assistance of believers in Britain in meeting some of their needs. The barrels of second hand garments were welcome, but they could only meet a minute portion of the refugees' clothing requirements and did nothing to address the primary needs of food, housing, employment and education. The refugees naturally longed for an assurance they could return to their homeland in the near future and this hope created a problem for a number of Christians, both national and foreign. Many believed that one day Israel would again be recognised as a sovereign State and thus, if the establishment of Israel in 1948 was the Lord's doing, the possibility of these thousands of refugees returning to their original homes, would depend upon genuine peace between Jew and Arab. We were caught between two conflicting sympathies. As one of our friends commented, "When I look at the prophetic Scriptures my sympathy is with the Jews; when I see the plight of the Palestinian refugees my sympathy is with them." That conflict of sympathies remained with us though we sought to the best of our ability to show true compassion for those who, in situations not of their own making, endured much suffering.

By this time we had local assistance for our language study and this, plus attendance at meetings in Amman and Mahatta, and a Saturday evening service in nearby Zerka, enabled us to make fair progress. Soon these activities were supplemented by visits to the town of Es Salt where, for many years, there had been a Christian witness. For some years the CMS maintained a hospital and an evangelical testimony while, in more recent days, workers from the 'Assemblies of God' had established a junior day school. The hospital had long ceased its activities and, whilst a school continued in modified form, there were now no expatriate workers. The Mission buildings, including the school and small living quarters for the head teacher, were well made of local stone but this, through dust and time, had weathered to a drab dark beige, and the woodwork also cried out for more than a lick of paint. The small company of Christians, the living stones to which the Apostle Peter refers in his first letter, had likewise been neglected and badly needed spiritual refurbishment and refreshment. Their numbers were swollen by a few Palestinian refugees but none among them were capable of taking any spiritual leadership. The little group turned to Roy Whitman for help, and in turn he suggested we participate in this particular ministry. Neither of us felt drawn to the area but, though it meant forfeiting some fellowship with believers in Amman, the need could not be ignored. So many a Sunday saw us up early to catch a bus whose hard seats and inadequate suspension ensured any vestige of sleep vanished long before reaching our destination.

The major part of the town lay scattered over the sides of a gloomy, rocky defile, an offshoot from the deep gorge which cleft the main mass of the mountain range. The inhabitants of Es Salt, who were mainly Muslim, seemed to take on the character of the rocks around them and, from every aspect, the place could be termed very stony ground. But the spiritual need existed and our visits, supplemented by Roy and others, began to revive the seemingly dying testimony.

Our increasing activities outside Amman highlighted the need for some form of personal transport. The only timetabled bus services were from Amman to Jerusalem via Es Salt, and Amman to Irbid via Zerka. The rest of the country depended upon the village busses with their one daily return run to town. Some villages had two or three service cars but, generally, they travelled only when they were full, sometimes meaning eight people in a six seater and possibly a sheep in the boot, though six plus numerous items of luggage would more likely be the norm. Even getting to Zerka, relatively near though it was, had its difficulties and unless one of the team had use of a car, evening meetings were out of the question. Roy could tell of the time when it would be the norm to travel by horse and how, in the mid 1920s, he had visited the majority of villages on horseback distributing Bibles. Arabs have long memories and many a time in a village someone would remember him and his previous visit. But the Whitmans did not live in the past; they knew the value of personal transport, though at that time only Dora could drive. However, seeing I could chauffeur him, we agreed a shared car could prove invaluable. This became a pressing issue as Roy, having left copies of the Scriptures in various places, desired to renew some of his previous contacts. So enquiries began for a cheap but suitable vehicle

Whether we got a suitable vehicle was always a debatable question. Suffice to say I overheard the Palestinian from whom it was obtained, make the comment that if he had known Mr. Whitman had a share in its purchase he would never have sold it to him! However, for the princely sum of £200 we possessed an early 1930s four door Morris Ten, plus a whole host of unexpected experiences. In the flush of new ownership pride we decided the car should be named and finally whittled the choice down to two: either Dorcas, a woman renowned in the early church for her good works; or, Phoebe, a servant of the church in Cenchrea near Corinth. Fortunately the latter was chosen, for mechanically the fast aging Morris was certainly not filled with good works. Those it had functioned reasonably well but the adverse circumstances of passing years, and coping with difficult terrain, took their toll. Steep hills placed stress on an already overworked first gear, whilst the low slung exhaust and well worn leaf springs came to grief on unmade roads. Many were the times we either bumped or roared our way back to Amman heading for our favourite repair shop, a one man affair run by an Englishman whose mechanic's course in the army had put him in the way of making a good living. Happily for us, he was ingenious in making do and mend.

Problems also arose from self appointed experts among the Arab believers ready to proffer help. On one occasion when we were visiting Es Salt I happened to mention the brakes were not too effective on the hills. "No problem," said one young man. "I can fix them in minutes," and, sure enough, he did. On the way home the car seemed to find the climb out of the town more arduous than usual and even on reaching the plateau, laboured as if heading into a stiff wind. Then a strange smell pervaded the vehicle and I spotted in the mirror a wisp of smoke. We quickly found a very hot rear brakedrum dripping the last of its fluid, and ourselves stranded once more. Our friend's fixing had nearly fixed us as well.

In addition to the occasional broken spring, punctured exhaust, deflated tyres, a run down battery and faulty lights, there were three more surprises. The first concerned a temperamental electric petrol pump which occasionally let us down. A friend in the assembly said he could cure it and promptly took the offending item home and, a few days later, returned it with the assurance, "It's as good as new." Well, almost it was. Along with the pump he handed over half a dozen small brass washers, casually remarking they had fallen out when he dismantled the pump but, as it worked without them, they were obviously of no importance. The pump worked, for about five minutes. A personal exploration of its inner workings revealed the washers' true function and, after a DIY repair, we were once more on the move. Our second surprise was when the hand-brake left its moorings as we were descending one of Amman's steepest hills. The foot brakes, as usual, were not holding too well and safety called for a little more restraining power. Maybe I pulled too energetically but, whatever the reason, a loose lever trailing a length of ineffective wire hung in my hand as we rapidly approached a sharp bend. I am sure we must have negotiated it in fine style. The third unexpected development could have spelt complete disaster. I had been visiting Irbid and, before returning home, agreed to take some friends to the village of El Husn. Being the rainy season some village roads were almost impassable but we bumped and bounced along the unsurfaced track without any problem. Then in the village we reached a stretch where the road near my friend's home had been churned into really gooey mud. Having made my farewells I tried to turn round but found the steering strangely unresponsive. It always had considerable play, and assuming this plus driving in mud to be the cause, I accelerated and turned the wheel intending to go left. Instead the car lurched to the right and another turn of the wheel brought us straight. Being completely mystified and, in peril of ruining my trousers (clothes were scarce in those days) I got down to see the steering linkage had come completely adrift. With a vital bolt missing, only one wheel responded to the steering; the other could just please itself. The thought of what might have happened if the bolt had vanished on a main road, or negotiating a hairpin bend, or in the midst of heavy traffic, did not bear contemplating.

Phoebe was not always a pain in the neck and a drain on our pockets. For many months she fulfilled a vital function as a servant of the church. Her help opened the way to regular meetings at Zerka and Es Salt and made possible visits to villages which otherwise may not have been reached. The car could not always be blamed if, on occasion, she looked forlorn with all four tyres down to their rims. Young fingers, maybe urged on by older ones, were sometimes busy while a visit was in progress, for what could be more exciting than hearing a sustained hiss from the tyres of a visiting foreigner? One could view the situation with complacency providing sympathetic village men were present to locate the culprits, and make them pump up the tyres. Phoebe also did valiant work in summer when shortage of water involved travelling to a stream some distance away for essential supplies; without her we would have been dependent on delivery by donkey.

'Phoebe' - another flat tyre!

The car was not our only new worker in 1948. In August a much more valuable colleague, in the person of Victor Dodsworth, arrived. We had met him in 1946 but never thought that one day we would be serving the Lord together. We had very short notice of the date of his arrival but were able to arrange for him to be met in Beirut by the Touryans, our Armenian friends in the early days at Jerusalem. The more difficult problems were how to accommodate him in our one bedroom home, and covering the cost of a trip to Beirut to assist him on his journey to Jordan. The first was solved by converting our wood store into a bedroom. This was a small unroofed extension at one end of the house formed by the outer wall of our bedroom and two walls of rough stone. Skillful plastering with a local cement consisting mainly of mud, a front wall containing both door and window, and a roof of corrugated iron, resulted in a comparatively dry, though primitive bedchamber. True it was draughty with the wind in a certain direction, the odd spot of rain found its way through joints in the roof and window frame, some insects made it their home too, and in springtime the odd plant or two would grow out of the mud plastered walls. However it provided a room for our new colleague.

Getting to Beirut to pick up Victor and all his luggage proved more difficult and was finally solved through our being granted the loan of a car. This was an old American 'Essex', which looked rather like a huge, comfortably furnished box on wheels. But what it lacked in beauty it made up for in usefulness. Its capacious body proved to be ideal for meeting someone with a pile of luggage. It was our first trip to Lebanon and, once we were through the tedious formalities at the Jordan and Syrian borders, and had negotiated the badly pitted road across the wastes of the Hauran, the whole experience was enjoyable. The journey over the Anti Lebanon and Lebanon ranges proved to be sheer delight after the barren, arid wastes of the Jordan plateau, whilst finding pockets of snow and rippling streams high on the slopes of Mt. Hermon was, after the scarcity of water in Amman, a positive tonic. Each succeeding mile, twisting through rocky gorges, brought new scenes culminating in the beauty of the plain of the Bekaa and, from the summit of the next pass, the initial breathtaking view of Beirut gleaming white against the background of the deep blue of the Mediterranean sea.

We discovered Victor's boat had arrived four days before and he had gone with the Touryans to Farayah, a summer resort on the approaches to Mount Saneen. There we found him, well rested after his sea trip and enraptured with the beauty of his surroundings. Part of his leading to the Middle East centred around certain Scriptures which spoke of the mountains and cedars of Lebanon so, understandably, he felt he had almost arrived at his destination. But within twenty four hours we were on our way with Victor's luggage snugly stowed in the boot and rear compartment of the Essex. His arrival began a period of mutual service during which we all appreciated, and benefitted from, the differing gifts and abilities God had granted to us.

The closing months of 1948 saw two significant developments. Firstly the way opened for the commencement of missionary work in the north of Jordan and secondly, various signs indicated the possibility of an addition to our family. The commencement of the evangelistic work in Irbid had an unusual background for it centred round the distribution of milk to refugees. The town lies on a plateau north of the mountains of Gilead and just over two thousand feet above sea level. Within a short distance westward the land plunges steeply to merge into the fertile plain surrounding the Sea of Galilee whilst northwards it is broken by the deep gorge of the Yarmuk River. Nearby is the ancient site of Lo-debar, whilst to the east the terrain, home for Bedouin tribes with their camels and sheep, gradually merges into desert sloping gently down over hundreds of miles to the border of Iraq. Irbid had been the last Jordanian town visited during our journey in 1947 when its predominantly Muslim character, as well as its strategic situation for reaching out to villages in the north, impressed itself upon us. The population numbered around ten thousand of whom about 95% were Muslim; the remainder being communicants of the Catholic, Greek Orthodox and Protestant Churches, the latter by far the smallest. But these statistics were soon out of date, for refugees from the districts around Nazareth and the towns of Galilee flooded in daily. Consequently poverty stricken habitations were springing up in the area and their desperate plight called for immediate help.

In an endeavour to meet the needs especially of children and nursing mothers, the United Nations Relief Agency opened a milk distribution centre under the direction of a Dr McLean. He and his wife were veteran missionaries who, after a number of years overseeing a mission hospital in Es Salt, opened a clinic, later to develop into a hospital, in Ajlaun. This principal town in Gilead was some twenty five miles away from Irbid, and the doctor soon discovered he needed help if the centre was to be kept open twice a week, and he asked if we could assist. Tuesdays and Thursdays were our only free days, so on those mornings we were up bright and early catching the bus for the long journey north. With the help of a few assistants vast quantities of powdered milk were liquefied and the doors of the centre would be opened to admit the anxious throng. The next few hours would be chaotic. The crowd had to be shepherded into some sort of order and there were always those who would press and shove to get first place. In the midst of the confusion ration cards had to be checked to ensure the right people obtained their allocated share, whilst arguments and pleas for extra supplies had to be met with a firm, but I trust gracious, No! By the end of the afternoon we were relieved to be back on the bus for home, when, as the miles slipped by, one's tired mind wrestled with the searching question, 'what were we accomplishing for the Lord by playing milkman to refugees?' But He soon revealed He had a purpose in it all. Unbeknown to us He was preparing the way for the beginning of a work which, in various aspects, continues to the present day.

It all began with a lady who had visited us in Amman, appearing at the milk centre. Her husband, a full time Christian worker, had recently died and now, with four children in her care, she was living in the Christian village of El Husn. Hearing we would be in town she came to greet us accompanied by another Christian lady who, with some of her family, had recently had a thrilling night journey escaping from Nazareth into Jordan. The ladies mentioned they knew someone who would be happy to welcome us in her home for a time of prayer and Bible study. Later we shared this information with Roy who readily agreed to join in the next visit to Irbid and assist in conducting our first meeting in the town. This led to a weekly service when some eight or nine would gather to pray, read the Scriptures and share the good news of the Gospel. As a result, within a few weeks the lady of the house had the joy of knowing for herself Jesus Christ as Saviour and Lord. Her husband, sympathetic and interested though he was, never as far as we knew, followed his wife's example. So, with the help of a couple of faithful ladies, who took an interest in a third, the work in Irbid commenced, but not without our knowing we were in an area where it might be fiercely opposed. An Arab believer who had moved into this town for the purpose of preaching the Gospel, had been expelled when his testimony resulted in a Muslim confessing faith in Jesus Christ as the only Saviour of mankind.

Concerning the addition to our family, previous experience taught us to view the situation with some caution, but as the weeks, then the months, slipped by without mishap there appeared to be every reason for making preparations for the coming event. These included deciding the place of birth. Three options were open to us: the Roman Catholic Hospital in Amman, the missionary hospital in Ajlaun, and the Christian Medical Centre in Beirut. Taking the advice of friends who were well acquainted with the facilities available in each place, we chose the latter. Meantime Marjorie consulted an English doctor who, through long residence in Amman, was more Arab than British in his outlook. He gave excellent advice on how to keep fit in the Jordanian climate, advice we definitely needed for the long, hot, dry summer, gave way to changeable weather; sun warmed days faded into bitterly cold nights; gentle breezes became fierce biting winds and dark snow clouds drew an impenetrable veil across deep blue skies.

Early January saw other clouds rolling in from the west, harbingers of the longed for latter rains as the initial brief downpours gave way to torrential rain, driving snow storms and bitter cold. Our small wood stove, smoky though it could be, was pressed into service but, even with the aid of a paraffin heater, it had a hard job to keep the cold at bay, whilst the odd leak from the roof did nothing to cheer the spirit. But the weather became the least of our concerns. Although we sought not to worry, the subject of finance took on a new dimension. We had enough to meet daily needs, but no way could we save towards the expenses involved in the birth of a child. With the months slipping by it was obvious one visit, at least, ought to be made to the Medical Centre in Beirut but this was beyond our present means, the payment of another year's rent being due in a few week's time. With Jordan being outside the Sterling area, gifts from Britain could only be remitted through a Government recognised agency. Echoes of Service were recognised as such but thirteen weeks or more, depending on the post, could elapse between communications. Experience had taught us the Lord used various ways to make provision but, with no remittance from Echoes in the offing, our prayers became more urgent! The Lord then gave us two pleasant surprises, the first being a visit from one of the elders of the Amman assembly who on leaving left a gift of five pounds from the church. We still had no idea how the larger need would be met and had to wait a little longer for the next surprise.

CHAPTER 14

In Joy and Sorrow

(1948-49)

Weeping may endure for a night,
but joy comes in the morning (Psalm 30:5).

As the days slipped by we continued to pray for guidance regarding a visit to Beirut and the answer came in a way we did not expect. The Armenian brethren in Beirut invited us to visit and conduct a series of meetings, and about the same time, the American friends who had advised us to make use of the CMC wrote offering hospitality. Believing this to be an indication from the Lord we should go, and simply trust Him to supply the needed finance, we arranged to travel about the middle of January. Funds became available and Marjorie saw the doctors at CMC, then fixed a provisional date for the next and hopefully final appointment. We explored Beirut, were not enamoured with it, then returned thankfully to the more unsophisticated atmosphere of Jordan.

Arriving home the matter of the year's rent still remained but, unbeknown to us, relief was already on its way. Believers meeting at Heliopolis in Egypt felt constrained to send a gift to Jordan to meet a specific need and forwarded to us an amount almost equal to one year's rent. Their covering letter gave no indication how they intended the gift to be used and to us it appeared to be an obvious answer to prayer. In acknowledging we mentioned how thrilled we were the Lord had answered prayer, both as regards timing and the amount. Many months later when passing through Cairo, we discovered their original thoughts had been towards the refugees! However, they were pleased it had met our specific need. We were happy to discover that our ignorance of their original intention had not diminished their interest in, and assistance to, the refugees from Palestine.

Back in Amman we continued to share in the outreach to Zerqa, Es Salt, and Irbid plus the occasional English Bible studies in our home. Our facility in Arabic gradually improved, though not to the extent of being able to give a full length address without an interpreter. We knew our value to the work would always be limited until we could dispense with that particular prop. So there still had to be a place in our programme for study. Victor's arrival took off some pressure for he willingly shared in the visits to Zerka and, during our time in Beirut, developed a keen interest in the work in Irbid.

Life was full and the weeks sped by, so much so, that April and the time for Marjorie's visit to Beirut, almost took us by surprise. We decided she should travel by plane a week or ten days before the baby was due, and I would follow by road as soon as local engagements permitted. Travelling by plane was not as straightforward as it sounds. Amman had a very small airport, formerly used by the RAF and facilities for passengers were very primitive. The only regular services were provided by an enterprising Englishman, who having managed to acquire three small planes, alternated their flights between Amman, Beirut and Cairo, weather and serviceability permitting. Marjorie's first ever flight was scheduled in one of these fragile looking machines, and she may well have wondered whether the discomfort and possible dangers of the road would be preferable!

The day of departure dawned and the weather took charge of the situation. Jordan's short Spring came very late that year. The heavy rains ceased but showers continued and westerly winds piled cloud upon cloud over the Lebanon and Anti-Lebanon ranges. The small five seater planes reached a very limited altitude and no pilot in his right senses would attempt the flight to the coast whilst Hermon and its attendant peaks were swathed in mists We made our way to the airport but the forecast remained dismal for hours to come. The next day, and the next, we repeated the journey, always hoping that if the weather improved the plane would take off. By the fourth day the prospect of Marjorie travelling by road loomed large and there were visions of the baby being born on the way but, by the fifth, the clouds lifted and, with very little notice, the pilot decided to fly. Dilatory passengers would have to wait for another fine day. Then, as the plane moved down the runway, the remnants of cloud disappeared and, soaring into a sky of limitless blue, the tiny craft with the westering sun glinting from its wings, gradually changed from a plane to a spot, then to speck vanishing over the horizon. From the ground it all appeared to be beautifully smooth but, in reality, it was a rocky, bumpy ride calculated to hurry any pregnancy to its end. Nevertheless, Marjorie arrived safely to a very warm welcome, but one deeply tinged with sorrow. A few days before this those with whom we were to stay had welcomed a tiny baby into their home, only to lose it within a matter of hours. Their kindness and unstinted hospitality at such a time witnessed to the depth of their faith and complete reliance on the God of all comfort.

A few days later I travelled by road, arriving in Beirut some thirty six hours in advance of Peter Gerald who put in an appearance at 8.30 on the morning of 2nd May, a fine bonny child weighing in at eight pounds exactly. Marjorie relaxed in the care of the Centre for a few days, and then for another week with our hosts prior to the journey home. Again I travelled by road, this time with a lot more luggage including a child's cot which our recently bereaved friends wished us to have. With the weather being more settled, Marjorie, with Peter snug in his own special basket, flew the following day. They endured an exceptionally rough journey over snow crusted mountains barely cleared by the plane.

Peter's arrival, from an Arab's point of view, increased our status. A boy had arrived, an occasion for hearty congratulations; had it been a girl there could well have been commiserations, at least from some. For our part we would have been equally thrilled and rejoicing at whatever the Lord gave. But, with our first born being a boy, we would now be addressed, not by our given or family name, but by an acknowledgement we were the father and mother of Peter. Thus Marjorie became Um Boutros and I, Abu Boutros. Our programme had now to take account of our new and precious arrival. Marjorie no longer had free time for visits to outlying places and, to enable her enjoy fellowship locally, I undertook some of the responsibilities connected with Peter. As he grew apace, the joy of holding him and seeing the dawning light of recognition in his lovely clear eyes, together with glimpses of those first fleeting smiles, was inexpressible. He brought life, love and joy into our roughly built home, and his presence strengthened the ties of love between us.

As the happy, busy weeks slipped by, there was much to encourage us in Zerka where definite spiritual growth resulted from the preaching of the Gospel. This work received additional strength with the arrival of a mature Christian couple from Nazareth. The Kawars had exercised a leading role in their local Christian fellowship and, with their arrival, the missionary from overseas could take a less prominent place. Letting go a work where there has been a tremendous amount of personal effort is not always easy but, when the Lord indicates the time is ripe to do so, blessing results from the seeming sacrifice. I must confess it took me some years to learn this lesson and accept it with grace! This was the case in Zerka when the Arab brother took responsibility and the work moved on to a sounder footing. At the same time we could reach out to other places and, not without some apprehension, that included the difficult town of Es Salt. The occasional visits were increased and, in due course, acting on a suggestion from Roy, we seriously considered making our home there. However, subsequent events made it clear the Lord had other plans.

Peter continued to make good progress, including the development of a powerful set of lungs and a healthy appetite. It was a great surprise on returning one evening from Es Salt to discover he had been listless most of the day. Periodically he brightened, took a little nourishment, then gave indications of stomach discomfort. The usual simple remedies gave no relief and, after a sleepless night, we made tracks for the local Catholic hospital. The queues were long and our anxieties increased as we waited for our turn to see the doctor. Eventually he examined Peter, stated he had dysentery, gave him a hefty injection, and declared he would be perfectly fit in two or three days. With no improvement and, after a second disturbed night, we were back early at the hospital seeking more help. Halfway through the morning the doctor saw us briefly and promised to see us later. Two hours or more later we felt we had to press for admission to the surgery, when the doctor floored us by stating there was nothing he could do and we had better take the child elsewhere. We returned home devastated, completely at a loss as to what to do. Our only recourse was prayer.

Just then someone suggested contacting Dr. McLean in Ajloun. We eventually obtained a line through to the Hospital, in itself a minor miracle considering the state of rural telephonic communications. He urged us to get Peter to him as soon as possible, advice in the circumstances easier to give than to follow. Ajloun was miles away over unmade roads and our car would never have negotiated the rougher parts of the way. But just before ringing off, Dr. McLean mentioned his wife and chauffeur were in Amman that day. If we could locate them, and if there was still room in the car, they would happily provide the needed transport. So, continuing to pray, I set off to town in haste hoping that in the crowded streets, I would find them. It appeared to be like looking for the proverbial needle in a haystack. But prayer was answered - I met Mrs. McLean and her driver, and found they still had two vacant seats.

Within a short time the journey to Ajloun commenced, a journey we would never want to make again. The rough road twisted wildly up hill and down dale climbing into the mountains of Gilead. In spite of the chauffeur's best efforts progress was painfully slow and the inevitable bumping, jerking and swaying added to the discomfort of a seemingly interminable journey. Peter, cradled alternately in our arms, lay quite still and his steadfast looks as he gazed trustingly into our eyes tore at our hearts as we felt our inability to meet his need. Within moments of arriving Dr. McLean examined him and at once diagnosed a blocked intestine. The only hope lay in an operation even though he feared it might already be too late. The Whitmans were visiting and, together with one or two friends, we met in the doctor's house to pray as the operation progressed. Then came a great surge of relief, and prayer turned to thanksgiving - a message from the hospital stated all was well. Later in the evening we met again for prayer, and the evening reading, 'Jesus Himself drew near', brought a deep sense of His presence. We truly felt the comfort of His nearness. Almost drugged by the anxiety and sleeplessness of the last three days, within minutes Marjorie and I were slumbering deeply and thankfully, happy at seeing Peter peacefully asleep in his tiny cot.

A hand shook my shoulder, and a whisper in my ear drew me out of the depths of sleep. Gradually, I sensed a shadowy form by my bed. The thin beam from a torch obscured my sight, but the doctor's voice jerked me into wakefulness and a glance at the empty space at the end of the bed gave meaning to his words. Jesus had indeed drawn nigh and taken Peter to Himself. A night nurse, noting a deterioration in his condition, had called speedily for help but all in vain. The doctor withdrew, and with him the light. There, in the dense darkness of the room, I tried to come to terms with what had happened. My heart ached, not only for myself, but for Marjorie who had now to face a very bitter blow. A few minutes later, in spite of all my endeavours at self control, my limbs shook as if with ague. I could hear Marjorie breathing peacefully and, wondering how I could possibly break the news, dreaded her waking. Suddenly she sat up. The absence of the baby's breathing warned her something was amiss and, in a quiet voice edged with anxiety, she asked, "Where is Peter?" Then her own special strength came to the fore. Her concern for my personal distress, compounded by my anxiety for her, overshadowed her own for a while. Together we prayed and waited for the dawn before deciding to make our way across the compound to meet with the McLeans. From the hospital porch we stepped out into a gloriously sunny morning which gilded the hills around and burnished the tops of dense pine woods, whilst the steep sided valleys remained deep in the morning mist. Tracing a path through the trees Marjorie suddenly grasped my arm and said, "Look at that!" There out of sun-baked ground, hard, barren and parched after the rainless months, peeped a group of autumn crocuses, a marvellous picture of resurrection, life out of death. We turned aside to sit on the pine-needle strewn mountain side and, looking across the expanse of valley to the towering hills beyond, and then above to the azure of a cloudless sky, we bowed to give thanks to the Lord who, in the midst of our grief had granted us such a wonderful promise of life after death. Peter was not dead, he had just gone on before. On the night of 13th September 1949 His heavenly Father had taken him unto Himself.

Gathering for breakfast we realised more of the grace of the Lord. Others who shared with us that meal had passed through the same sad experience. Roy and Dora's first and only son had died at birth, whilst the McLean's only daughter, one year old, had been dropped by her nurse with fatal results. Their very presence brought a measure of consolation and strength. There was no frantic searching for words of comfort, but the opening verse for our morning reading, 'we walk by faith, not by sight' could not have been more appropriate. Later in the day, gathered by the doctor's home together with some of the Arab staff, Roy conducted a simple but very poignant service before we laid to rest in a corner of the hospital compound, the little body whose spirit had passed into the presence of the Lord, there to wait the reunion of the glorious resurrection day. We cannot say we did not weep, but the wonderful sense of the presence of the risen Saviour, and the encouragement of His words strengthened our faith.

Within a few days we were back in a home which seemed to be strangely quiet. The very genuine sympathy of the Arab believers helped tremendously, even though one or two expressed the view we were under the judgement of God. Within a few days our morning reading began with, 'whom the Lord loveth He chasteneth', and we knew the loving discipline of the Lord is far different from judgement for sin. The situation was easier for me than Marjorie, but I felt convinced we had a mutual need for a break and change of scene. I was out and about whereas she had time on her hands and this, plus the strains of the past three years began to take their toll. There had been the parting from loved ones, the miscarriage and hospitalisation on the voyage out, the adjustments of living in a foreign land, the trauma of the evacuation from Palestine, the stress of living in cramped and hot conditions in Egypt, followed by dangerous days in Jerusalem, the further move to more primitive conditions in Jordan, the confinement in Beirut, the joy of a home enlightened by Peter's presence and then his sudden fatal illness. Apart from one very hot but enjoyable week in Alexandria, there had been no holiday throughout this whole period. Having sought the Lord's direction, we were convinced it would be right to consider a visit to Britain, a move encouraged by the Whitman's.

As this became known in Britain, some adverse comments began to arrive suggesting we could not take the strain and had decided to turn back. We appreciated people meant well, especially the lady who wrote saying that after coming home we would never return, and urged us not to leave the country. But we were confident the Lord was directing us and later learned that there were other reasons why we should be in England at that time. Gradually, in answer to prayer, gifts began to arrive, we packed up our belongings and stored them in the old mission premises in Es Salt as we envisaged living there on our return.

Our house rent had been paid for a year in advance but the possibility of a refund from the landlord was more than remote. However, a few weeks before the date for our departure, the Whitmans found themselves faced with eviction from their home. Their shack, for it really was little more, had been given by an Arab Christian to the Amman assembly and for years, it had been considered as a provision made for Roy and Dora. In those days the assembly had no legal right to own land and the property was in the name of one of the leading brethren who later left the fellowship. With the influx of Palestinians leading to a sharp rise in land prices, he sold the property to a Muslim neighbour. Our place was far from ideal but a lot better than the shack which had been sold, and the day before we left they moved in. The Lord had provided for His children just at the right time and that, to us, is one of the wonders of miracles. Very often, the crucial matter is not what happens, but the actual time at which it happens.

The day of our departure dawned bright and clear with just a sharp nip in the air to remind us winter with its cold, rain and snow had almost arrived. The early rains of October had settled the summer's dust, tiny streams tumbled and sparkled over the stones of once dry river beds, a faint sheen of green clothed the brown hillsides and minute desert plants reached up towards the light. In the crevices of a sheltered wall tiny mauve cyclamen gave promise of new growth, a delightful foreshadowing of the carpets of wild flowers, with their riot of reds, blues, pinks and green. But now our faces were turned towards England's green and pleasant land. Changes had abounded since we left home, especially with the creation of the Welfare State and Labour's swift nationalisation of the railways, mines, utilities and most heavy industry. As we settled in our seats for the flight to Cairo, we began to wonder what conditions would be like at journey's end.

Within three weeks sufficient funds had arrived enabling us to enjoy the luxury of travelling by air. From Amman the flight path skirted the length of the Dead Sea with the mountains of Moab standing out stark and grim in the blaze of the morning sun. After crossing Jordan's southern border, it passed over the waste of Sinai where the monotony of the desert was occasionally broken by the long black tents of Bedouin, surrounded by flocks of sheep and herds of camels, creating a mosaic of white, black and beige against the tawny earth. Miles later came the ribbon and lakes of the Suez Canal, with the adjacent well irrigated fields and gardens, merging into the dirty yellow of the huge sprawling city of Cairo. An overnight stop there with friends stretched into days until BOAC finally caught up with itself and had a plane bound for London. After the rush, bustle and noise of Middle Eastern traffic London was positively peaceful!

Emotions ran high when we alighted at Nottingham's Victoria station, and Marjorie's family approached to envelop us in the warmth of their welcome, one, however, accompanied by a shock. Her mother looked ill and worn. In the excitement and bustle of the moment words were few for journey's end was a mere three miles away. Within the last hours we had travelled by plane, bus, train and car and now, finally, we were home. Anxious queries concerning mother's health were met with the assurance of her being only slightly off colour, an assurance belied by the hue of her cheeks. The doctor gave no reason for alarm and the family assumed winter's onslaught had been debilitating and a period of rest would prove a sufficient remedy.

For us, life now took on a new complexion. We were missionaries on furlough which meant embarking upon a period of almost incessant travel. The Middle East, and the newly created State of Israel, held a fascination for many Christians. Many believed the return of the Jews to Palestine, followed by the creation of Israel, indicated the near return of the Lord Jesus. Therefore, even though we emphasised our work was in Jordan and not amongst the Jews, invitations to give a report on missionary work amongst Jews arrived from many parts of the country. We found this embarrassing seeing as we had no contact with the State of Israel. Nevertheless, we could, and did, give an update on general conditions in the Middle East and appreciated every opportunity for reporting on the missionary situation in those predominantly Muslim lands.

There were many misconceptions concerning the Middle East. Mention the word 'Arab' and immediately people equated it with 'Muslim'. Few appeared to realise that scattered throughout most of the Arab lands there exist communities who in spite of the dangers and pressures surrounding them, have for centuries kept the name of the Lord Jesus alive in the midst of a hostile and powerful Islam. They have various identities: Greek Orthodox, Greek Catholic, Maronite, Copt, to mention but a few names which were current long before Islam. In spite of many of their beliefs being based on the traditions of men, and their following forms of worship reminiscent of the Old Testament priesthood, they have maintained their faith in the Bible as the revealed Word of God. Furthermore, they have never denied the truths concerning the birth, death and resurrection of Jesus Christ. Most maintain a sincere belief in the person of Christ as God's Son, in His true humanity and deity. But that salvation from sin's power and judgement depends upon personal faith in Christ Jesus as Saviour is generally unknown. For the majority, maintaining the Christian life means doing your best, keeping the Church festivals, going to confession and receiving absolution from the priest.

By late spring, we were convinced that planning for our return should begin in spite of the continuing ill health of Marjorie's mother. This illness placed a great strain on her father and it was obvious that Marjorie's support would be tremendously advantageous. Gradually we realised we had two options. We could delay our return to Jordan indefinitely, or I return alone and Marjorie would join me later. Much as we disliked the thought of the latter option, we decided to take it - the first of a number of occasions when dual loyalty, to the work and to the family, led to our taking different paths. The need for booking a passage became imperative, and an increasing amount of luggage ruled out any thought of going by air, so I contacted a shipping company dealing with the Mediterranean ports whose ships carried eight to ten passengers.

They anticipated a sailing for Beirut somewhere about the end of June and I booked.

Getting our goods together then became a priority - a 'mixed cargo' including an above normal amount of clothing, and certain items considered to be useful for our personal needs and the work. The baggage also included two baby cots of canvas and aluminum tubing for the Ajlaun Hospital as a remembrance of Peter, and a token of gratitude for all their loving help. With the health of her mother deteriorating, Marjorie needed to concentrate more on her parents' affairs. A few days later, surrounded by cases and packages on the familiar platform of Victoria station, we filled the moments with inconsequential conversation trying to help each other forget the pain of parting. I am sure both of us felt in low spirits though within a few days, the loneliness of separation was overshadowed by the hope of re-union.

Arriving at Marylebone, the unexpected appearance of a helpful porter facilitated the task of getting my bags and packages to a taxi rank and, within a few minutes we were on our way to what is now known as Dockland. Late in the afternoon, the huge dock gates swung open to allow our vessel to glide into the fast flowing Thames and head for the open sea. On that first evening most passengers disappeared to their cabins early and, alone in the twilight, watching the Thames recede and the lights of coastal towns grow dim, it became impossible to avoid a touch of melancholy. The shadowy coastline faded into a blur, the distant lights gradually vanished, the boat swung westward to face the English channel and I could not help wondering how many years would pass before I would see that coastline again. According to the shipping Agents, Alexandria would be the first scheduled stop and Beirut the second so, wind and wave permitting, ten days should see us there. The tenth day passed but on the eleventh, Egypt's low flat shore line hove into view broken in the distance by a serrated edge which gradually expanded and evolved until the outlines of the vast city and port of Alexandria could be discerned. But then came news of another delay; after Alexandria the ship would call at Tripoli before going on to Beirut.

I had arranged for a missionary to meet me in Beirut and now I sent an urgent message for him to meet me at this new destination.

Fortunately it got through and, as the boat dropped anchor off shore at Tripoli, I had the pleasure of seeing my friend's estate car on the quay. Soon we were on our way, through Damascus, across the plain of Hauran and the Syrian-Jordanian border, through the desert area around Mafrak until I eventually had the pleasure of receiving a warm welcome from the Whitmans, now well settled in our old home. What a flood of memories it evoked and how thankful I was for the sanctuary created for Victor, but now providing a home for me.

CHAPTER 15

To Pastures New

(July - December 1950)

My soul shall make its boast in the Lord; the humble shall hear of it and be glad (Psalm 34:2).

Waking in unfamiliar situations can be confusing and only gradually did I make sense of my new surroundings. The bare whitewashed walls, the corrugated iron roof, the beige rush mat partially covering a grey concrete floor, the dust motes dancing in a ray of light streaming through a chink in the rough wooden door, all jerked me awake to the realisation I had returned to Amman. Familiar sounds began to penetrate; the raucous tones of car horns, a lorry's klaxon, cries of vendors indicating the world was awake once more. The sound of a distant whistle, and the floor's slight vibration, announced the approach of the morning train, and reminded me it was high time to rise. Roy and Dora's hospitality had provided me with temporary accommodation and, for a while, my daily programme would be governed by their household arrangements.

On that first day I ought to have been thrilled at being back but, with the house containing a host of memories, many linked with Peter, I had difficulty adjusting to the new situation. Also, in view of changes since we left for furlough, I was not sure of the best way of using my time. We had intended to live in Es Salt and had stored some of our things there ready for the move. The seeming lack of interest on the part of the American Mission who owned the school building, to evangelistic work in the area, had appeared to leave the way clear for others to undertake this task. However, they decided to renew their commitment and now a Jordanian had been employed to serve as pastor.

This closed the door to that area for us and for a while I devoted my time to language study, helping the local church in Amman and its offshoot in the Mahatta area, whilst recommencing a weekly visit to Zerka. Within a few months the population in and around Zerka had increased considerably, mainly due to an influx of refugees, and there was plenty of scope for evangelistic work there. The Zerka church, as it was called by the Amman brethren, grew steadily with evidence of spiritual renewal in the lives of some, whilst in others a dramatic change took place and antagonism to the Gospel gave way to a definite commitment to faith in the Lord Jesus. Two illustrations come to mind.

The meetings were held in a simple home where both the husband and wife had been true lovers of the Lord Jesus for a number of years, but their lives differed little from their neighbours. His military occupation and the absence of Christian fellowship, meant it was easier to go along with the crowd rather than take a positive Christian stand. Opening their home for the meetings resulted in a change, for it led to a renewal of faith, a stimulation of zeal and regular periods of Bible study. Their increasing desires after holiness became plain the first time we met for the Lord's Supper. The time of worship had hardly begun when the wife, in tones of some distress, said she did not feel worthy to partake of the bread and the wine. Earlier that morning Mrs. Hani had been involved in an unseemly row with neighbours and harsh, angry words had been spoken. Previously this would not have troubled her, but now her deeper commitment to the Lord had impressed the need for Christians to be holy in word and deed. So feeling her testimony had been marred, and her Saviour dishonoured, she had visited the neighbour and humbly apologised, asking forgiveness for her part in the scene The apology was refused with a further spate of angry words and the brave attempt at reconciliation failed. "Now," Mrs Hani asked, "could she break bread seeing her apology had been refused; was she not out of fellowship with the Lord as long as her neighbour refused to be reconciled?" Our Arab brethren warmly welcomed her to the table and, for me, the incident has remained as a challenge. Am I as sensitive as I ought to be concerning coming to the Lord's Supper with nothing on my conscience to hinder worship?

Perhaps it is not surprising this deepening love for their Saviour led to them moving to the southern town of Aqabah where they were instrumental in developing a work for the Lord in that fast growing port. Aided by occasional visits of believers from Amman they witnessed faithfully and with good effect. Others also from that Zerka group have, over the years, scattered far and wide and it is encouraging to know that those first meetings, held in the simplicity of a primitive home with the light of a flickering oil lamp, have resulted in the greater and inextinguishable light of the Gospel spreading far beyond the confines of a small Jordanian town.

In due course the group in Zerka outgrew the house and erected a brick meeting room. It was the simplest of places and in those early unsophisticated days, the floor continued to provide the seating for many. Simple it may have been but there were times of spiritual blessing and my next memory embraces an evening of special joy. A few days before, at the mid week prayer meeting in Amman, a woman graphically portrayed the problems facing her since her conversion from a sordid life, including involvement in witchcraft. Her new found faith and joy were not shared by her husband, however; in fact his antagonism drove him to acts of violence, even threats of death if she continued to meet with evangelicals. That night she made an urgent request for others to pray for her to be faithful in following her Saviour. Personally we knew nothing of her background or place of residence and so were surprised to find her in the Zerka meeting on Saturday evening. There, unknown to any of us, was also this woman's husband, Salem, ready to vent on her the full extent of his wrath if she dare oppose his wishes. After I had preached the Gospel, Jarius, my interpreter, added his own comments and made a brief appeal. He challenged any who felt convicted of their sins, and were conscious of their need of deliverance from the wrath of God, to openly confess their desperate need and pray the prayer of the tax gatherer of old, "God be merciful to me, a sinner." The brief silence which followed his comments seemed charged with tension, heightened for a moment by the commotion of someone standing, then relieved as a voice cried to God for mercy and forgiveness. Amongst the amens which followed that prayer, none could have been more hearty than that of the woman who but a few minutes earlier, had been wondering what awaited her on returning home. Salem, who had entered with antagonism in his heart and hatred against his wife, left rejoicing in the knowledge of sins forgiven, of peace with God and a consciousness of the dawning of a new relationship with the one he had threatened to kill.

The joy of seeing someone making an open confession of faith in the Lord Jesus is always linked with caution for they are but babes in the faith and targets for Satanic forces which would seek to cause them to stray. What would happen in Salem's case; would the going be too tough, the pull of the old life too strong? A year must have slipped by before I visited Zerka again to spend an evening with the thriving church. I had hardly set foot in the door when a man I could barely recognise embraced me. So changed was he from the rough, sullen, person of a year before. Salem welcomed me with the words, "My father in Christ!" and embraced me as a brother in the family of God.

By this time, Victor had moved to the area of Irbid and made his base in the village of El Husn. His outgoing personality endeared him to many and he soon had a coterie of teenagers and an open door to a number of homes. El Husn's population consisted mainly of two 'Christian' tribes divided by an ancient blood feud normally kept in check by an uneasy truce. Victor, unaware at first which side people were on, happily made contacts wherever he could. At the same time friends in the village introduced him to relatives in Irbid and these, plus the contacts we had made in earlier days, laid the foundation for an ongoing missionary effort in the town. An Assyrian doctor helped immensely by opening his home for Bible studies, and the appointment of a keen Christian to an important post in local Government gave further encouragement. Victor's accommodation consisted of one scantily furnished, poorly equipped room which served as kitchen, dining, reception and bedroom. Lighting depended on small paraffin lamps, water came from a nearby rainwater cistern and toilets were a hole in the ground shrouded with bits of canvas nailed to a wooden frame - fine in summer, but something of a nightmare in winter if the untreated drinking water took its toll, and the hens had already occupied the place for the night.

The prospect of Marjorie joining me within a few weeks faded. Her mother, having undergone surgery, recovered sufficiently to leave hospital. The surgeon gave no hint of a fatal disease, whilst the general practitioner only prescribed pain killing drugs and advised rest. Only after a distressing relapse did the truth surface - mother had inoperable cancer. The fact it might be months before Marjorie could return did not alter the need to find a home for us. Having decided the market town of Irbid would make a better centre than one of the villages, I began searching for a suitable home there. At first I thought this would be a simple matter but soon ran into difficulties, partially because our requirements were very unusual for the local situation. At that time a local family, of very moderate means, could live quite happily with three rooms plus a small kitchen. But now we were in need of something more spacious.

In addition to sharing it with Victor, a lady from Scotland, who had been commended to missionary service in Jordan would, initially, be living with us. Three bedroom homes were scarce and the matter complicated by our being foreigners and considered to be very rich! Every week when I visited we prayed hard, and searched diligently to no avail. Then one week we decided fasting should accompany prayer and set aside the following day for that purpose. First we allowed ourselves a drink and then spent the morning in periods of prayer and meditation. Lunch time came and, as we experienced little difficulty in avoiding food, we thought our time of fasting was proceeding well. But round about 3 pm temptation entered in the form of a heavily laden tray of delightfully cooked food from one of the neighbours. They had no idea we were trying to fast, it was just a friendly gesture by an Arab family who felt two men could hardly cater for themselves! This kind act placed us in a difficult position. To refuse it would have been an insult, to try to dispose of it secretly a risk, to partake of it a breaking of our agreement to fast. But we decided the only way forward was to give thanks heartily and eat. I am sure the Lord understood, though no guidance came concerning accommodation!

By now the oppressive summer heat, accompanied by constant

empty, brazen skies made one long for a sight of clouds and a refreshing shower. Harvesting had long since finished and the dry, barren ground was turned into a huge dust bowl. Village ponds were almost dry and wells running low. No piped water existed outside Irbid and villagers depended on rain water collected in huge underground cisterns during winter and early spring. Visiting homes in the height of summer had its dangers for there was no guarantee the water, in the customary welcome drink, had received any form of purification. Sometimes a jug, which had all the appearance of being filled with a weak form of lemonade, consisted of the latest drawings from a depleted well and, on a scorching hot day, the temptation to slake one's thirst proved difficult to resist. Lettuces, tomatoes and certain fruits always presented a hazard unless they had been thoroughly washed, or dipped in a solution of permanganate. But with all the care in the world digestive troubles were difficult to avoid.

My weekly trips continued but my energies began to flag; the bus journeys became tedious and interest in any form of activity diminished. I had little appetite for Dora Whitman's ample meals and even less for our own at El Husn. An onset of intermittent headaches, an occasional temperature, a certain amount of weight loss, short periods of intestinal trouble and often restless nights made life unpleasant. As the symptoms were similar to those experienced during my Army days in Iraq, I assumed they were due to the heat and, once the cooler weather arrived, life would return to normal well-being. But a visit to Dr. McLean at the Mission Hospital in Ajlaun soon led to the diagnosis of severe amoebic dysentery and, within a few hours, I had the tender ministrations of nurses, the comfort of a hospital bed, but also very painful injections. Lying there feeling rather sorry for myself, I began to wonder which was worse, the disease or the cure and, with Marjorie unlikely to return for months, life had lost its rosy hue.

About the fourth day the situation changed. Victor put in an appearance looking as if he were the bearer of good news; and so he was. He brought a telegram announcing the totally unexpected news of Marjorie's imminent arrival in Damascus. The only problem was that this exciting event was due within the next forty eight hours and in no way could I be fit to travel to meet her. Victor, ever helpful, offered to go and with that I could relax and revel in the anticipation of her arrival. In my selfishness I never stopped to think of her family situation; only later did I know of the difficult decision she had been compelled to make. The knowledge that Marjorie was on the way gave me a much needed fillip and, by the time she arrived at Ajlaun, I felt ready to leave! Within a few days we were back in Amman sharing that ex woodshed-turned-bedroom originally prepared for a single occupant. Now furnished with two single beds and a minute chest of drawers it left little room for movement, but the prospect of a move to the north counterbalanced the inconvenience.

The journeys to Irbid recommenced and each visit included a period of house hunting. Occasionally we heard of a place which seemed as if it would meet our needs, but there was always a snag. It might be a tumble down shack, or three tiny rooms in a courtyard, or a half built structure which would be finished immediately(?) if only we would pay a hefty sum towards its completion. As the weeks slipped by we could not help but ask ourselves whether we were seeking to move in the wrong direction? Finally we felt convinced we needed a positive sign from the Lord, a definite indication Irbid was right. Therefore before our next visit we simply asked the Lord that, if He wanted us in Irbid, please would He provide a home by noon that day. On arrival we shared our thoughts with Victor and then set out to walk, enquire, and look. The morning slipped by with the usual result and, having exhausted all probable leads, we retraced our steps to the town centre intending to return to Amman by the midday bus. Victor, having some business to settle at a nearby Bank which closed at noon, hurried off whilst Marjorie and I secured seats in the rapidly filling bus. Just as the driver began to warm up the engine, Victor appeared at the door beckoning us to leave at once. He hurried us to the Bank, almost breathlessly mentioning someone there knew someone else who might know of a place to suit our needs.

The Bank clerk gave us the details and, from his description, the place sounded very promising, but then came a snag. The owner lived some miles away and the clerk had no idea when he would be in town. However he gave us the address of a shop whose proprietor could arrange for us to meet the landlord at a later date.

A few minutes later we located the shop, one of a row of typically open fronted establishments lined with shelves crammed with goods. We found the solitary chair in front of the counter occupied by a dignified looking person, presumably a customer, though, judging by the seeming emptiness of the place, it looked as if he would have to wait a long time to be served. As we entered, another figure whom we assumed to be the proprietor emerged from the inner gloom, and in answer to our query, indicated that the gentleman sitting at the front was none other than the man we sought! He agreed to show us the place and we knew our search had ended.

The detached, single storey dwelling could not be termed palatial; but it was new, stone built, and had enough rooms to meet our needs, though none would accommodate much in the way of furniture. It had the benefit of being linked to the town's water supply, but no guarantee there would be any in the pipes. It was about two hundred yards from the main highway, almost in the centre of a new development, and the front door opened directly onto what would be the street. Electricity had not yet reached the area but this was no loss – the house was too far from the generators.

The Muslim owner impressed us by the dignity and graciousness of his demeanour, his courteous attitude towards Marjorie and friendliness to Victor and myself. Therefore, when all formalities of business had been completed and we turned to go, there were handshakes all round. Unfortunately, our introduction to the culture of Islam had been somewhat defective, and Marjorie also stretched out her hand. For a moment he looked startled but, after another moment of hesitation, arranged his cloak to completely cover his hand and then extended it towards her. When more conversant with Islamic custom, we realised how gracious he had been to do that, instead of turning away offended by the prospect of defiling himself by touching a woman's unclothed hand.

We returned to Amman fully convinced the Lord had opened the way for the move to Irbid. The next few weeks were hectic as we collected our belongings from Es Salt, purchased basic necessities for our new home and then, early in January 1951, on a bitingly cold though sunny day, moved once more to unfamiliar surroundings. As the shadows lengthened and twilight deepened,

the muezzin's voice proclaiming the greatness of Allah and calling the faithful to prayer, echoed across the town; a reminder of the forces which would oppose the unique claims of Jesus Christ our Lord. Suddenly we felt very lonely, inexperienced, insufficient for the task to hand, and cut off from the warm Christian fellowship of the believers in Amman. But we encouraged ourselves with the Lord's words, spoken so long ago to the tiny group shortly to face a hostile world with the message of the Gospel, "Lo I am with you always even unto the end of the age." We then finished tidying our new abode, commended ourselves to the Lord's care and settled down to rest.

A new phase in our missionary experience had now begun. But before January ended, the news arrived, half expected, from Marjorie's father of her mother's homecall. Her initial anguish at having to leave her mother in October had passed its climax, and was now mitigated somewhat more by the knowledge that her suffering had ended and a new life had commenced in the presence of the Saviour whom she loved. Her favourite hymn, "Just as I Am" was played at her funeral and the singing of it now continues to bring back memories of a truly lovely person.

CHAPTER 16

Fresh Ventures in Irbid

(1951-52)

The Lord thy God shall bless thee...in all the work of thine hand (Deut. 16:15).

The shrill voices of excited children milling round our front door, penetrated to the tiny kitchen long before the breakfast dishes were cleared and preparations for the Friday gathering completed. Nine-o-clock had not yet struck but some forty children were clamouring for entry and the commencement of another unusual, and possibly chaotic, morning. Nearly two months had slipped by since we were first aware that our days would end under the sound of the muezzin's strident voice and begin, in the pale light of dawn, to the refrain, "God is great, Mohammed is His prophet, arise, prayer is better than sleep." Our little team had been increased by the arrival of Essie Brown, a trained physiotherapist, who desired to make use of her profession in the service of the Lord. Our contacts in Irbid had increased, partially due to the arrival of more refugees. The town engineer and his wife, young and zealous believers, made their home available for meetings and the number attending gradually increased. This was encouraging but we knew there would be a limit to church activities as long as they were confined to a young couple's newly furnished lounge. Such an arrangement excluded the possibility of any activity amongst children and youths, and we couldn't take the liberty of inviting Muslim adults into someone else's home. So the only solution was to invite the children into our home, even though this might lead to opposition from Muslim parents.

The question then centred around how to stimulate the interest of the children in the locality. The only other Christians we knew in the area were a Greek Orthodox family and we hoped, through their two children, to reach a wider group. Meeting these youngsters in the street I stopped to chat and, after inviting them to come to our home the following Friday, suggested they bring some friends with them. So early on the Friday morning a lively tattoo on our front door, and the raucous shouts of an excited mob, announced the children's arrival, and I wondered what sort of message had been conveyed by our two young friends. Anyway there was no time to analyse the situation, our first children's class had arrived and the situation called for speedy action. Hurriedly, and trusting the door would take the strain as the pressure on its lower panels increased, we finished breakfast, let the young hopefuls into Victor's bedroom which doubled as classroom, and endeavoured to bring order out of turmoil.

Having no idea how our invitation had been reworded, we were completely unaware of their anticipations. Knowing of the unfortunate experiences of others, we felt it wise to make clear that material gain had no place in our activities! Fortunately we were sufficiently advanced in Arabic to gain the children's attention and did so by the time honoured method of teaching them a chorus. Victor possessed a concertina which gave a lead but, in retrospect, I shudder to think what a cacophony of noise emanated from that room as a crowd of children, with completely untrained voices, sought to grapple with a simple western tune. But the children remembered the words and, being used to learning by rote, also committed to memory a Bible verse. Furthermore, not only did they come back the following week but brought others with them. The pattern of that first day repeated itself for many months, always with an attempt at a chorus, a verse to learn and the recounting of incidents from the life of Jesus. Whatever tales the children told on returning home, none were prevented from coming again.

As numbers increased we ran two groups, first admitting the girls, and after they trooped out, the boys who for most of the time had been clamouring round the doors or climbing up to peer through the iron barred windows. Naively we thought the girls would disperse, but they took their cue from the boys and the second session was as noisy as the first. The children's classes, in spite of their turmoil, continued for almost a year by which time many Scripture verses had been learned, along with accounts of the life and death of the Lord Jesus. It was a bold effort to reach Muslim children, and through them their parents, with the good news of the Gospel and only a coming day will reveal whether the seed sown bore fruit. Years later we did learn how the news of these classes had spread through the town. One of the stories, widely recounted, was that we invited the children to pray to Mohammed and nothing happened; but when responding to a request to pray to Jesus they were showered with sweets!! With such stories circulating, and in the light of other rumours which came to our ears much later, it was something of a miracle we survived unharmed in that particular area, especially after our contacts, quite unexpectedly, spread to an older age group.

After a few weeks a group of menacing looking teen-agers began hanging around the place taking note, or so we thought, of the children who had attended. But one Friday morning, just as we were enjoying a much needed coffee break, a hearty banging on the door announced their intention of seeing us. Their opening comments indicated the reason for their interest in our establishment, though they did not necessarily reveal the true motives for the visit. "We understand," said one, "you are a teacher of Christianity and we want to know what Christians believe." With coffee forgotten they were invited in and, there and then, began the first of many sessions endeavouring to explain the truths concerning Jesus Christ and His teachings. They were high school students and I took their request at face value and put aside all thought they might have come to argue, or with the ulterior motive of involving me in comments which, construed as insulting Islam, could lead to dire consequences.

As they had asked to learn about Christianity we laid down the terms of our discussions. First we placed before them an Arabic Bible asking what their opinion of us would be if we, as Christian teachers, denied anything contained in what we believed to be God's inspired word. They hesitated to answer but further questions elicited the answer they would consider us to be hypocrites. We stated that we believed the Bible to be God's truth and would have no need to go outside its pages for instruction in Christian belief and practice. They readily agreed to this though at the time we were not sure why we had been led to be so emphatic about the matter. Later we were grateful for that agreement because, when the visitors sought to turn to Koranic statements, we were able to lead them back to the Scriptures without getting involved in argument. When the first group of visitors left we wondered if they would ever return, but every Friday they came in increasing numbers - always in groups of three or four, one after another, until on some Fridays there was a continuous period of discussion from 11 am. till late in the afternoon. These young men had no objection to receiving literature and we hoped this would reach a wider circle than the groups meeting in our home.

There was good reason to believe the Gospels were read. Nearly eighteen months later I stopped to give a cadet officer a lift and almost immediately he asked if I recognised him. I could only afford a quick glance for even on the almost deserted roads of north Jordan wisdom dictates that one concentrates on the road. He said I ought to know him seeing he used to come to the house to talk about Christianity. Then he added, "You gave me a Gospel, remember?" I apologised, pointing out he had certainly changed since I last saw him and, after congratulating him on his obvious advancement, asked if he had read the Gospel. He assured me he had and then asked if I had more to give him. Happily I could, trusting these would also reach further than the immediate recipient.

So the weeks of 1951 slipped by with a little band of believers meeting twice a week in a private home, while the work amongst young people, remained centred on ours. But all the while, even though outwardly all seemed to be going well, we were conscious of an undercurrent of suspicion and distrust. Apart from our little team of four we knew of no other westerners living in the town and in view of the political situation, the reason for our presence was suspect. By this time a truce had been declared in Israel but hatred seethed against the Jews, especially as many scores of refugees arrived in the area of Irbid with tales of deprivation, hardship and terror. Poverty abounded and, whatever might be thought of the rights and wrongs of the situation, there could be no denying the fact that under one pretext and another many Palestinians had been forced from home and possessions. The hatred spilt over against the British and Americans.

The Arab - Israeli war had brought an influx of men into the Arab Legion and, whilst the majority were adherents of one of the Muslim sects, quite a number were members of the Orthodox and Catholic churches. The Muslims had opportunities for their daily prayers and the Friday sermon, but no provision had been made for the Christians and this had become a cause for complaint. General Glubb, who always had a deep concern for the welfare of his troops, was prepared for the Christians to have their own Chaplain but he faced a problem, which church tradition should be represented? The Orthodox would not be happy with a Catholic service, the latter would have baulked at the former, whilst any from an Anglican tradition might have been embarrassed at either. The best solution seemed to be to appoint someone whose ministry, being free from any particular liturgy, would consist of straightforward teaching from the Bible. Finally Roy, who was well known to the General and some of the Church leaders, received an invitation to undertake this responsibility. Roy asked me to join him as chauffeur, and during the next few months we visited most of the Arab Legion camps in Jordan and on the West Bank. Roy developed his own programme and this information was included in the Legion's daily orders. Most of the troops were happy to have an excuse for a duty free period, and consequently most of the meetings were well attended - so much so, it became clear Muslims were appreciating having extra time off as well! Many a Muslim, possibly for the first time, heard truths concerning Christ and Christianity and had the opportunity of correcting some of the misconceptions which he had held over the years. Camp visiting days were long and tiring, more so if they ended with an evening service calling for many more miles of travel, often over rough unmade roads. It was at the end of such a day the suspicion we were enemy agents appeared to be confirmed.

Roy had been conducting a series of evening meetings at the Ajlaun Hospital prior to travelling to Damascus and Beirut. The last day of the series included a visit to a distant Army unit resulting in arriving in Ajlaun just in time for the service. A time was fixed for the beginning of a service but never the end, consequently it was very late when we faced the dark road home. As we rocked, rattled and rumbled down the hill from the hospital Roy casually mentioned he still had to write a report to Command Headquarters. But there was no need to worry, he would plan it during the journey home. In five minutes he was fast asleep, all thoughts of the report forgotten unless it be in his dreams. Arriving home, there was a frantic scribbling of notes and, finally, a realisation that as he had to depart by 6 am. a readable hand written report could not be finished on time. Marjorie came to the rescue by typing his notes and a long night session began. I had to be up by 5am. to drive Roy to the Jordanian border to catch the bus, and so retired at midnight. Marjorie finally crawled into bed about 2.30 and, unbeknown to us, lingering, listening neighbours crept away to spread the rumour of midnight subversive activity on the part of the foreigners. What else, in their estimation, could those conversations and the click-clack of a machine mean other than communication with the enemy Israel. To ignorant and over heated imaginations it must have had all the elements of a classic spy story.

Had we known of these suspicions it would have been less of a surprise when on 20th July, a very agitated friend informed us of the assassination of King Abdullah, and warned us not to leave the house. Within a few minutes of his departure, armoured cars of the Arab Legion were roaring up and down the roads creating plenty of noise and dust but, as far as we could see, without any real purpose. Later when the facts of the case became known we understood why. The King, attended by General Glubb, had visited Jerusalem for the Friday prayers at the Mosque on the old Temple area. As he entered a few paces ahead of his guards, shots rang out and the King fell mortally wounded, killed by an assassin secreted behind the main door. The guards, much to the annoyance of General Glubb who realised the man must have been working in concert with others, shot the murderer and, in so doing, hindered the discovery of the real perpetrators of the crime. King Abdullah was very popular with the Jordanians, but less so with Palestinians who thought, maybe with good reason, he secretly desired to come to terms with Israel in order to add the West Bank to Jordanian territory. His murder sent shock waves throughout the country, especially as many thought it could be a prelude to civil strife. That strife reared its ugly head a few years later but for the time being the army, under the firm hand of General Glubb, kept the situation under control.

For the next few months no unpleasant incidents disturbed the even tenor of our lives. Numbers at the childrens' meetings continued to increase, divided fairly evenly between the sexes, and still with only two from an Orthodox Christian home. Muslim young men visited regularly on Fridays, whilst three or four who had a Christian background, felt free to drop in at any time. Their friendship proved invaluable, especially as they were by no means shy in pointing out our errors, both cultural and verbal.

At this time our little family increased by one as a young girl from Ajlaun, Martha, joined us to help in the home. The help was as much for her family as ours for, like many others, it was large and penurious. Later a younger sister, Rifqa, took her place and whilst their families had some financial benefit both girls obtained far more spiritually as they came to know Jesus as their Saviour and Lord. Then too a Muslim neighbour very earnestly spoke of a night vision in which Christ had revealed Himself and told him to seek counsel from the Christians. Victor and I listened attentively to his tale and, noting the eager way in which he listened to the story of the Cross, were impressed by the way he readily acknowledged his need of forgiveness and peace with God. Then came the disappointment - it turned out to be a blatant lie in the hope of obtaining material aid. Without doubt another useful lesson, warning us not to jump too quickly to conclusions, needed to be learnt.

Then came the moment when a hurdle of reticence was overcome, a restraining fear of inadequacy went, a verbal barrier was broken and the need for an interpreter ended. Living in Irbid, where the nationals rarely spoke English, meant we had made significant strides in understanding and communicating in Arabic on a social level. But to preach to a group of adults, where blunders would generate amusement, and broken grammar give rise to scornful criticism, required a boldness which eluded me. Victor and I took it in turns to lead the mid-week Bible studies and these, on the night so clearly remembered, were centred on the typical teaching of the Tabernacle in the Wilderness. To illustrate the lessons we had a small model and, on this particular evening, the brazen altar, standing at the entrance to the Court was to form the basis of our study. With the model ready, the room well filled with an enthusiastic group, and my notes prepared, the meeting could have commenced - except for one problem; the regular interpreter had not arrived. The group grew restless, some began to chat amongst themselves, others looked uncomfortable and a couple asked, "Why don't you give the lesson?" The situation left me with no alternative but to do it. So feeling horribly nervous, and with what many term a 'Nehemiah prayer', I launched into this most unlikely subject for a first endeavour. For the next forty five minutes I spoke on the lessons to be learned from the brazen altar and its equipment. There could hardly have been a better example of jumping in at the deep end, but the experience and the friendly, encouraging comments of the group, combined to assure me the Lord had loosened my tongue in His service.

Then came the day Victor set off for England, with the physiotherapist accompanying him as far as Cyprus. A sense of loneliness returned as we faced the pressure of the work alone. At such times, lacking the encouragement and strength of fellow workers, words similar to those of Isaiah 41:10 take on a deeper meaning: "I will strengthen thee, help thee, hold thee." We realise again that help is from the Lord alone.

CHAPTER 17

A Developing Ministry
(1952-53)

Neither he who plants is anything, nor he who waters, but God who gives the increase (1Cor. 3:7).

Towards the end of 1951, Dr. and Mrs. McLean relinquished hospital work in Ajlaun due to their advancing years. However they had no intention of retiring from Christian service and considered opening a medical work in Taibeh, a village a few miles west of Irbid where an ex-patient lived. We knew this man by name, the familiar one of Ahmad. During the fighting over the partition of Palestine, he had suffered a wound which affected his lower limbs, and was transferred to the hospital in Ajlaun as a long term patient. Almost immediately he made clear his antagonism to the Christian faith. Attempting to disturb the ward services, arguing with the native evangelist, being disagreeable to the staff, and breaking as many rules as possible, Ahmad made himself a thorn in the flesh to those responsible for the good running of the hospital. He tested their humility, meekness, and longsuffering. The quality of their lives gradually made a deep impression and his attitude softened. He began to heed the daily service, started to pray for physical healing and to show interest in Christian literature. Evidences of his prayers being answered, and the significance of what he read, were two principal factors in leading to his conversion. One book he read, *The Balance of Truth*, had been so effective in convincing Muslims of the truths concerning Jesus Christ, that it had been banned in Arabic countries and only a few copies were still in circulation. From books and tracts Ahmad turned to the Scriptures and was convinced of his spiritual need. He trusted the Lord Jesus and commenced to witness of the reality of his new found faith.

In due course Ahmad, though permanently lamed, returned to his family. The staff could not help but wonder how one so young in the faith, and uninstructed in the Scriptures, would be able to maintain a Christian witness in a mainly Muslim environment. There was a small Greek Orthodox community in the village but, bearing in mind the antipathy of the Christian minority to the Muslim, the question remained as to whether they would receive him. This antipathy of Christians to Muslims puzzled us in our early days in Jordan, but as we came to learn more about the Islamic faith, the course of its history, its culture and its attitudes towards Christian minorities, we began to understand the reasons. It was, therefore, not surprising that when the McLeans visited Taibeh they wondered whether Ahmad had been able to make an open declaration of his faith. They need not have worried. On locating the cluster of buildings which housed his extended family, they found him in the courtyard teaching a group of children choruses he had learned in hospital. Obviously, through their vocal efforts, however inharmoniously, Ahmad had found a way of making known his own faith.

A change affected also us and the work at this time - we lost the use of our meeting place. For some time this had been the home of Jameel, the town engineer, but, for family reasons, this became impossible. The obvious alternative was to move the meetings to our own home. Unfortunately this idea ran into an unexpected problem - the believers' fear of the Muslims. They refused to come as a group to our quarter, especially if it involved being there after dark. The two or three who were prepared to come assured us no strangers would and, as one of our main objects was to reach people with the Gospel, our home proved to be far from ideal. The message was clear: move to, or nearer, the Christian area and we will come. But such a move would have been counter-productive forestalling any hope of reaching Muslims. We decided the problem would only be solved when we found neutral ground, somewhere with a Christian presence and yet not inimical to any Muslim who desired to visit. So early in 1952, we found what we needed in a complex of three houses not far from the town centre. The largest house contained a spacious guest room which would be ideal for the meetings and the living quarters were adequate for our purposes. The front faced an extensive area of open ground flanked on the left by a few small houses and on the right by the road to El Husn, whilst at its base a line of buildings screened the high road and the main entrance to the town. The landlord, Abu Samaan, a native of El Husn and nominally a Christian, occupied one of the two smaller houses forming the rear of the building. His presence brought both problems and protection, the stories of which need to be told in their proper context.

When we changed homes we had a glimpse of the Muslim's detest for foreign Christians. Behind our original home lay a tiny patch of ground where we had cultivated a few flowers to create a spot of beauty. A needy Palestinian refugee with gardening experience had taken loving care of that little plot for us and found delight in turning its barren, somewhat stony, surface into a tiny oasis of green bordered with plants of various hue. Just after we left, a crowd of youngsters, unhindered by any of the neighbours, swarmed over the wall and destroyed the garden utterly. Every vestige of green was uprooted, tiny shrubs torn apart, plants trodden down, stones from a neat path scattered - the wilderness reigned once more. It was a mindless act of vandalism but, sadly, one of a piece with the historical record of Islam's tendency to destroy and reduce that which is fruitful into desert. The ruins of ancient civilisations in the Middle East and North Africa, the remains in Mesopotamia of vast irrigation systems, which once turned parts of Iraq into verdant and fruitful land, bear a bleak testimony to this.

Within a few days the regular pattern of meetings recommenced and the benefits of the change were soon apparent. The guest room became the official meeting room with adequate seating for forty; even forty five at a squeeze! Numbers gradually increased as believers felt freer to bring friends and to invite casual acquaintances. The small group of believers formed the nucleus of a local church and, as such, felt their responsibility both in witnessing and sharing the expenses of maintaining the centre. Whilst the meeting room was a part of our house we wanted it to be their meeting place. They, and we, desired it to be free from the common accusation that the missionary, and the missionary's money, controlled the situation. The church paid a rent appropriate to the size of the room, the cost of necessary equipment was covered from their weekly offerings, hymnbooks and Christian literature were obtained and provision made for covering the expenses of visiting speakers.

Yet another change involved our friend Essie Brown, the physiotherapist. Before going on holiday to Cyprus, she had made weekly visits to the Hospital in Ajlaun. There her training proved invaluable and she became one of the channels God used to bring the Gospel to Ahmad. On returning from Cyprus she renewed her visits to Ajlaun and then, partially due to the new situation there, made another move, this time to Jerusalem. There she found opportunities for serving the Lord in the exercise of her spiritual gifts and professional skills. So, once again, we were on our own with a threefold responsibility, shepherding the growing group of believers, seeking to make new contacts in Irbid, and endeavouring to develop the outreach, originally commenced by Victor, in El Husn.

The pace of life increased. In addition to a regular pattern of meetings, new contacts in the town created opportunities for visiting other villages. In those days it was not seemly, or wise, for Marjorie, an unveiled foreigner, to move around the town unattended, so general shopping fell to me. This provided plenty of scope for conversation and discreet distribution of literature which, at times, had positive results. Over a cup of coffee a shopkeeper might show some interest or even suggest we might like to visit his village. The suggestion might merely be the result of Arab courtesy but it could lead to a village where, possibly, the Gospel had never been preached before. In making such a visit the support of one or two young men from the local church would not only be an encouragement but of great benefit. Their facility in language compensated for our deficiencies, and their faith was strengthened as they became active participants in witnessing. Such visits had their problems, and moments of tension. Visiting a home with the intention of renewing an acquaintance, it could be filled with Muslims who were not merely anti-Christian but suspicious of a foreigner's intentions. Polite but impassive faces would convey these thoughts. General discussions had to be frank, but a-political, until some comment opened the way for something of spiritual significance to be expressed.

Sometimes the problem was in reaching the village, many of which were approached only by rough tracks more suitable for mules than cars. This meant a bus to the nearest definable spot and walking. A young Christian invited Victor and me to his village, cheerfully assuring us it lay but a short distance from a bus route, and he would happily take us on his day off. Late in the afternoon, after a bone-shaking ride over unsurfaced roads, the bus stopped at a wild, lonely spot where the only village in sight was an excellent example of a city set on a hill which cannot be hid. It appeared to be no more than a mile way and, as the bus rattled away enveloped in a cloud of dust, we started off in good heart over a narrow stony track to cover that 'mile'. However, our guide had failed to mention that a deep ravine lay between us and our destination! That mile was more like two whilst the steep gradients on the far side made it seem in excess of three! As we breasted the final slope with aching knees, short of breath, thirsty and wondering if the effort would prove to be worth while, our young friend told us if we only possessed a car a roundabout track would have brought us there in a few minutes!

The extended family gathered round to welcome home their son and his friends. With typical hospitality they ensured our thirst was quenched with well brewed tea. In a devious way questions were asked - who were we, what did we do, were we married, how many children did we have, did we get a good salary? all of which provided an informal atmosphere in which to witness to our faith. As the evening wore on, a sudden commotion and loud squawk of a scrambling hen, brought the assurance that preparations for the meal had begun. In due course a low table, graced with chicken, rice, cheese, bread and olives, was placed in the centre of the room and we squatted down to eat. By this time weariness made the thought of bed enticing but where remained a mystery. In due course local guests wended their way home leaving Mum and Dad, a clutch of children and ourselves to settle down for the night. The process was simple, the elders stripped off a robe, the children a garment or two, we divested what we thought necessary and managed a rinse in bowl of water. A row of mattresses was laid across the length of the single room and, with the oil lamps extinguished, we bedded down in comfort.

Dawn saw us gathered again around the table. Goat's cheese, hard boiled eggs, dishes of olives, humuz, zarta and oil, encircled a pile of freshly baked flat bread, and plenty of hot weak tea. We made a hearty breakfast before facing the ravine's steep and rocky track. Panting and puffing over the final crest we saw in the distance a cloud of dust, and put on speed to try to catch the bus. But all to no avail, the driver must have taken our vigorous waving as a morning greeting, and he simply rattled merrily on and left us standing a hundred yards from the road. Finally we hitched a lift back to Irbid's comparative luxury.

Visits to nearby El Husn were made more regularly. For centuries it had been a Christian village but the long running blood feud between its two main tribes hardly testified to a vital, life-changing faith. A few homes were open to us and one in particular anticipated frequent visits. Like many it bore the marks of poverty. The outer courtyard, populated by a few scrawny hens, was unpaved, its main mud brick walled room bare of furniture, whilst colourful locally made rugs only partially concealed the dinginess of a grey concrete floor. Deep recesses housed a quantity of brightly coloured single mattresses and cushions ready to be arranged around the walls in lieu of chairs. Very comfortable those mattresses were if one could recline but, for sitting cross legged, they became a penance for the uninitiated westerner. Previously unidentified muscles began to complain, the only relief being an occasional stretch of the leg, an action which could be attended by cultural problems. A carelessly extended leg might result in the sole of one's foot pointing directly at another person and causing deep offence; or, in the case of a lady, the exposure of an ankle could be a breech of decorum. Marjorie has never forgotten the hastily produced towel to cover legs and feet as she stretched for a little relief.

Poor that dwelling may have been, but it was home to one of the brightest Christians one could hope to meet. Nyim was completely blind. When barely six years old a gun accident robbed him of sight. In his teens he had been given the opportunity to attend the

British Syrian Mission blind school in Beirut and, possibly it was there he came to know Jesus as his Saviour. The Um Samweel family introduced Victor to him and from then on the home was open for Christian witness. With Victor absent in Britain we went as often as possible and our arrival rarely went unannounced to the neighbourhood. Within a few minutes a primus stove, covered by a small pan, would be roaring in a corner of the room, the odour of roasting coffee beans would begin to pervade the air and, shortly, rhythmic pounding began as they were ground to powder. Within a few minutes neighbours would drift in and, by the time the first cup was being sipped, it would be standing room only, at least for the children. Conversation would then flow freely, but gradually fade, as the Scriptures were opened and the way of life proclaimed.

Reaching El Husn did not present much problem. The all weather road deteriorated as soon as it reached the town boundary. From then on it was a dirt track leading across a wide expanse of level land; green with young corn in early spring, golden at the time of harvest, brown, barren, dry and dusty in late summer heat, but in many parts sodden and transformed by early rains into deep patches of heavy mud. An ancient bus, supplemented by a few service taxis, plied between Irbid, El Husn and regions beyond but timings were virtually non-existent. For a westerner, this could be an irritating situation. Sometimes it was quicker to walk than wait.

The use of local transport may have been interesting, and the pedestrian exercise healthy, but we were not sorry when the situation changed. Someone sent us £200 earmarked for a car and in due course we got a fairly spacious Plymouth saloon with a front bench seat. Carrying six was no problem, though double that number of children were squeezed in at times! It looked in fairly good condition, possibly because layers of paint concealed most of the rust. The engine pulled well, especially on the flat, and whilst the gear box rattled it never let us down. Other parts did. One time, admittedly when heavily overloaded, a sudden jerk sent a loose water pump through the radiator with interesting results. On the whole it proved to be a good vehicle, for the price, and did us yeoman service for many months. Like the majority of cars in that part of the world it had been patched up with non standard items, a fact which came to light when someone, having shut a door rather vigorously, was surprised to see the glass fall out. In low gear over rough roads, or on climbing a steep slope, it had a tendency to boil and many a time there were opportunities to survey the countryside through clouds of steam. A four gallon tin of water became standard equipment and the need for lubricant boosted the shares of the oil companies. But it was our own car and we were grateful for the Lord's provision.

On Victor's return from furlough in 1952 changes continued. He arrived, almost penniless, after travelling overland using local rail and bus services. He had bought a copy of the European train timetable and planned his own route. He now shared our home for a few weeks and his cheerful enthusiasm was a tonic but, before long, he moved again. Before going on furlough Victor had frequently visited the hospital in Ajlaun but now he transferred some of his energies to the new work in Taibeh. During the war years he had served in the Army Medical Corps and had a keen interest in the work of Dr. McLean and the recently opened clinic. He also enjoyed a very friendly relationship with Ahmad and together they bore a fine Christian testimony. He maintained a keen interest in Irbid, and on Sundays, after conducting a morning service in the village, would come over to us to share in the breaking of bread and evening fellowship. We took it in turns to preach and, even under the most appalling weather conditions, he would endeavour to be present. One dismal Sunday the lowering clouds threatened more rain on an already water logged earth. By midday the downpour had begun and, realising it was unlikely any vehicle would get through on the Taibeh road, we felt sure Victor could not come. But about 4pm. a rain soaked figure lurched, rather than walked, through the front door. It was Victor's turn to preach and, rain or no rain, he intended to fulfill his responsibility. We had been right in assuming no vehicle could get through so he decided to walk. First the rough muddy track led down into a deep valley, then weaved its way up a steep hill towering above the Jordan valley, finally to reach the main road. There, already soaked, he began the winding uphill way to Irbid anticipating a lift from some friendly driver, but none would stop. By the time he reached Irbid he had covered fourteen miles over very difficult terrain, so it was no wonder he lurched! That, however, showed the measure of the man; a responsibility must be fulfilled.

1952 was full of activity, and sometimes many miles of travel. Marjorie's father, in company with a friend, had decided to spend a month with us and we were to meet them at Beirut. But their passage was on a cargo boat operated by a minor shipping line and this was diverted to the northern Syrian port of Latakia. This would add many miles to our return trip but a friend, who offered to travel with us, guaranteed a night's lodging at his home about thirty miles short of the port, so we thought the trip could be accomplished in two days. The outward journey was a nightmare due to lengthy delays, atrocious weather and poor roads. Late in the evening, tired, cold, hungry and damp we began to wonder if the journey would ever end. Then came the moment of relief, a few feeble street lamps, a blur of houses and we were there. What a lovely welcome we received, and how much we appreciated the warmth of the room and the bowls of hot water to soak our tired feet. Restored after a good night's rest we were early on our way, only to be pulled up by the police who, quite belligerently, demanded why the car was unlicensed. I had completely forgotten the number plate had fallen off the previous day, and had difficulty convincing them we were not smugglers or car thieves but innocent tourists. Finally, after insisting on seeing the license plate attached, they waved us on our way.

Arriving in Latakia we saw the boat lying off shore and rolling heavily in the swell. The port boasted no harbour - goods and passengers were off loaded into small craft. The sea was too rough for small boats to tie up to the ship and it would be some time before passengers could disembark. We were faced with the problem of finding accommodation again and it was then we had one of those lovely surprises the Lord loves to give. The American Mission had a boarding school in town and we wondered if they could direct us to low cost accommodation. Understandably we were greeted with some reserve but, after realising we had mutual friends, they relaxed and welcomed us in, the outcome being a delightful two days' stay waiting for the seas to subside. Unbeknown to us, there was a young pupil there named Wadiah who would later be, with her husband, a valued colleague in both Lebanon and France. On the third day the passengers who were bold enough to risk the transfer from ship to boat, landed and we were on our way home. That journey was enlivened by the comments of our passengers as they faced a completely new world and culture, and by a brief brush with the Syrian authorities because I had forgotten to get an exit visa. The month's visit left us with some vivid memories, the most important being the pleasure of hearing Marjorie's father openly confess his faith in the all sufficiency of Christ's redemptive death on Calvary.

During the final months of the year a literature ministry was added to our activities. Before leaving Jerusalem in 1948 we helped the Nile Mission Press to close their work in the old City. As a consequence a fairly large stock of material, in Arabic and English, had been left in store where it was of no use to anyone. By 1952 we were convinced the literature ought to be recovered and could now see at least one good reason for our being allowed to stay in Egypt in 1947. From that time we had a very good relationship with the manager of the Nile Mission Press, and he also knew of the help we had given in Jerusalem. So our letter requesting permission to take over the stored material received a favourable response. The Mission entrusted us with the stocks and, having transferred them, we began to work out methods of distribution. In retrospect it was a very small effort with literature but it helped to lay the groundwork for a far wider ministry in days to come.

Irbid was off the beaten track for tourists but we still had many visitors, some of whom were gifted speakers and we certainly appreciated them. Others were touring and just passing through on their way to the Holy Land. We entertained missionaries on their way home from Pakistan or India, others from Cyprus and even further afield from England and America. One couple caused us some anxiety. On Christmas Day two strangers appeared at our door and, surprise, surprise, they had come from the land Arabs would not include on their maps - Israel. Only when they mentioned their names and Nazareth did we realise the unpleasantness they could have experienced on their journey. Outside Jerusalem anyone mentioning they lived in Israel could be guaranteed, at the very least, a cool welcome, especially if they were Americans, as our visitors were. Mr. and Mrs. Medrow were astonished to discover such animosity existed, which only served to highlight the fact that, in Israel, there was little appreciation of the Arabs' resentment against those they blamed for the loss of their land.

The Medrows had translated Emmaus Bible Correspondence courses into Arabic but then discovered a snag. No Arab land would receive mail from Israel and thus the prospect of reaching the Arabic speaking world was nullified. The solution to the problem lay in basing the work in another Middle Eastern country and they decided to seek our help. Their problem was how to contact us, obtain our agreement to develop the work, and hand over the translated material. The Christmas season supplied the answer. For that period the Jordanian government granted permission for Christians in Israel to make a pilgrimage to Bethlehem, and the Medrows crossed the border for that purpose. Then, not realising their permit covered only a restricted area, nor how far they would have to travel, they decided to catch a bus to Irbid. How they got through without any problems we do not know. The Bible correspondence course contact was fruitful, for over the years we saw it grow to embrace eighteen Bible courses distributed to many hundreds of students in numerous Arab lands.

The Medrows became good friends, but it is possible their visits did more than any others to confirm the impression we had dealings with Israel. Being ignorant of the trouble it could cause, they not only mentioned their links with that country, and in particular Nazareth, but, on one occasion, turned up in their own car with American number plates bolted over those of Israel! It nearly gave us a heart attack! But for the time being we were able to continue our work, more or less unhindered, and unaware of the cloud hanging over us.

CHAPTER 18

In Journeys Oft

(1953 - 55)

The Lord will guide you continually (Isaiah 58:11).

At the beginning of the new year, we were planning a visit to Iraq. In various ways our contacts and experiences in the Middle East were expanding bringing with them a realisation of the complexity of its racial mix. Most people append the name Arab indiscriminately to the inhabitants of North Africa and the broad swathe of land from the Mediterranean to the Persian Gulf, without realising the national and cultural differences that exist. The true Arabs of the Arabian peninsula, descending from the ancient tribes of Ishmael, have little in common with the Palestinians and Lebanese whose roots go back to Caananite and Phonecian times. The Syrians (the Aramaens of the Old Testament) likewise differ from their neighbours in Iraq, where historical antecedents lie in the ancient Assyrian and Babylonian empires. The characteristics and culture of the Egyptians, grounded in a civilisation whose origin is shrouded in the mists of time, set them apart from those of Tunisia and beyond where the Berbers once held sway. From the time of Alexander the Great most of these nations have known periods of domination by European powers and whilst, today, they rejoice in their own sovereignty, traces of the cultural norms of the occupying forces remain. The unity which results in them all being termed Arab, rests upon a common language and an almost common religion. The Muslim conquests of the seventh century AD absorbed the entire area but, in spite of adversity and persecution, some 5% of the population still have their religious roots in one of the early Christian traditions. But whatever their nationality, all are included in the promise that 'whosoever calls on the name of the Lord shall be saved' and are embraced in the same question, 'How shall they hear without a preacher?' It was in response to that challenge that we accepted an invitation to visit Baghdad.

Captain Arthur Trebble, a pilot with Iraqi Airways, had accepted the post with the Lord's service in mind. He and his wife Violet and their three young children lived in a spacious house on the outskirts of Baghdad and within a few weeks Bible studies were commenced in their home. It was obviously an effective ministry for it was not long before they had the joy of seeing a number committing their lives to the Lord Jesus. Hearing we were engaged in a similar ministry he invited us to visit with a view to conducting a series of evangelistic and teaching meetings. It proved to be an interesting and spiritually profitable time which one hoped would lay a foundation for a growing work. Sadly the political situation finally led to the Trebbles having to leave the country.

Within a few days of our return from Iraq we commenced a period which seemed to be full of visitors, together with new opportunities for reaching villages with the Gospel. The first of our visitors were, once more, the Medrows. They had come to inform us that the first Arabic Bible Course was with a printer in Arab Jerusalem, and an Arab brother would take delivery. However, they hadn't arranged for the three thousand copies to be transported to Irbid, a task I eventually accomplished on the bus. Lugging those parcels on to the bus, and then from the terminus to the house, may have been good for the muscles but a strain on the temper! However, in the spring of 1953 the first few Correspondence Course students were enrolled, beginning a ministry which would touch, and is still touching, thousands of lives.

Our next visitor, a missionary based in Cyprus, provided an opportunity for a week of special meetings which were not only well attended but provided moments of interest and even excitement. Like most visitors he spoke by interpretation and as Costa Deir was also visiting he undertook this responsibility. It was a difficult task, for the speaker used long, complicated, sentences and tended to be dramatic in his presentation. When speaking of the Children of Israel being delivered from Egypt he excelled himself. Graphically he depicted the raging seas, described fervently the overwhelming of Pharaoh's army, and then them 'gnashing their teeth at the bottom of the sea'. I was so lost in trying to envisage this that I never did know how Costa dealt with that one. It was, I believe, the same night when Costa suddenly asked the speaker to pause and allow him to make a few comments. He then explained that the events which had been described took place thousands of years ago and had no link with recent affairs. He had noticed that a number of Muslim strangers were present who seemed to be on the verge of a riot. The visitor's reference to Israel and Egypt they took to be about Egypt's defeat at the hands of the Israelis in 1948. Consequently, as the destruction of the Egyptian armies appeared to be told with great satisfaction, they became more and more agitated. With eyes blazing they were preparing to erupt, at least verbally. Costa's well timed intervention calmed the situation but it highlighted afresh the need for care when presenting historical situations which have a modern parallel.

Costa's evangelistic gifts were an invaluable help. Being a Bible Society colporteur he was well supplied with a good selection of the Scriptures but, being anxious for them to be distributed, he must have given away more than he sold. He strongly believed in sowing the Word. His response to that injunction was to leave Gospels wherever he considered there was the remotest possibility of them being picked up. Many a time copies were left by a village well, placed amongst the corn at harvest time, or even amongst the stubble where the gleaners would gather. I had reservations about the effectiveness of such unorthodox methods, but my doubts disappeared when I saw a demonstration of their value.

On a swelteringly hot day in the middle of June we were on our way to a small Bedouin encampment. In one of the loneliest of spots Costa left three or four portions of Scripture near the road side. A short while later we were reclining round a charcoal brazier, in the comparative cool of a goat's hair tent, sipping scalding bitter coffee from minute china cups, whilst black robed Bedouin gathered around plying us with questions. Outside the heat haze shimmered and the air resounded with the bleating of sheep. Suddenly came the sound of hurrying feet and a young lad burst into the tent. Waving a little booklet he excitedly broke into the conversation, "Look what I have found!" and immediately all eyes were riveted on him. Costa, recognising it as a copy of the Psalms, stretched

Bedouin tent

out his hand to take it and, saying he knew it and it was good, began to read. Voices quieted and stillness reigned as he led the assembled shepherds, verse by verse, through Psalm 23. For the next few minutes those men, who as far as we knew, may never have seen even a portion of the Bible, listened intently as Costa read and spoke of the most wonderful Shepherd of all who gave His life for the sheep. It was a great experience sitting with that small, very attentive, crowd, knowing too that beyond the dividing curtain some of the women folk with the children, would also hear the word of life. Someone there must have been literate for Costa left the booklet and, if I remember correctly, portions of the Gospels as well. One could not help but wonder how often they might be read and be used to lead someone to seek the Lord.

As soon as Costa finished, a hubbub of conversation broke out only to be checked as a young lad, bearing a large ewer of water and a towel of uncertain hue, entered to wash our hands. Like Elijah's servant of old he poured water over our hands, we all shared the towel and, a few minutes later, the brazier was removed to be replaced by a huge brass tray bearing piles of flat bread and, in a shallow cauldron, a steaming pile of rice liberally dotted with pieces of greasy looking mutton. We were urged to gather round but not before the contents of a large bowl of melted grease had been poured over all. It was only the second time I had been to such a meal and, this time, I could be thankful the skull did not adorn the pile, thus negating the possibility of being offered one of its eyes.

Eating implements were non existent: each man simply plunged his right hand into the hot sticky mess, rolled a portion into a firm ball then, with an adroit flick of the finger, threw it into his mouth. Balls of rice were rapidly flicked into many mouths, strips of mutton torn off and quickly consumed, grunts of satisfaction emitted and the huge pile diminished before our eyes. I can't say either of us ate too well. My little balls of rice were never quite firm enough, disintegrated half way to my mouth and the flick of a finger took most of the rest over my shoulder!

That particular month saw visits to a number of villages two of which, for very different reasons, remain fixed in our minds. One appeared to consist of a single, very extended, family of Orthodox Christians. We had been assured of a warm welcome so, piling into the Plymouth, we rattled our way there. After a relaxing evening with opportunities for presenting the claims of Christ, we were urged very strongly to come again. Two or three weeks later we did and the welcome was especially warm, even including the mention of an evening meal, though, with no sign of preparation, we wondered at what hour they dined. The answer to that query came some half an hour later when, as we relaxed on their makeshift verandah and viewed the peaceful countryside, the evening calm was suddenly shattered by a commotion in the courtyard below. A scared looking hen was running, literally for its life, chased by one of the women. Soon we were squatting on stools round a low table, graced with the bird's remains, goats' cheese, olives, humus and sundry other items, sharing the family meal. Only as the evening progressed did the reason for the invitation become apparent. Gradually, the subject of health entered the conversation. We spoke freely of the good work being done by both the Baptists, and Dr. McLean and Dr. Dorey, in their respective areas.

But the conversation took a different turn when one of the village elders suggested we arrange for a hospital, or at least a clinic, in their village! We could only point out the impossibility of our being able to organise or operate such a project. But the pleading went on until the senior elder made an offer. If we would arrange things as they desired, they would ensure the whole village would convert to the Protestant faith. When we managed to convince them we were not in the business of buying, or bribing, anyone to become an evangelical their ardour for us vanished. In fact, a few youths loitering near the car, shied a few stones as we départed one of which sailed through an open window and caught Marjorie on the head, fortunately without any serious damage.

The other visit had a vastly different ending. Anis Shorrosh introduced us to Naji, a serjeant of the Arab Legion and nominally a Christian. The suggestion was made that we should visit his village and he, happy to have the opportunity of being with his family, readily agreed. Accompanied by Costa we spent a very pleasant evening there and on the way home something unexpected happened. Our serjeant friend had been more influenced by the Gospel message than we realised and, as I drove, he and Costa were deep in conversation. It became clear from his comments the Holy Spirit was convicting Naji of sin and righteousness and judgment to come. Before arriving home he had trusted the Lord Jesus as his Saviour and, from that moment, there began a tremendous change in his life. The change was soon noticed in the Muslim regiment to which he was attached; we saw it month by month in his speech and attitudes. A few months later, when the regiment moved down to the Jordan valley, even the villagers noted the quality of his life, so much so that one stopped him in the street to ask, 'Why are you so different from all the other Christians we know?'

Costa Deir, national evangelist

Then the month of Ramadan commenced and increased religious fervour placed restraints on our visits to Muslim villages. Costa was to be with us for just one more week and being anxious to make full use of his days, suggested another method for the distribution of Scriptures. Public transport between villages was often limited to one daily bus to town, though some of the larger villages had a service car which, generally, only travelled when full. This meant there were always pedestrians happy to obtain a lift, not least during Ramadan, when hunger and thirst took their toll. So each day we roamed the country roads and on overtaking someone, often carrying shoes or sandals over his shoulder to prevent undue wear, would stop and offer a lift. It was rarely refused and, while I drove, the stranger would chat with Costa whose cheerful, extrovert nature soon broke down any restraint. By the time we reached the outskirts of a village the passenger would have satisfied his curiosity concerning me and extended a welcome to his home. Costa would politely refuse, on the grounds of it being Ramadan and a daytime visit might not be convenient, and then present his new acquaintance with a portion of Scripture. Throughout that week we became familiar with our local roads and many Scripture portions were distributed, accompanied by a witness to the Christian faith.

On one occasion Costa brought a few of his friends to stay. Then two or three more arrived and were bedded down in the meeting room but, as they ate heartily before retiring, little remained for breakfast. Housekeeping funds were nearly finished and we wondered if we dared expend them on food for the guests, knowing it could only be at the expense of forgoing some necessary item; for example, milk powder which we sorely needed. But there had been no need for us to worry. While we sat at breakfast sharing with our guests all that Marjorie could provide, a knock on the door announced another visitor. A missionary friend had called, simply to bring a gift - a small barrel of dried milk sufficient to last us for several weeks! Our friends left and we turned to praise and thanksgiving for present provision and the many other times when the Lord had met our needs. His ways are of His own devising and we can but sit back and marvel.

We had several lean times financially during 1953, for our frequent visitors placed a strain on our meagre resources. Then the Lord provided another surprise. One day a very official looking envelope arrived from a London solicitor asking if I wished to contend a will. Apparently an aunt had died and, without mentioning specific names, had left a legacy for 'the children of her two brothers'. Knowing this aunt had not been in touch with our side of the family for years I replied stating I felt I had no claim on her estate. In a few days the matter was forgotten, so it was a great surprise when later we received cheques of £100 for myself and £50 for Marjorie. This bounty not only supplied the rent but enabled us to take two weeks' holiday in Lebanon, the first for nearly three years.

In addition to such problems and opportunities we came across opposition from an unexpected quarter. By this time we were well aware of the antagonism of Islam but had forgotten the possibility of opposition from the Church of Rome. The Nuns in the Catholic school forbade the children to come anywhere near us and threatened penalties for any who dared attend the meetings. The priest in El Husn went one step further. He told the boys in his school the Scriptures were forbidden to them and any copies they had should be burnt. As a result four Bibles, and possibly a number of Gospel portions, were gathered together and destroyed.

The new year 1954 had its measure of unexpected experiences. The first occurred in our local police station. I had occasion to visit to try to help a young nominal Christian who had got himself into trouble. Foolishly he allowed his antipathy to Islam to erupt into verbal cursing and had been speedily bundled off to prison. Some of his relatives asked if I could intercede for his release and, the least I could do, was to go and try. The serjeant, who was new to the town, asked why we were in Irbid and, in the midst of my explanation, another Muslim policeman butted in. He, apparently, had attended Gospel meetings in Haifa and proceeded to tell the serjeant what we believed. Amazingly, the serjeant himself began to give a fairly clear idea of the way of salvation. He told the story of two people on their way to Heaven, both of whom knew they needed a passport to enter. Only one had his with him and the other asked if he could have a portion. At this juncture the serjeant, who had a piece of paper in his hand, tore off a strip, then continued. The man with the bit of paper reached heaven but was refused because when the bits were displayed they formed the word 'Hell'.

As I knew a version of the story I could not help but wonder what the serjeant would do with the piece of paper still in his hand. I half expected him to crumple it up and throw it into the waste-paper basket. But he picked up the thread of the story saying, "The other person went on to the door of Heaven and was allowed to enter," and then added, "Why?" Here he unfolded the piece of paper revealing the Cross. "That," he said, "is how the second man entered in." The rest of the men standing around listened intently and, without demur, accepted my offer of Gospels and tracts, whilst the serjeant asked for a Bible. The following day I had the pleasure of fulfilling that request and could but pray it would be read with spiritual profit.

The weeks slipped by full of activity and by April we were conscious of the need for a definite break. Before the end of the month we decided to visit England and, hearing one could travel from Cyprus to London for £25, we checked our finances, decided we could afford it, and began preparations for leaving in June.

Our route was Damascus, Beirut, then a flight to Cyprus, to catch a boat to Venice then overland by train to England. Our few days in Cyprus spent in the company of Jack and Gladys Morris, formerly missionaries in Egypt, were most enjoyable. At that time the problems between Cyprus and Britain, over the subject of sovereignty, were spilling over into acts of violence but, in spite of that, we found the place restful and relaxing after the tensions of the Middle East. Consequently, by the date of sailing we were beginning to unwind. That, however,changed when we boarded, especially for Marjorie who found herself sharing a cabin with three other ladies, two of whom had two young children apiece, and a third whose main luggage appeared to be a huge cheese. Travelling in what would be termed steerage the cabins were near the waterline and there was no hope of opening the portholes. The combination of the lady insisting on giving her cheese a daily airing, the other ladies succumbing to sea sickness and the washing of dirty nappies leading to the blocking of the basins, meant the atmosphere was heavy and redolent ... I shared a cabin with only five others, some of whom had failed to deal with their socks for a long time. Not surprisingly, we spent most of the daylight hours on deck! Fortunately the sea did little more than provide a comfortable, gentle roll and this, plus suitable medication, kept seasickness at bay as we headed for Venice.

At this juncture our ignorance of the city struck us and we realised we really were 'innocents abroad'. We would have two nights and a day to spare before catching the train but where to locate accommodation suitable for our means, and how to get there, remained a mystery. As we leaned over the rail and discussed the situation, a Lebanese with whom we had exchanged an occasional word, approached to ask how we intended reaching our hotel. He became, metaphorically, an angel in disguise for he speedily solved our dual problem. He not only knew of a cheap hotel near the railway station but, being familiar with the watery methods of transport, and their rightful costs, saved us the expense of a taxi by hiring a gondola and sharing the fare. We deeply appreciated his kindness and, at the same time, saw it as another gracious act of the Lord meeting a definite need.

Had our time schedule permitted it would have been easy to linger in the fascinating city of Venice, but early on the second day, we boarded the train for the next leg of the journey home. The flat landscape of northern Italy was uninspiring though glimpses of distant mountains gave promise of spectacular scenery once we had passed Milan. However darkness fell just as the train began the picturesque route through the foothills and commenced its twisting climb to the summit. Couchettes had not been included in our budget and, with the crowded compartment subject to constant movement, the possibility of sleep was minimal. This didn't bother us, we were on our way home and excited by the thought. By mid morning with Calais behind us, the white cliffs of Dover came into view and, not long after lunch, we were steaming out of Euston en route to a new home in a new area. My sister and mother had moved to the village of Wollaston near Northampton and this became the main base for the whole of our furlough.

A batch of mail waited our arrival including invitations to various meetings and missionary conferences. In a manner reminiscent of our first furlough we soon had a fairly full programme for the next six months and travel within Britain began in earnest. In retrospect we appreciate we made a mistake, often committed by missionaries on furlough; no time was set aside for an initial holiday to recuperate. Life became one long round of conferences, meetings, visiting relatives and travelling, resulting in our being as tired when we returned overseas as when we arrived home. But we were young, enthusiastic, zealous in what we believed to be the Lord's work, and fearful of being unfaithful servants. Many years were to roll by before the lesson was learned, that the Lord is quite content for His servants to rest awhile.

Comments on this particular furlough would not be complete without a reference to a most memorable engagement. We were invited to take joint responsibility, as padre and wife, for the Yorkshire Assemblies' Sunday School Camp at Marske near Redcar. We had taught in Sunday Schools and spoken at children's meetings, but the thought of guiding Bible studies and a series of evening services, geared to an age range from three to eighteen was, to say the least, daunting. Having duly prepared, but still feeling much trepidation, we set off for Leeds to join the buses for Camp and the start of a very exciting week. Most of the children came from the Leeds, Bradford, Halifax area with a few from Doncaster, Sheffield and York, the common denominator being the broadness of their dialect, the boisterousness of their spirits and their determination to make the most of freedom from parental restraint.

It was a very happy camp with lots of fun both within its perimeter and further afield on the lovely sands but, more importantly, it proved to be a time of rich spiritual blessing. Marske Camp was a highlight in the lives of many young people and time proved the reality of their conversion. Lives were definitely changed and one of our encouragements on subsequent furloughs, even up to thirty five years later, was to meet one and another who would remind us that at Marske they had come to know Jesus as their Saviour. One obeyed the call to an overseas mission field and, no doubt, others have been used in many ways to further the kingdom of God.

One other event retained its clarity - the renewed, but short-lived hope of an addition to our family. Maybe the pressure of our programme was too demanding and prevented Marjorie obtaining sufficient rest, or there could have been some other physical explanation. Whatever the reason, there was no doubt of her miscarriage on Christmas day. We were both deeply disappointed but, having acknowledged the sovereignty of the Lord, and come to the conclusion that, if for some reason our service for the Lord required our remaining childless, we endeavoured to be content. We thanked the Lord for His over-ruling and yielded our united lives afresh into His hands. It took some weeks for her to regain strength and she was barely fit to travel on the day when, having again experienced the trauma of leaving loved ones, we turned our faces eastward once more.

Having located a cheap flight to Cyprus we decided to fly in preference to another sea voyage. 'Skyways' (I believe that was the name of the firm), an enterprising private company, provided overnight economy flights from the fledgling airport of Stanstead to Cyprus via Malta. Their plane was an ex RAF transport and had certainly seen better days. It was noisy, seemed to vibrate in every joint and, as planes still flew at comparatively low altitudes, gave a very bumpy ride, especially as we slowly circled over Malta before finally meeting the runway with a hefty bounce. Some passengers made half joking comments about crash landing but it seemed one traveller took the matter seriously for he failed to turn up for the next leg of the flight to Cyprus! We reached Cyprus on the 17th March, flew into Beirut on the 18th, and on the 19th passed through the airport in Amman. From there it was but a two hour car ride, through a multi-coloured countryside where a profusion of spring flowers and patches of winter sown seed maintained a precarious hold in shallow rock strewn soil, on to Irbid and a period of more totally unexpected changes.

CHAPTER 19

Opposition and Expectation

(1955-56)

His faithfulness will be your shield and rampart
(Psalm 91:4).

The last few months of 1954 had seen a hardening of attitudes against Christian missionary effort in the north of Jordan, possibly due to the influence of the Muslim Brotherhood which had a strong following in the area. According to Victor, the Government had on three occasions instructed Costa to refrain from going to villages selling Gospels and preaching to Muslims. Believing he should obey God rather than man, Costa continued, resulting in his being summoned before the courts where, supported by the prayers of many of his Christian friends, he had both courage and wisdom to testify to his faith. In court he based his defence on the fact that he was a son of the country, the birthplace of most of the prophets and the birthplace of Christ; and if the court could show him a law, framed by the Government of Jordan, forbidding him to speak of Jesus, he would submit. The court dismissed the case but it was the first of a series of attempts to restrict the proclamation of the Gospel. Before the end of the year Victor had written to tell us that the Ministry of the Interior had brought pressure on the Gilead Mission in Taibeh, by requesting a document to be signed stating there would be no preaching of the Gospel outside a recognised place of worship. The request was refused, visits to villages continued and, in spite of the attitude of the Government, and opposition from nationalistic movements, Muslims still continued to attend evangelistic services. The fact that the Gilead Mission conducted an excellent medical work from its base in Taibeh may have softened the attitude of the authorities. By the time we returned nothing had been done to hinder the missionary work in Irbid; in fact by the end of March there had been an encouraging increase in the numbers attending the services.

On our return the house had a drab, dreary, deserted look and a thorough spring clean was needed before unpacking boxes, arranging furniture and making the place look and feel like home. We began to pick up the threads of the work and come to terms with some of the changes which had taken place in our absence. There were new friends to meet both in the church and within the missionary fraternity, especially amongst the Americans in Ajlaun. But we noted many nationals had adopted new attitudes towards Westerners in general and the British in particular, mainly due to the increasingly serious refugee problem, for which Britain and America were blamed. Even those who devoted time, energy and finance to assist refugees found themselves in difficulty. The Ministry of Interior banned an American Mission working near Jerusalem which had made generous donations of clothing to all in need who attended their services. Unfortunately this gave the impression one had to be a Christian to get help and many Muslims were professing Christianity simply to get garments. This incensed Muslim leaders who made protests in influential quarters.

In Irbid, a retired missionary from the British Syrian Mission, was providing clothing, food and free education for a number of refugee children. She faced the threat of having her work closed, due to tighter regulations against the distribution of Scriptures to Muslims. Miss Fitzpatrick made no secret of the fact that Bible lessons were included in the curriculum, but she was always careful to comply with the law against the distribution of Christian literature. But one day a visitor left a pile of Gospels on one of the desks and a number of pupils helped themselves and, no doubt, displayed their acquisitions at home. The result was a visit from a very angry and discourteous School's Inspector who brusquely demanded to examine the pupils to see if they had been indoctrinated. As he rifled through one of the pupil's bags his temper was not improved on finding a Gospel. He followed this with a series of questions, the answers to which only increased his anger. Thoroughly irritated he passed to the last room of older children and sarcastically asked,

"Can anyone pray"? "I can, sir!" said one girl and, maybe hoping in some way to humiliate her, he ordered, "Pray then." She stood, placing her hands together and bowing her head, prayed spontaneously, simply and sincerely in the name of Jesus. Turning to the door he strode out, with Miss Fitzpatrick trotting after him eagerly inviting him to join her for coffee. Turning to her he refused and furiously demanded that all scriptural instruction and preaching, should cease forthwith. However he had not considered how his discourteous behaviour, and obvious anger, had tried the patience of the Irish lady before him. As he ranted on, she drew herself up to her full five feet, and emphasising her words with an admonitory finger, burst out, "I will preach, and preach, and preach!" As each repetition was accompanied with a step forward the Inspector could but retreat and leave the premises. No more was heard of the threatened closure even though within half an hour the incident was widely known.

These attempts to curtail some of the aid aimed at relieving the plight of Palestinian refugees was, in part, politically motivated. Some politicians endeavoured to use the refugee situation as a lever to bring pressure on the United Nations, hoping that it would force Israel to allow them to return. But for us there was much to encourage for, paradoxically, the authorities granted residence permits to all the missionaries, at least in the north. In addition, before the beginning of May the local church in Irbid had been registered with the Government. This helpful step resulted from the local church in Amman applying for registration which, when granted and confirmed in the Gazette, covered the whole of the country. One of the great advantages of this official recognition was that the work, registered as a Jordanian religious body and not a mission, would not be summarily closed down. The medical work in Taibeh, however, was still known as a mission and there was some uncertainty as to whether it would be subject to restrictions. At this time also Mrs. McLean's health broke down and, shortly after returning to Britain for treatment, she died leaving a big gap in the lives of those who had known and loved her. Dr McLean returned to Taibeh for a few weeks but decided he could no longer continue. This left Dr. Dorey and a nurse, Dorothy Bird, to carry on the clinic. Victor too, gave valuable assistance and, at the same time, maintained the spiritual side of the work.

A most important change for us was foreshadowed towards the end of April. Marjorie's health had improved considerably and she had put on weight. This seemed to be a good sign. She worked on as busy as usual until, one day, strange stirrings within raised a question and the time came to seek medical advice. In fact, if it hadn't seemed so ridiculous, Marjorie would have voiced the opinion she was pregnant. But the miscarriage at Christmas seemed to make this impossible. So, a visit to Taibeh and a chat with Dr. Dorey who, at the close of her examination, simply burst out laughing. Marjorie was nearly five months pregnant! There had been no doubt about the miscarriage, and we could only come to the conclusion there had been twins on the way, but her health had not permitted the carrying of both. As we looked back on the early days of the year, the reason for her sickness and tiredness became apparent. We wondered later what would have happened had we known. Would we have returned to Jordan at that time, let her do all that heaving and hauling while we renovated the home? Would all the entertaining, visiting and general running around have stopped, the whole of life's pattern changed? In spite of everything she was well and, at last, we could look forward to Peter's successor. Life changed for us as we began to prepare for parenthood, and future plans were coloured by the prospect of the responsibility of a family.

The exciting news that within four months our baby would be born, speedily gave way to the realisation that no preparation for its arrival had even been contemplated. All we could do was to let the Lord know the need and wait to see how He would work. Naturally we shared the news with family and friends at home without, of course, making any reference to finance. In response, letters containing many a good wish began to arrive, among them one from the Women's Missionary Fellowship asking if there were any items they could supply. Thankful for such an unexpected offer, Marjorie sent off a short list of necessities and waited to see the result. The WMF's response went far beyond anything we had asked for and, within a few weeks, the local Custom's Depot asked me to call and clear a bulky parcel. Every item had to be inspected, and commented on by a group of Custom's officers who, in true Arab style, expressed their fervent wish the baby would be a boy, and then passed the lot through without charge. Then next week another parcel arrived and the week after another, then still a fourth, and the men began to wonder how much equipment the foreigner's child would need! But they were very kind and, even though they possibly considered the amounts excessive, made no charge. One benefit of these constant visits was the opportunity to explain why we were in their country. The Lord opened doors for witness, and gave further evidence of His readiness to supply abundantly for every need.

The country's internal political situation became increasingly unsettled during May and June. The young King Hussain had succeeded his father, Abu Talab, and the firmness of his authority was beginning to be felt. But at the same time, the security of the country still rested in the hands of the Arab Legion under the control of General Glubb Pasha, and his position as the main advisor to the King, infuriated some of the Palestinian leaders. Many of these saw General Glubb as a hindrance to their aims of recovering their homeland and were anxious to see his authority broken. A few junior officers, because of their increasing nationalistic fervour, were also desirous of seeing an end to all western influence in Jordan's affairs. These men, being contemporary with the King, had no difficulty sowing in his mind the thought he would never be king in his own right as long as the Pasha had any influence. Their advice prevailed and, within a few months, King Hussain took the sudden dramatic action of dismissing from his post the man who, out of love for and loyalty to his adopted country, had spent a lifetime seeking to help create the independent State of Jordan; and who with the aid of his beloved Arab Legion, had maintained within its borders peace, stability and a measure of prosperity. The General was given a few hours to prepare for his departure before being escorted to the airport and flown to Britain. These events were portents of things to come and one could already sense a groundswell of dissatisfaction which one day would bring the country to the verge of civil war.

By now the way had opened for us to reach further afield, and Jerash, the ancient city of Gerasa, had been added to our meeting schedule. The Bible Course ministry was also on the increase. The Medrows had forwarded two new courses, and another was being written specially for Muslims. Our stock of Christian literature in Arabic had also increased and from time to time we visited groups of believers on the East and West banks, seeking outlets for distribution. Encouragement to continue this part of our ministry came from hearing a young believer give his testimony. He began by saying that more than a year ago he had asked me to give him a Bible as he could not afford to buy one. I believed him and responded to his request. Some time later while reading in the Old Testament, the Lord convicted him of his sins and his need for salvation and cleansing. This led to his conversion, a changed life, and a desire to witness for the Lord. We were also encouraged to continue evangelistic services for though little results appeared, we knew of some who were led by the Holy Spirit to trust the Saviour.

Ahmad of Irbid was one of these. During his earlier visits to the services we could not help wondering if ulterior motives lay behind his interest. He was very poor and he would not have been the first to show interest in Christianity for material gain. He earned his living a hard way. Day in, day out, he moved around the market and cafes dispensing a kind of liquorish drink from a large container firmly strapped on his back, from which a brass spout protruded over his shoulder Clanging together two metal cups he would attract attention and, in response to a customer's request, would bend forward to fill tiny cups or glasses carried in a brass tray attached to a belt round his waist. The excessive heat made it arduous and exhausting work, for which the rewards were very small.

Ahmad listened intently to the Gospel message but had great difficulty in accepting its central message. He would often say, "What I hear is good, and would be very good, if only the preacher would omit any reference to the death of Jesus. Doesn't he know the Koran denies the death of Christ?" He was prepared to acknowledge Jesus as a holy man and one to be reverenced. In fact on one homeward journey he knocked down a fellow Muslim because he began to curse the name of Jesus. But the preaching of the Cross was, for him, truly a stumbling block. But week after week he continued to attend and one day he confessed openly the

Lord Jesus as his Saviour. He joined with us in the prayer meetings and the sincerity of his prayers and the change in his attitudes, made it obvious his life had been touched. If there had been any ulterior motives they had certainly vanished. In fact, instead of requesting help he would occasionally bring a gift of a huge ripe water melon to show appreciation.

His faithful witness was expressed on one occasion in a rather unchristianlike fashion. One morning disturbing news reached us. Ahmad had been involved in a brawl, arrested by the police and was in prison. Later in the day we heard of his release and the reason for the arrest. He had been sitting in his room quietly reading one of the Gospels when a friend called to see him and, in due course, showed curiosity in the book in Ahmad's hands. On hearing it to be the Christian Gospel he began to curse the book and, in his rage, snatched it and tried to tear it to pieces. This was too much for Ahmad who simply grabbed the fellow by the neck and threw him bodily into the street. There the man began to cause a commotion, yelling and screaming that Ahmad was an infidel. This soon attracted the attention of the police who dragged Ahmad off and locked him up for the night. The next day the station serjeant, endeavouring to discover the cause of the trouble, asked the obvious question, "Why did you throw him out?" to which Ahmad simply replied that the man had tried to destroy John. Having no knowledge of the 'Gospel according to John' the serjeant jumped to the conclusion that a man called John was being attacked, and Ahmad had acted in his defence. Therefore the fault was not his but that of the other person who had tried to injure John! So he released Ahmad, cautioned him to keep the peace, and there, apparently, the matter ended. Only later did I discover it had a tail piece.

A short time after this I visited the Station to obtain the officer's signature on our applications for new residence permits. After signing he suddenly asked if we had any books in Arabic which would explain the Bible as he had a copy and wanted help in reading it. It was a pleasure to be able to pass on to him a very good commentary on the Gospel of Matthew, a pleasure compounded by discovering it was Ahmad who, seizing the opportunity provided by being brought before the police, had made that Bible available.

Among these encouragements were concerns. Primarily there was the need for local brethren who had a gift for preaching the Gospel. We knew rising nationalism prevented some from attending meetings addressed by a westerner. It was obvious that numbers always increased when it was known a Jordanian, Palestinian, or Egyptian would be the speaker. But such gifted men were available only a few times in the year and, consequently, the majority of the speaking continued to be the responsibility of Victor or myself. In Irbid some of the brethren were showing much promise and we had high hopes they would, in due course, take over the work. However, events dictated otherwise.

Another concern was how to cope with the situation when Muslim youths attended the meetings. Generally they were well behaved and did little to disrupt proceedings, but their presence was resented by nominal Christians who would accuse them of attending for ulterior motives. The Orthodox and the Catholics were emphatic in their belief that Christ was 'for the Christians alone', an attitude which amazed those of us who believed that 'whosoever calls on the name of the Lord shall be saved' means exactly what it says. One evening a youth from an Orthodox background violently accused the Muslims of spying on the girls, an accusation which might have had some truth. Incensed by his outburst the Muslims gathered on the road to beat him up, and the situation looked decidedly ugly. We advised him to wait a while then quietly go home some other way and let the matter rest. However, he had been threatened and insulted so he went to the police and lodged a complaint, doing the very thing we were anxious to avoid - providing the police with an excuse for saying we were disturbing the peace. But they took no action and we heard no more of it.

It was not only the nominal Christians who were suspicious of the Muslims. Even true believers had doubts concerning Muslims who claimed to be converted. We ourselves had to agree there were great difficulties for a Muslim to truly become a follower of the Lord Jesus, but we believed anyone who made such a profession should be given the opportunity to prove its reality and not be stumbled by a negative attitude. Sadly, this did happen to Ahmad in Irbid at one of the midweek prayer meetings. In his prayer he emphasised his personal faith in the Lord Jesus, but a mature believer visiting from Zerka acted very unwisely and let Ahmad know he doubted his profession. But Ahmad continued and there was every reason to believe the validity of his testimony

The hot dry weeks of June were followed in the next month by even hotter and dustier days. We now went to Ajlaun, to the American Mission Hospital, where in a secluded corner of the grounds, lay Peter's resting place. In these hospitable quarters, we went to relax as we looked forward to his successor. Within a few days Dr.Lovegren forecast the baby's arrival could be within a week. However the week went by, and the next, and there was talk of action to hasten the arrival, but a fall, which could have had serious consequences, obviated that. Having finished a load of washing Marjorie took it to dry on the roof where odd bits of projecting concrete were a hazard for unwary feet. Returning with the empty basket she tripped and fell full length. Attempting to rise she discovered her legs had completely locked and could not even crawl to the steps. She could only wait for someone to become aware of her absence. In the meantime the thoughts of injury to the baby flooded through her mind, only to be calmed by the realisation the Lord was in control. Nearly half an hour elapsed before I realised there was something wrong and discovered the situation she was in. I carried her downstairs and settled her in bed, able to praise the Lord that a more serious fall and broken bones had been avoided. Two days later, 23rd August 1955, Stephen Andrew arrived safe and sound, a miracle baby. In spite of a miscarriage, many hundreds of miles of travelling, much heaving and hauling of heavy weights, and the final fall, his lusty cries announced he was truly alive and well. Life for us could never be the same again; his presence was bound to have a profound effect on all our subsequent decisions.

But baby Andrew was not the only one to bring changes into our routine; our colleague Victor did the same. Shortly after this he told us of his intention of going to England in the autumn, then surprised us by adding it was doubtful if he would return to Jordan. His Army medical training and recent involvement with the clinic in Taibeh, had given him a deep desire to be more fully involved in a ministry of healing. Now, with encouragement from Drs. McLean and Dorey he had set his mind on a doctor's degree. Initially this was shattering news for us, as we had come to rely deeply on his friendship and partnership in the Gospel. In many ways we were as different as chalk and cheese but this only meant we complemented each other and the work benefitted. Victor had been an excellent companion and, while we differed on a few things, there had never been a harsh word or unpleasant argument. He had spiritual and personal gifts which would be sadly missed and, as I could see nothing but loss resulting from his decision, I found it hard to accept this to be the Lord's leading. But Victor had no doubt about the matter. He had every confidence he was acting in obedience to the Lord's direction and, in due course, the medical degree would be obtained. Within a year of leaving Jordan he secured a University place and it is a tribute to his diligence that, in addition to setting up home and being constantly involved in Christian service, interrupted by periods of ill health, he passed successive examinations and obtained the necessary qualifications. Victor and his wife Biddy went on to serve the Lord in Tanzania, and later in New Zealand, where Jordan's loss became others' gain.

Marjorie, Andrew and Douglas, 1956

CHAPTER 20

End of an Era

(1956)

You will call upon Me and go and pray to Me
and I will listen to you (Jer. 29:12).

Victor's departure raised an important question. How could we maintain the testimony in Taibeh as well as in Irbid? Our old banger had gone the way of all old steel and we had to rely on public transport. In the case of Taibeh this consisted of one ancient bus which, as usual, made one daily return run into town. This negated any possibility of maintaining a regular pattern of services in both places unless we could make use of the Gilead Mission's jeep which had to be readily available for the medical work. Faced with that limitation it became apparent that the only workable solution would be for us to make Taibeh our base. So early in October, shortly before the winter rains made havoc of the roads, we moved to our new location, much to the satisfaction of Dr. Dorey and nurse Dorothy Bird who enjoyed having more company, and another male about the place.

The sprawling village of Taibeh consisted of an assortment of low built houses and lay at the head of a plateau which sloped away to the west then steeply down into the Jordan Valley. The unpaved and rock strewn road from Irbid wound across a couple of ravines and for much of the way was negotiable in all seasons. However, the final approach, whether from east or west, lay across an area of deep earth, firm and hard in summer, glutinous mud in the depths of winter. The village was a hotch-potch of little lanes, dusty or muddy according to the season, connecting three main streets, likewise unpaved. Neither electricity nor piped water had reached the area; water was brought from a few rain filled wells, or drawn from a family's own deep cistern.

The Mission compound, situated at the western end of the village, provided an uninterrupted view of the the Judean hills, dominated by Mount Tabor. They would stand out boldly against the evening sky and, as the dying rays of the setting sun illuminated the ridge, many refugees from Nazareth must have looked longingly at Tabor and visualised their home town on the farther side. Five buildings dotted the compound; we took over one vacated by Dr. McLean. The other buildings housed Dr. Dorey and Miss Bird, Najeeb, the Mission's driver, and Ahmad, the gatekeeper, while a long low building, directly accessible from the road, contained the surgery and a waiting room which, on Sundays, served as the chapel. Staff who helped in the clinic or worked in the garden, lived in the village. Cisterns dug beneath the main buildings were divided into two sections, one fed by drainage from the concrete paths for regular use - almost clean after the settling of sediment! - and the other by the overflow from the roofs. This was supposed to be fairly safe for drinking, providing it had been boiled or treated with halozone tablets. Pumping water from the cisterns into tanks on the roof had to be done by hand, a daily task allotted to a man from the village, providing he came: if he didn't it fell into other hands, sometimes mine!

We had no problem in making Taibeh our base without any interruption to the work. The Bible Correspondence Course ministry was maintained and the services in the village and Irbid, with occasional forays further afield, continued. Here Andrew thrived in the country air, being petted, but not spoilt, by the ladies on the compound. He also made his presence known in the church services for as soon as the congregation began to sing - or rather, attempted to do so - he gave vent to the loudest of howls resulting, eventually, in his being excused attendance.

The move to Taibeh coincided with the onset of heavy rains which were a blessing as they guaranteed our water supply for the hot summer months and benefitted the kitchen garden. But they caused problems from their effect on unpaved roads, leading to the danger of being bogged down in some lonely spot two or three miles from home. During daylight the problem presented little difficulty, at least for the wary driver, as the muddiest sections and the deep tracks left by heavier vehicles, could be discerned. Night time, however, was another matter as we learnt during our first few weeks in the village. After a long and tiring day, night had fallen before we turned off the main road for the last stage to the village. We had Andrew with us, snugly wrapped up against the cold, but becoming fretful as his feeding time had long since passed. Najeeb, the Arab driver, skillfully negotiated obstacles but progress was tediously slow until the last rocky stretch was passed and the rutted track ran straight and level across the cultivated plain. With less than two miles to go, and knowing we were anxious to get home, Najeeb put his foot down for a final spurt. I warned him to ease down and take care of the boggy parts, but he cheerfully assured me not to worry for he never got stuck. He turned his head to make himself heard and within seconds there came a juddering and a shaking followed by a sudden halt. He had run out of a rut into a morass of mud and, by the time we were out of the jeep, the front axle had almost reached an earthy resting place.

With a few sacks and a shovel of sorts, we set to work trying to get the wheels to grip but they just spun on top of the sacks, driving them deeper into the mud. Our predicament left us with no alternative but to walk to the village to get help. Najeeb needed to stay by the vehicle to assist the rescuers. I could not leave Marjorie and Andrew so, we set off with Marjorie carrying our bag, and myself with Andrew folded firmly in his cot blanket and sheltered from the wind by a fold in my coat. It was a cloudy, moonless night, and even a slight diversion from the road could take us well wide of the village, so wisdom dictated following it as closely as possible. We squelched ahead, slipping and slithering over the uneven ground, and at times stumbling into patches of mud reaching above the ankles, from which our feet withdrew with even a louder squelch. We were encouraging each other by saying we would soon be home when, suddenly, there was a resounding flop. Carrying the case and unable to help herself, Marjorie had fallen full length into the mud. With my free hand I helped her up and was about to express sympathy, when she burst out, "That's another pair of stockings ruined." A few minutes later, mud bespattered, hungry and thirsty we were home and dry and none the worse for the experience. Andrew had slept soundly all the way, secure and unconcerned in the shelter of my arms. This has often reminded me of those everlasting and stronger arms which enfold the Christian through all the journey home.

The creation of the nation of Israel, and the ever increasing problem of a disaffected refugee population, prepared the way for trouble. We had our first brush with anti-western sentiment in Taibeh when a noisy mob gathered at the police post some hundred yards away from the compound. A goodly number of men and youths could be seen milling around the place and, being curious to know the reason for it all we went out to our front porch to see developments. After a few minutes the crowd, now swollen by recent arrivals, changed from a dense mass to form a long line, some seven or eight abreast, moving menacingly in our direction. The blurred sound of many voices, now accompanied by the muffled tread of numerous feet on hard packed earth, changed to a steady rhythmic chant, growing louder with every step, and could soon be recognised as cries calling for the downfall of imperialism and colonialism, the end of British influence and the destruction of Israel. We had no idea of what the marchers really intended to do, though two or three of the local staff spoke of them coming to stone and invade the compound. They urged us to go inside, but it seemed to us wiser to stay and see how things developed. In any case, what could we do to stop the marchers, or alter their intentions; we committed the situation to the Lord, then waited for Him to show us how to act. We watched the procession coming nearer, its shouts getting louder as the leaders reached the wall opposite our front door. The foremost ranks then turned along the outside of the wall to make for the main gates which Ahmad had locked before disappearing from sight. Some of the mob began to pitch a few stones which fell harmlessly short of the house. The leaders were now almost at the gates with the bulk of their followers hard on their heels, and it seemed nothing could prevent the excited crowd fulfilling whatever they had in mind. But, suddenly, and somewhat breathlessly, six or more of the village elders appeared, arrayed themselves in front of the entrance and an excited argument between them and the instigators of the trouble broke out. Slowly the authority of the elders prevailed, the chant gradually lessened, and slowly the crowd dispersed. A few hotheads vented their frustration by shouts, and an odd stone, but the heat had been taken out of the situation and we could go inside to thank the Lord for His protection and peace.

Later we discovered the reason for the elders' involvement and, also, one of the factors leading to antagonism towards us. Apparently the lone police serjeant at the post, sensing the possibility of trouble, called the ring leaders together to try to persuade them to desist. When they insisted on marching he contacted the elders and warned them, in no uncertain terms, they would be held responsible for any damage or injury caused. The thought of the repercussions which might affect their own pockets and persons, stirred them to action. The antagonism arose from a rumour that the Mission was in league with the Jews and supplied them with information. Most of us were puzzled to know how such a rumour developed until we heard someone had reported having seen us signalling to the Jews on Mount Tabor. Then we realised what had happened. A small window in the study gave an uninterrupted view of Tabor. Normally this room was not used in the evenings but occasionally one of us would pop in for a few minutes. Each time we had to carry an oil lamp. As we looked for a book or sat for a few minutes to write, this would be moved from one side of the room to another. The curtain would rarely be drawn and anyone with an interest in keeping watch on the place, and with a mind already full of suspicion, could easily assume the irregular appearance of a light to be a form of signals.

My next direct encounter with violence had little to do with my nationality. A few weeks after the previous incident, a protest against the Government led to a call for a strike aimed mainly at paralysing transport throughout the country. This made life very difficult for village people, especially those who depended on the daily bus to town for work or marketing. The owner of the Taibeh bus decided to ignore the ban, though threatened with violence, and the bus left as usual. The vehicle was hardly half way through the village when a barrage of stones broke a lot of glass and wounded the driver in the head. He was brought to the clinic but the nurse could do no more than dress the wound and declare he needed hospital treatment in Irbid. Najeeb declared he would go if I went with him and, knowing a circuitous route which would avoid passing through the village, we started as soon as possible. The road ran past the edge of another small village some two miles away but I assumed the folk there would have no intimation of our coming and, providing we kept moving, we could be through in a few minutes. In typical Najeeb style, he declared, "Oh they won't bother me, I'm Arab!" and slowly drove on as if he were out for a leisurely Sunday trip. But a mob was waiting, with stones in hand, ready for our coming. Najeeb stopped, put down his window and began to shout at the mob, waving his arms in tune with his words. For a moment or two an ominous silence reigned, almost fearful in its intensity, broken only by some muttering from our wounded passenger. Some yards of waste land lay between the mob and the edge of the road, so a quick dash would have got us past, but still Najeeb hesitated. A moment later they began to surge forward, and only then did he take off at an exemplary speed. A few stones reached the car making various dents and broke some glass but, none of us were any the worse for the experience. Irbid was quiet on our arrival and our passenger soon safely deposited at the hospital.

We made for home as soon as possible. Trusting that by this time Taibeh would prove to be the quieter of the two villages we decided on this shorter route, mainly because we knew the schools were operating and, with speed, it would be possible to arrive home while the majority of youths were in class. We came near the edge of the village, with barely a minute or so to spare before the main school would close, and had just drawn level with it when Najeeb made one of his famous mistakes. He chose a wrong part of the rutted road, still miry from the winter rains, and the front of the wagon sank slowly down. I got out to investigate whilst Najeeb tried reversing, but the wheels simply threw up a small fountain of diluted mud, and the car sank gracefully another inch or so. Then a bell sounded and a minute later a stream of youngsters, followed by older youths, came pouring out, obviously in high spirits at the moment of release, and there we were like sitting ducks. A number came round laughing and joking, but sympathy for our predicament must have prevailed - for a group of older boys gathered round and hauling manfully, lifted the station wagon onto safer ground. I found it an interesting example of the volatile nature of the Arabs in general. In the morning those same youths, egged on by zealots, would have been happy to join the mob in the other village to stone us but, by the end of the day, it was helpful friendliness.

As 1956 began to unfold, life in Taibeh continued on its ordered way whilst in Irbid the small local church also made steady progress. Numbers were not large, but those who considered themselves members were faithful to the meetings. The small meeting room was usually comfortably filled for the evangelistic service on Sundays and, whenever I visited further afield to El Husn or Jerash, our friends in those places would bring in their neighbours. Blind Nyim in El Husn was very good at this, so much so, there was rarely spare sitting space on the mattresses ranged around his main room. Nyim also remained faithful to the meeting in Irbid and, rain or fine, would be there; often having to walk both ways led by a much younger member of the family. In fact, the meeting seemed to be going so well we began to think the time had come for us to move on to other areas. These thoughts were strengthened by a certain verse which, taken out of its context, was brought before us in various ways. One morning the text on our daily calendar read, 'I will work a work in your days which you would not believe, though it were told you.' It seemed to speak directly to us and we wondered why. Did it mean the Lord had a work for us to do far more reaching than that which could be done in one small part of Jordan? A few days later the same verse came in our regular Scripture reading, and again one evening in a book of morning and evening readings, then shortly afterwards on another calendar. We prayed the Lord would help us to discern His will, but the thought of leaving Jordan never crossed our minds.

Whilst all was peaceful in Taibeh the same could not be said for Irbid. Periodically there were minor demonstrations against the Government, as well as protests against the activities of the United Nations Relief Agency as I discovered in a rather dramatic manner one Sunday in March. After the morning service in Taibeh and immediately after lunch Najeeb drove me into Irbid where we were surprised to see a lot of commotion at the junction with the El Husn road on which our home was situated. By the time we reached the turn we were amongst a crowd of excited folk and, as we stopped someone, completely unknown to me, thrust his head through the open window and hastily said, "Don't go up that road today!" and then vanished. Up that road were four or five newly built garages used by the United Nations Relief Agency as warehouses for relief supplies. What seemed to be a vast crowd milled around them, not far from our house, and a station wagon was burning, smoke billowing in the breeze. I told Najeeb to drive on to be clear of the crowd and then considered our next move. We had come to town with the specific purpose of joining with believers for the Sunday afternoon and evening meetings. If during the next two hours the situation quietened, people would be arriving expecting me to be there, so this ruled out an immediate return to the village. But I needed, somehow, to get into the house. We appreciated the warning but, believing the mob were directing their anger against the United Nations, I thought no one would bother if they saw me. Najeeb would have been happier to cut and run, and I didn't feel all that brave myself. We took a parallel road and, gradually worked our way round to our landlord's home directly behind ours. There I left Najeeb and the jeep and, having walked round the side furthest away from the mob, had only about twenty five yards in full view of any before turning into the small courtyard fronting the house. Trying to walk normally I passed the length of the front of the house, turned back into the gate, completed the last six yards to the porch, went up the four steps to the verandah, paused to unlock the door and entered without, apparently, anybody realising I was there. The tumult of the mob, which had been almost deafening at times, was now muted and, thankfully, I relaxed.

My moments of relaxation were rudely disturbed by a loud banging on the door. There stood our landlord who seemed to be somewhat pale and very upset. He informed me the mob were threatening to burn the house down as soon as I arrived and, possibly being more concerned for his house than me, begged me not show myself. Then like our other unknown friend he also vanished. This certainly gave me something to think about and, heeding his warning, I suppressed the natural desire to watch the exciting events outside and kept clear of the windows. I was therefore surprised when a few minutes later the front door, which I had left unlocked, opened and who should appear but Um Samweel. Her opening words, "Hello, it looks as if we have a party outside today," would surely have equalled any British understatement. I couldn't help but feel her comment rather missed the mark, and hastened to inform her our home was supposed to be part of the celebrations! Having dismissed the idea with a shrug of the shoulders, she sat down to chat whilst the noise outside increased as the size of the mob increased, squashing the hope that more of our little company would arrive. Again I was proved wrong - within ten minutes ten more had made their way through the crowd, all of them being desirous of remembering the Lord in the breaking of bread. By now members of the Arab Legion had arrived to protect the United Nations property and were making attempts to disperse the crowd. The rioters endeavoured to hold their ground, but when the soldiers began to fire over their heads, they gave up and retreated.

With noise and confusion outside we gathered around a table, prepared with the emblems of bread and wine, in a lovely atmosphere of peace and unity. I glanced round the little company and saw in it a practical expression of the oneness which exists between those who are truly brethren and sisters in Christ. There were Jordanians, Palestinians, Armenians as well as an Egyptian doctor and, if my memory is correct, at least one Assyrian, and myself from Britain. One or two of them were blessed with this world's goods and comfortably off, others lived on the poverty line. There was a mixture of education, and possibly political persuasion, but as we took the bread and wine we did so as truly one in Christ. Barriers of race and worldly position were broken down, the love of Christ predominated. For me it was a most memorable time of worship and, as I thought how this little company had made their way through the turmoil to share with me, the real foreigner, this time of remembrance, I could not help but be deeply moved,

By the time our service ended the soldiers had accomplished their task. The wide open space in front of the house was devoid of life and the damaged warehouses and ruined vehicles were the only evidence of the riotous mob. Najeeb having relaxed in the landlord's house, made an appearance with the news the town would be under curfew from six-o-clock. This left us no option but to return to Taibeh as soon as possible. For a short period afterwards

Irbid was saddled with an evening curfew until, gradually, the situation eased and life returned to its usual languid pace. I went into town on Sundays but, for two or three weeks, made no attempt to hold evening services nor to visit outlying villages. In due course our normal programme returned and there was a good attendance at most of the meetings, though we were disappointed by the lack of response to the claims of the Lord Jesus. But our responsibility demanded faithfulness to our calling, leaving spiritual results with the Lord. It was helpful to remember that when the farmer sows his seed the harvest does not come overnight - this rule often applies to the sowing of the seed of the Gospel.

A case in point is that of blind Araxi. Araxi came from an Armenian family and though Christian in name, had never come to the point of accepting Jesus Christ as her Saviour. She enjoyed our informal services but did not feel particularly concerned about the evangelistic content of the message. Occasionally she had an uncomfortable feeling that, in order to have complete assurance of forgiveness for sin and enjoy the peace of God, there was something she ought to do, but then would simply shrug it off. Months slipped by until one prayer meeting night Araxi came with a beaming face and obviously had something to share with us. It seems that during the previous night she had a vivid dream in which she was conscious of following a path which led to some very desirable place. The path dipped down into a valley and ended on the banks of a wide flowing river. No bridge or ford could be seen even though a path wound away from the farther side up and up towards the place where she longed to be. In her dream she longed to know how to get across, when a faint figure appeared on the other side and, pointing to a certain spot, quietly said, "That is the way across." Plunging in she found it to be shallow with firm ground beneath her feet all the way to the other shore. Immediately on waking she recalled her need of the assurance of sins forgiven and peace with God and, in a flash, became convinced she knew the way. Christ had died on the cross for her sins; all she had to do was to thank Him for that fact and, in faith, accept Him as Saviour and Lord. She now wanted to confess to all in the prayer meeting that she was a committed follower of the Lord Jesus. Later she desired to be baptised as a witness of her faith but, on the day appointed, her brother, furious because of the step she had taken, locked her in her room. Many years were to pass before she could fulfill that desire. There were others like Araxi who attended services for months without any apparent influence on their lives but time proved they had not listened in vain.

In Taibeh, Ahmad exercised a very faithful witness, not only in the village but also further afield; so much so he became a target of Muslim antagonism and, being called an apostate, was threatened with death if he did not desist. As a result he confined himself to Taibeh but never wavered in his adherence to the Lord. The Gilead Mission itself faced certain difficulties, partially due to the need for a male doctor. Dr. Dorey faithfully maintained the clinic and child welfare service but without fulfilling the wider ministry formerly envisaged. In spite of her being well qualified, men were reluctant to be treated by a woman, while the lack of skilled personnel frustrated the possibility of developing clinics in other villages. With the work in Irbid being helped by local brethren we were happy to make visits twice a week, but by April there were a number of changes there. A keen member had obtained work at the Ajlaun hospital so his valuable help had been lost. One of Abu Ibrahim's sons also joined the hospital staff whilst he himself decided to take the rest of the family to Beirut. Another faithful and much appreciated member announced his intention of studying medicine in the United States and would be leaving within a few weeks. It seemed we ought to move back and give more time to Irbid.

A full, and in many ways momentous, year had passed since our return from furlough and now the time had come to reflect on the many evidences of the Lord's guidance, provision and protection. We definitely believed we could say, 'hitherto the Lord has helped us', and were still where He would have us be. Emotionally there had been some times of stress, we sorely missed the companionship of Victor, and the strain of maintaining and seeking to develop the ministry in two places brought its own spiritual pressures. We were aware of those spiritual adversaries of which the Apostle Paul spoke, and faith passed through its times of testing. The devil is very good at seeking to sow doubts in the mind and we were not immune from such attacks. Our faith was tested by the paucity of the response to the preaching of the Word of God. If we were proclaiming the truth, and if the work of the Holy Spirit included convincing men of sin, righteousness and judgment to come, why could people continue to listen and not seek the Lord? Where was the fault? - it could not be in the Scriptures seeing, as we truly believed, they were divinely inspired. Could it therefore somehow be in us? Was there something in our lives hindering the long desired blessing? This and other thoughts would crowd the mind until driven to seek the Lord in prayer and, sharing with Him the doubts and fears, we left them all with Him.

But one great need seemed as if it would never be met, namely reinforcements to replace the loss of Victor and Essie Brown. Much as we appreciated the warm fellowship of local believers we missed the support of fellow workers who would share in and help extend the missionary enterprise. Unbeknown to us the Lord had this matter in hand. At one time I had mentioned to a well known Bible teacher who led tour parties to the Holy Land, that Jerash, one of the best sites on the East Bank, seemed to be ignored. He took me at my word and not only included Jerash on his itinerary but invited us to meet the party there. While strolling though the ruins one of the visitors asked if we were looking forward to the arrival of new workers. To his surprise I had to admit complete ignorance of the matter! He informed me that a young couple had been commended by an assembly in Larkhall near Glasgow to the Lord's work in Jordan. He added that they were married a few days after their commendation and, as far as he understood, were already on their way out by sea. Neither he, nor we, could understand why there had been no communication from either their assembly or themselves. So immediately, we had the prospect of a young couple arriving complete with bags and baggage in Beirut and wondering what to do next. Later it transpired they had been in touch with Victor who, in the midst of his busy schedule, had not thought to mention the matter to us. He had, however, given the Miltons the address of the Tourians and hoped they would be on hand to meet them.

A few hours after we heard of their arrival, Najeeb was on his way to Beirut to collect them. We appreciated having them with us and were thrilled as we envisaged a much younger couple becoming immersed in the work. Also it was encouraging to know that, if the Lord was preparing us to move elsewhere, they would be able to carry on in our place. Jim and Molly were good companions, with a lovely sense of humour and a friendly disposition. They soon buckled down to language study and did their utmost to become acquainted with local culture, thus laying the foundations for a rapport with those they had come to serve. Being well grounded in the Scriptures Jim happily spoke by interpretation, though Jameel sometimes found his accent something of a trial. Occasionally after a sentence Jameel would look baffled, cast a questioning glance at me, and then struggle on usually with a correct interpretation if not a translation. The only time I remember him being stumped was when Jim, speaking from the Psalms, said, in a broad Scots' accent, something about 'iron entering the Psalmist's soul'.

The hope that the Miltons' arrival would bring a period of mutual service was blocked by unforseen circumstances. During the summer came rumblings of further trouble and an intimation from the British Consul of possible danger. Halfway through August we received a red alert, together with advice that the British who had no vital reasons for staying should leave the country. We could think of a number of reasons for staying but, we felt a responsibility towards our new co-workers facing their first experience of physical trouble. Naturally, we were also concerned for Andrew's safety and saw, therefore, valid reasons for heeding the official advice. I visited the Consul in Amman to check on the situation and discovered that the Foreign Office had warned that, if their advice went unheeded, there might be difficulty in reaching the coast. What a quandary to be in. How could we preach about trusting the Lord fully in all circumstances, and of the Angel of the Lord 'encamping around them that fear Him', when on the hint of trouble we packed bags and left? How could we expect local believers to face difficulties if we disappeared and left them to face trouble on their own? Surely, we reasoned, even as the Lord had wonderfully preserved us in the dangerous situation in Jerusalem, He would do it in Irbid. But, even though seeking to rely on the many promises of God, we could not help feeling a sense of unrest.

Two factors finally decided our move. First Um Samweel visited us and, after discussing the political situation, added that if there were to be any trouble with the British, it would be better for the local believers if we were out of he way. This shed a different light upon the matter. The church members were identified with us and, as long as we were present, any antagonism would be directed against the group as a whole. Our leaving would be making life easier for them.

I must confess it still appeared to me as if we were running away and we prayed earnestly for the Lord to give us definite direction. As we prayed our thoughts were directed to the British Consul in Jerusalem, a former missionary during the troubled times in Eritrea, a good friend and one who would understand fully our situation. We asked the Lord that, if it was right for us to leave, please would He give us a sign by Bob advising us to do so. In spite of the primitive telephone system, I managed to get through to Jerusalem from the local Post Office and, whilst realising it would be impossible for him to say anything confidential, acquainted Bob with our problem. He paused for a moment, then suggested Marjorie and I should go to Lebanon for a few weeks' holiday. The Lord had answered prayer and, trusting Him for all needed provision we, in company with the Miltons decided to visit Lebanon.

CHAPTER 21

A New Era Commences

(1956-59)

Behold, I will do a new thing, now it shall spring forth: shall you not know it? (Isaiah 43:19)

When on 5th September 1956 we left Irbid, we had no idea this step would determine our area of service for the next twenty years. Early in the day we set out for Amman to catch the plane to Beirut. Our intentions of travelling by car had been frustrated by my discovery that due to some entries on our passports we were on a 'black list' for Syria and would not be able to drive through. Jim and Molly travelled by road for what proved to be a very frustrating and tedious day. It was their first experience of travelling by service car on their own and they had to jostle their own way through the crowds for both passport and Customs' clearance. Having done this they still had to wait, and wait, while other passengers had their luggage searched or, having unexpectedly met old acquaintances, decided to stop for a lengthy chat. By the time they arrived, weary from the tedium of travel, we had been some hours in Beirut and were able to welcome them to our temporary lodgings in an unfurnished apartment rented from some American missionaries.

Finding more suitable accommodation became our priority but the problem was where to start looking in this bustling and unfamiliar city. We soon found there was no need for anxiety on this score. Within a few hours we heard some friends of ours, Jack and Monica Blockley, who had left Amman before us, were now living within ten minutes walk from our lodgings. They had rented a small one storey villa and were happy for us to share their home. They had also made friends with a lady who owned a three storey block of flats one of which, being furnished and available for rent, enabled the Miltons to have accommodation as soon as ourselves. The truth of Paul's words, 'My God shall supply all your needs', had again been proved true.

At this stage we still thought our time in Beirut would be fairly short, and looked on our stay as being an unexpected holiday. The cool of Lebanon's brief autumn had supplanted the summer heat and this, plus the beauty of verdant orchards, tree clad hills and grey tinted, snowcapped mountains, rising like a magnificent backdrop behind the city, and the wide expanse of deep blue sky reflected in the sea skirting its feet, were all a refreshing change from the arid heat and barren plains of northern Jordan. But we could not help feeling a tinge of unease.

We detested the noise and rush and commercialism of the city, as well as the high rise flats dominating many of its streets, neither did we feel at home with its inhabitants. They were so different from the Jordanians we had come to love. The absence of the unsophisticated rural atmosphere negated the feeling of belonging which usually arises from being in harmony with one's surroundings. Here we were strangers, and merely visitors amongst a multi-lingual, multi-faith society in a region of the Middle East which had been heavily influenced by Western, and especially French, culture. We were in a milieu which considered no foreigner could possibly speak Arabic, and where to be fairly fluent in French, English or maybe German, was considered a symbol of being educated. As a result, the foreigner who tried to make use of Arabic in the markets, shops, post office or Government departments, would be met with a look of blank surprise and receive a reply either in French, which we could not understand, or in atrocious English which was frustrating.

No wonder we longed for our little home in Irbid, with its feeling of belonging, even though we were relieved to be free from the tensions which had surrounded us there. In fact we were becoming an emotionally mixed up couple. There was the relief from strain, but a profound dislike of Beirut and, to cap it all, bewilderment as to what the Lord wanted us to do. Our faith commenced to pass through one of its times of testing, and it was many weeks before we had any assurance of being in the right place.

Nevertheless we found one place where we would feel at home in the realm of Christian fellowship. On a previous visit to Beirut I had fellowshipped with the Armenian assembly and also visited two Arabic speaking meetings. One of these had been commenced by a German missionary about the turn of the century, the other by two Christian couples, refugees from Israel, who, had been associated with an assembly in Haifa. It was with this latter company we found our spiritual home. I had visited them in company with Roy Whitman, a trusted friend of Munir who was one of the founders of the work. This initial introduction now smoothed the way to our being received cordially. Munir, and others, assured us that they would be happy if I took an active part in the ministry. I deeply appreciated this but as plenty of spiritual gift already existed in the assembly, there seemed to be little I could contribute. However, the Ashrafiyeh assembly of some fifty believers became the place where we enjoyed warm Christian fellowship and discovered a sense of belonging.

From birth Andrew had never been a good sleeper and his tendency to wake between 1 am and 2 am, usually for a two hour period, had one of us out of bed until at last, there was a relaxed stillness and closed eyes. Sometimes he would only relax in our arms and, during one of these nocturnal sessions as I paraded the room, the Lord spoke of the future. As I walked and prayed, "Lord, what do You want us to do?" the words, *'the vision is yet for an appointed time; but at the end it will speak and it will not lie. Though it tarry wait for it because it will surely come'*, suddenly rang in my mind. At the same time Andrew dropped off to sleep and, laying him in his cot I slipped back to bed thankful for what I believed to be the Lord's command to wait. But to wait for what? In the morning I shared the experience with Marjorie and together we read those words in Habakkuk 2:3. For us, verse 2 indicated the line of ministry we were to undertake. In Jordan we had already been interested in the distribution of Christian literature, including the Bible Correspondence Courses, and the statement, *'Write the vision and make it plain on tablets that he may run who reads it'* (KJR) was, for us, a clarion call to a literature ministry. But where? That had yet to be made plain. Neither of us advocate the practice of taking verses out of context to make them fit one's circumstances, but we believe that the Lord does speak clearly through His word outside the context in which it is written.

Four weeks had now elapsed since we left Irbid, and another five were to drag by, before the reason for our being urged to leave became apparent. On the night of 30th October we wondered why there was an increase in air activity and, on the following day, discovered the Americans had been leaving Jordan in a hurry. On the same day news broke of an Israeli attack on Egypt's strongholds in Sinai, whilst Britain and France attacked Egyptian positions hoping to regain control of the Suez Canal. Why Britain was involved in this activity has, in the main, been forgotten, so the events which resulted in this drastic action are worth recalling.

The Suez Canal runs for 100 miles from Port Said to the town of Suez on the Red Sea. It was planned by a Frenchman, Ferdinand de Lesseps, and developed by the French Suez Canal Company. The excavations began about 1858 and the canal opened for traffic in 1869. Six years later when the Khedive of Egypt was in need of finance, the British prime minister Disraeli acquired a major shareholding for Britain. In 1888, under the Convention of Constantinople, the canal was opened to all nations. It was administered by a company with offices in Paris controlled by a council of 33, ten of whom were British. In 1914 Egypt became a British protectorate, and a certain amount of British influence over Egyptian affairs remained even after independence had been achieved in 1936. In 1952 a military coup led by General Neguib and Colonel Nasser forced king Farouk to abdicate and Nasser became prime minister and later succeeded Neguib as President. The Egyptians strongly resented the foreign influence in their country and the fact that a major source of revenue, the Canal, was under international control. In 1956, when USA and Britain cancelled their offers of financial aid for building the Aswan High Dam, Colonel Nasser responded by nationalising the Suez Canal. In an attempt to reassert international control over the waterway, Israel launched her attack in Sinai and British and French troops landed in the Canal Zone a few days later. There is little doubt their efforts would have succeeded but for the interference of the USA which threatened to block all financial aid to Britain, at that time struggling to recover from the economic effects of the war.

The outbreak of this conflict explained why we had been advised so urgently to leave Jordan. It also killed any prospect of our making a return to Irbid and effectively prevented us from retrieving any more of our personal possessions. In the event our friends in Jordan sold some items for us, thus providing a small fund which enabled us to make a fresh start. We were grateful for this, though deeply regretted the loss of all our wedding presents which, having survived the war and thousands of miles of travel, had become a precious link with the past.

The realisation our stay in Lebanon would be prolonged made us seek better accommodation, and we were able to rent a two bedroom flat some fifteen minutes walk from the Blockleys. Living in a groundfloor apartment of a block of flats, bordered by two fairly busy streets was a new experience for us, and we hated it. I had been asked by the British Syrian Mission (later the LEM) if I could teach Scripture to a senior class, and so had the relief of a daily walk and some respite from the noisy, hot and oppressive atmosphere of the area in which we lived. For Marjorie, with a very active eighteen month old, life was much more difficult. The high humidity began to have its effect on her health and lack of sleep also played its debilitating part, partly due to the penetrating hum of activity in an area which never seemed to sleep, and the blaring of radios from flats which definitely were not asleep. It was all so different from the quiet nights of Jordan pierced only by the bark of a dog, the occasional howl of a jackal and the Muezzin's call to early prayer. The radios jarred our tautened nerves the most. There was one individual who regularly turned the music on full blast between 1.30 and 2 am.

For Marjorie this was a particularly difficult time, not merely due to living conditions which could be borne, but because of the absence of any positive contribution she could make to the Lord's work. Her call to full time missionary service had been as clear as mine, so it was hard not to be involved in any purposeful ministry. But once we knew our return to Jordan would be severely delayed we realised there could be a sphere of service for her, the restarting of the Bible Correspondence Courses from Beirut. Abu Ibrahim made another trip to Irbid to collect more courses and related material and, on his safe return, Marjorie began renewing contact with existing students. We were, however, faced with one vital deficiency; our stock of suitable booklets to enclose with the lessons, or for following up those who showed special interest, was meagre and the prospect of obtaining new supplies was bleak. On the outbreak of hostilities in the Canal Zone, many Britons in Cairo, including the manager of the Nile Mission Press, had been arrested and interned. The authorities then sequestrated the Mission press and buildings, ruling out the possibility of obtaining Arabic material from Cairo for some time. We could see clearly the necessity for Christian literature to be printed in Beirut, but how could we be involved in such a project? Some months were to pass before that question could be answered.

At this juncture we were faced with a completely unforeseen prospect. Arthur Trebble with whom we had stayed in Iraq, flew into Beirut at regular intervals and occasionally we met him at the airport for a brief period of fellowship. Our situation interested him though he never hinted that he, and others in Baghdad, were endeavouring to obtain entry permits for two missionaries to reside in Iraq. So it came as a complete surprise when, in a tone of delight, he announced that permits had been granted, and invited us to move to Baghdad. The coolness of our reaction must have disappointed him but the suggestion ran counter to the way the Lord appeared to be directing us. The Bible Correspondence Courses had been recommenced and, for numerous reasons, Beirut seemed to be a better centre than Baghdad both for this ministry and any other form of literature outreach. Nevertheless the two visas were not wasted. The Miltons, as soon as they heard of the open door to Iraq, expressed the conviction this was the place where the Lord would have them be. Within a few weeks they were on their way and we were happy for them, knowing their Arabic studies would progress more rapidly in Baghdad, whilst Arthur and Violet Trebble, together with the local believers, would give them all the encouragement they needed. Time was to prove the decision was right, especially as subsequent political changes in Iraq, leading to a change of Government, would have precluded any possibility of developing a literature ministry there.

We did not have to wait long after turning down the invitation to move to Iraq before we reached the next stage in the unknown road. The home Council of the Nile Mission Press, deeply concerned about the cessation of their work in Cairo, sent a representative to

Lebanon to assess the possibility of recommencing in Beirut. He contacted us and asked if we would be able to assist. We saw this as a challenge and, on receiving a formal invitation from the NMP Council, agreed to recommence their ministry under certain conditions. In view of the obvious advantages of using local printing facilities we required an assurance they were not expecting us to manage a printing press. Then, as we looked directly to the Lord for provision, we could not become paid members of their staff, with all that would imply. Also, being the Lord's servants we must be sensitive to His guidance and be prepared to move elsewhere if He so directed. Having made our position clear, we agreed to assist them in their literature ministry until they could send out their own appointed worker. They accepted these conditions and within a few weeks the work of the Nile Mission Press commenced its new career. The initial project was very small, arranging for the translation, printing and distribution of Scripture Union notes, but, within a few months, a number of books, some reprints, others new, together with a series of tracts and booklets, were off the press and in circulation. Much of this was due to our having an excellent assistant, Tewfiq Khoury, for the checking of manuscripts and proof reading.

Tewfiq had an interesting history. A priest of the Syriac church he had discovered through reading the Scriptures, the truth of justification by faith, and thus his personal need of Jesus Christ as Saviour. This truth and its subsequent effect on his own life, became the main emphasis in his teaching. For him the Syriac church was still his spiritual home; he had no thought of leaving and certainly no intention of fellowshipping with the despised Protestants. But before long his preaching resulted in conflict with the hierarchy and he was defrocked. The lack of official certificates which would have proved his proficiency in languages and other subjects, made it impossible for him to obtain secular employment, and Tewfiq moved to France. In Paris he found a small group of believers whose fellowship he could enjoy and, while with them, was baptised by immersion as a true follower of the Lord Jesus. Within a short time he obtained employment on one of the radio stations and all seemed set for him to enjoy a well paid career. But that was not the Lord's will for him. One day in the midst of his work the words,

'What are you doing here in France? Why are you not in your own country witnessing for me there?' seemed to echo in his mind. He resigned his post, booked a passage, and arrived almost penniless, and virtually friendless, in Beirut.

A few days later Tewfiq met one of our missionary friends who, hoping we could make use of his obvious linguistic skills, introduced him to us. We had already had a number of so called experts pleading for work so my initial response was very cautious. Most of the applicants sought to show their expertise by being very critical of other peoples' standards of Arabic literature. Therefore, Tewfiq did not endear himself to me when, picking up a manuscript being prepared for the press, he adopted the same attitude and plunged into a dissertation on what he believed to be its grammatical deficiencies. My missionary friend went to great lengths to assure me of Tewfiq's ability and, more for his sake than anything else, I handed Tewfiq the manuscript of a proposed Christian novel and, mentioning a ridiculously low fee, suggested he check it before it was passed to the Publications Committee. Just as he was leaving something prompted me to pay him the fee in advance and, having done so, I wondered if he would appear again. Three days later he was back with the work, not merely finished, but judging by its looks, to a great extent rewritten! That particular book not only received the warm approval of the Committee, but became one of the most effective in bringing many to personal faith in the Lord Jesus. Tewfiq joined us in the work and from the beginning proved to be a loyal and hardworking colleague. His efforts proved to be invaluable in establishing the work of the Nile Mission Press in Beirut. We became close friends, and only then did he tell me that the first day we met he was penniless, hungry and dejected. I felt ashamed for, now being fully aware of his worth, I realised my offering such a low fee had really been an insult. But also it brought a sense of gratitude to the Lord for prompting me to pay it in advance. Moreover it taught me a lesson, namely to be slow in judging a person's motives and quick in showing compassion to those in need.

Much to our joy we were now more fully occupied. The Bible Course ministry gradually progressed with contacts being made in Egypt, Sudan, Jordan, Iraq, Syria and Lebanon. The number of courses translated and ready for the press also increased, including one on the Gospel of John and another on Mark. At the same time we had a good relationship with the local Arab assembly and, though at times we felt the tug of Jordan, began to feel at home in Beirut and had every reason to be content. The work of the press moved ahead steadily and with the help of advisory and publications' committees, formed mainly of nationals, the foundations for a stable work seemed to have been laid. During the next few years this ministry passed through many ups and downs, but today continues as a vital, vibrant ministry based in Cyprus under the direction of the Middle East Christian Outreach.

By now it was high summer and within a fairly short time we were suffering from the enervating effects of Beirut's heat and high humidity whilst asthma caused me to relinquish my part time teaching at the British Syrian Mission. The continuous city noise, added to the intensity of the summer's heat, made it almost impossible to obtain a good night's rest. They also ensured Andrew's lengthy, wakeful moments continued and, eventually, we came to the conclusion a cooler clime was becoming a necessity. A trip into the hills convinced us of the advantages of living outside the city and in August we rented a cottage in the pleasant village of Beit Meri, some 2,000 feet above sea level. This straggly village whose roots were planted in Graceo-Roman times, was home to Christians and Druze who, in spite of ancient bitter feuds, now seemed to live in happy harmony. Its mixture of dwellings, ranging from humble cottages like ours to palatial new homes, lay on both sides of a pine clad ridge, one side presenting glorious views to the coast and on to the horizon, whilst to the east a vista of canyon-like valleys, and scattered villages clinging to precipitous slopes, formed the foreground to ever rising barren land, culminating in mountain peaks where winter's snow lay thick for months. A forty minute bus journey deposited us in the centre of Beirut, whilst service cars would cut the time by half. The cool nights, undisturbed by any raucous noises, ensured unbroken sleep, and the physical and emotional benefits of the move were soon apparent. After a day spent in the bustle and humid heat of the city, it was a relief to step out of the bus into the pine scented air, and walk home to the tune of cicadas celebrating the arrival of the evening hour. Andrew also benefitted and began to show his adventurous spirit by climbing over every item of ancient ruin he could find.

1957 moved peacefully towards its close and the new year opened, with little signs of the internal conflict which, in the near future, would drive an abiding wedge between Lebanon's two main communities and plunge them into all out civil war. An extended visit from close relatives provided us with an opportunity of a return visit to Amman, Jerash and Jerusalem. It was a memorable visit, for being Easter, our minds became riveted on the events enacted in Jerusalem so many centuries ago. There was the unforgettable experience of a midnight walk through silent dimly lit streets, out through the Eastern gate, retracing the steps of that little band who faithfully, though fearfully, followed their Master down and across the Kidron valley to enter the darker shades of Gethsemane. To stand in silence close to the place where the Saviour had knelt, prayed and, in the intensity of His agony, sweated as it were great drops of blood; then to look towards the darkened city and imagine the torch lit crowd, hastening down the hill, bent on His arrest, heightened appreciation of the events on that night of His betrayal. Voices were muted as we bowed in prayer, worshipped and wondered why He could love us so. That wonder increased in the morning as we walked the via Dolorosa, the way the Saviour trod from the judgment hall to Calvary. For those who truly loved the Lord, it was a fresh and poignant reminder of the price He paid in order that 'the handwriting of requirements that was against us' might be obliterated. Moving though these two events had been, they were but a prelude to early Easter morning at the Garden Tomb where, with hundreds of others, we joined in joyful praise celebrating the Lord's resurrection, and bowed again in worship as we recalled His glorious triumph over sin, death and the grave.

A few weeks after that Easter the first signs of internal dissension became apparent in Lebanon. The abortive attempt by France, Britain and Israel to retake the Suez Canal had generated within the minds of Egypt's leaders the desire to be the dominant power in the Middle East. This led Egypt to join with Syria in forming the United Arabic Republic, in which they hoped the predominantly Christian country of Lebanon would be included. For a long time a considerable proportion of Lebanon's Muslim population had resented the dominant position of the Christians, both in Government and economic affairs. Now, in response to the torrent of propaganda emanating from Egypt, they began to press for change. In certain areas of Beirut, huge posters bearing the image of General Nasser, began to grace the streets, whilst smaller ones decorated doors and windows. By May, civil unrest had turned to outright violence resulting in occasional gun battles, strikes in shops and industry and, at times, Government imposed curfews. According to Lebanon's constitution the head of state always had to be a Maronite Christian and the head of Government a Sunni Muslim, whilst seats in Parliament were allocated on a percentage basis relative to religious strength. With adherents of Christian denominations outnumbering Muslims they had long held the majority of the seats but immigration from Palestine, along with the Muslim birthrate, altered the balance and the demand for greater Muslim control over the country's affairs increased. Add to this the various political ideologies within each group, and it is not difficult to discern the seeds of the troubles which erupted and continued for the next six months.

In spite of curfews and strikes I managed to make the daily visit into town. Both Tewfiq and Abu Ibrahim did the same, but in doing so, faced very difficult and tricky situations in order to ensure the literature ministry continued. We also managed to attend the Arabic Sunday services, usually followed by lunch with the resident staff at the British Syrian Mission's girls' school. Travel was sometimes difficult and the journeys could be accompanied by a touch of excitement. At one period a certain Muslim sector became a no-go area and a number of Christians of differing persuasions had been kidnapped. The road through it was our quickest way home, but for weeks we made a lengthy detour until at last we heard it was open. We had been to the Mission school for lunch and then, being assured of the route being open, made tracks for home. The wide road seemed unusually empty and quiet. We sped along quite happily until, suddenly, a road block loomed ahead and a moment later, surrounded by a gesticulating group of armed men, we were directed into a maze of narrow streets where a further group demanded we stop. One doesn't argue with trigger happy individuals and, on being roughly requested to produce evidence of identification, we handed over our passports. A guard commandeered them whilst two or three others hung around, no doubt to prevent any effort to move. It possibly didn't occur to them we were not likely to vanish without those precious identity documents! I wondered about a number of things: how long would they keep us? would our passports be confiscated? if so, would this be the time when we disappeared from view for a while? Eventually, getting impatient I got out of the car and, after chatting for a moment to one of the guards, demanded, as firmly as possible, the return of our passports while praying the Lord would intervene. We were grateful He did. A few minutes later an older person appeared, thrust the passports into my hand and told us to make ourselves scarce without delay. We needed no second invitation to do so! I recollect that, as we hit the highway, shots rang out but we did not stop to see if they were in anyway intended for us.

Tension in the country increased in July when a rebellion in Iraq, fomented to some degree by dissidents influenced by both Russia and Egypt, toppled the monarchy. King Faisal 2 and his immediate family were assassinated, the elderly pro-British Prime Minister, Nuri Al Said, was caught by an angry mob while trying to escape dressed as a woman, and brutally murdered. Expatriates, especially British, found themselves in difficult, often dangerous, situations. The day the troubles commenced Jim Milton's quick thinking saved him from potential harm. Returning from town, a chanting mob pouring down the street warned him of danger ahead. Promptly jumping onto a providentially passing bus, he subsided into the only empty seat and relaxed. But a moment later his peace was shattered, the crowded bus erupted into an almost hypnotic chant of 'down with imperialism, down with the English'. Jim thought he could well be out of the frying pan into the fire, until he realised his slight build and Arab headdress had prevented him being marked out as a foreigner. He therefore promptly joined in with the chant and, being a Scot, had no difficulty in clapping in rhythm with the rest, loudly proclaiming, 'Down with imperialism, down with the English.' Fortunately his seat was near the door and, when the bus neared his home, he did not linger! Within days arrangements had been made for the evacuation of women and children. Molly, together with Violet Trebble and her two boys, returned home. Jim, and many other Britons, were placed under house arrest for a number of weeks, then ordered to leave the country.

The rebellion in Iraq encouraged many Lebanese who were supportive of the anti-Government factions, to envisage a speedy change in the country's constitution. Sporadic bouts of fighting, complemented by numerous strikes, continued in Beirut and various parts of the country until later in the year. The Government fearing Egyptian influence had grown to the extent of inciting all out rebellion, then invoked the activation of a defence agreement with the United States. This led to Marines making a sea-borne landing south of the capital, and this formidable presence on the outskirts of the city, restored a semblance of order. For the rest of the year the Lebanese army maintained check points on a number of roads, and introduced night time curfews at the least sign of trouble.

During the last weeks of 1958 life returned to near normality, with New Year's eve being celebrated in the usual raucous fashion as every church bell added its note to the cacophonous background of ships' sirens, blaring car horns, over indulgent revellers, and the roar of a city which would not sleep. For us there was a more personal reason for celebration. As the first hours of 1959 began, it was not the strident noise of a city but the cry of a hungry two day old baby, which kept us awake. On 29th December, at the Christian Medical Centre, our very precious daughter, Elisabeth Ruth, had joined the family and was now determined to make her presence known.

Another kind of birth also occurred in 1958. Two young Americans while studying the book of Acts, were gripped with the account of the birth of the church and the method of its growth, and believed they had discovered a pattern others had missed. They were also influenced by a book on New Testament Churches written by a missionary to South America. In fact both these Americans, and the missionary author in South America, were reaching the same conclusions as Darby, Muller, and many others early in the nineteenth century. Both the young men were keen on outreach to students, as well as to the expatriate community in general, and felt an English speaking church could be commenced in Ras Beirut. With the nearby American University attracting a multiplicity of foreign students, a mission field lay to hand, and they envisioned that keen Christian students, on returning to their own lands, would duplicate similar churches. It was a pleasure to assist them in this effort and in so doing see Ras Beirut church, as it was eventually called, born. During the next few years this grew into a vital testimony to a constantly changing congregation. The last time the visitors' book was used it bore over a thousand names of various nationalities and its ministry had touched the very young, the old and all ages in between.

With Elisabeth Ruth having arrived safely we lingered in Beirut no longer than necessary. Before the end of the first week in January we were back in Beit Meri where Andrew, though thrilled to have a sister, expressed surprise at her complete indifference to the dinky toys he endeavoured to woo her with! So he reverted to doing his own thing, including wandering in and out of our neighbour's house where he soon picked up simple Arabic expressions, so much so that on one occasion, when we seemed to hesitate in replying to a question, he proceeded to tell us the content in English – a good example of how, in learning a language, it would be helpful to become 'like a little child'!

The stress of the past few years now began to make itself felt and our thoughts turned to the possibility of a visit to England. Five years had slipped by and there had been no real period of rest and relaxation. The last few months had been far from easy and now, with two young children to care for, the need for a complete change from the pressures of the work became apparent. We let our families at home know we expected to be with them by the end of May, but before the end of January our tentative plans had been overturned. Halfway through the month the weather changed, and the latter rains began in earnest and a stream began to flow through the house. The landlord refused to do anything until the rainy season ended and so forced us to make an unexpected decision. Marjorie and the children would fly to England as soon as possible where her sister and husband would provide them with a temporary home. I would plan to travel sometime in May, by which time we hoped someone would be available to oversee the work and there would be accommodation for us all in England.

Finding someone willing to supervise the literature ministry was not easy. The one person who would have been most suitable, and whose Mission would have agreed to his helping, died in an air crash towards the end of 1958 and I knew of no one else in the country. Finally the need was met through the cooperation of an American Baptist missionary resident in Jordan. George Kelsey, a close friend of the missionary who had been killed, was keenly interested in the work his friend would have been doing and agreed to make regular visits to ensure it did not falter. With that matter settled I set my sights on finding a cheap passage home sometime in May, only to have my programme upset again. The Nile Mission Press held an annual report meeting in London, usually preceded by a meeting of the Mission Board. This was scheduled for April and they decided I ought to be there to give them an up date on the situation. By the time their plans reached me it was impossible to complete my responsibilities in Lebanon and be in London in time without resorting to air travel. With that arrangement made, I stored our goods, packed my bags and, shortly after dawn on the day of the meeting, boarded a plane which landed me in time to be in London at the appointed hour.

Before leaving Beirut we had received invitations to various missionary conferences and these steadily increased. All were important and we were grateful for the interest shown in the Arabic speaking lands. But one visit was possibly the most important made during that furlough. We received an invitation to visit the Isle of Wight, from Noel and Margery Allen, friends since our Jerusalem days in 1947, who were now managing a Christian Guest House in Ryde. They fixed a date in August and we looked forward to the pleasure of a complete change and rest in new surroundings. Also amongst the guests there were Will and Zoe Foster, now fully recovered from their unpleasant Egyptian experiences. Not surprisingly, conversation tended at times towards the Middle East and the value of Christian literature as an evangelistic and teaching tool, not only in that area, but westward to North Africa and south eastward to the Sudan. Then another friend from Jerusalem days appeared on the scene. Dr.Graham Gillan, who had been with me on the foray into Jordan, had emigrated to Canada but was now on a visit to Britain. Discovering where we were he also decided to visit Ryde for a few days. For the first time, after nearly twelve years, the seven of us, all sharing the same concern for the Lord's work, had the opportunity for a Middle East forum and we made the most of the situation.

With the summer behaving as we feel summers should the days were spent out and about exploring unfamiliar places. At the end of the day, the quiet and beauty of the garden lured us out to relax whilst we shared together experiences of the past and thoughts for the future. One evening Graham ended the session with a string of searching questions, culminating in a final challenge which we found impossible to ignore. His questions elicited comments concerning the necessity for extending the range of the Bible Correspondence Courses, the lack of certain types of Christian literature and, above all, the crying need for another Christian bookshop in Beirut. Apart from the Bible Society there were only two retail outlets for Christian literature, one housed in a church building near the town centre, and the other in an apartment in the suburb of Ras Beirut. The former, linked with the Near East Christian Council under the supervision of a delightful Lebanese Christian, stocked a wide and mixed range of material, some with a liberal bias. The latter was the brainchild of a very godly Missionary from Australia who for years envisioned opening Christian bookstores in every major town in the Middle East. For various reasons, that vision had not made much progress, so the need for well stocked premises with good display facilities seemed to be obvious. In response to our comments on the situation Graham simply said, "Why don't you do something about it?"! Here was a challenge to faith; also a reminder that awareness of a need often brings the responsibility of meeting it. Why don't you do something about it? Why not indeed? We could think of reasons why we could not, but the challenge brought wakeful hours that night.

A new day brought no relief from the challenge, nor was it minimised by a question from Noel Allen. He was not present the previous evening and had no idea of the possible effect of his words. "Have you," he asked after breakfast, "ever considered opening a bookstore and commencing a publishing ministry to include material not covered by the Nile Mission Press?" His unanticipated query came as a further indication of the Lord guiding us in that direction. We felt the problems and complexities of such an enterprise made it impossible and yet, paradoxically, could not avoid the conviction of this being, for us, the way ahead. One problem looming large in our discussions was that of finance.

Since first yielding to the Lord's call we were convinced He would, in answer to believing prayer, provide all the funds necessary both for ourselves and any project He called us to undertake. In various and sometimes unusual ways this had proved to be true and we believed He could, and would, do the same for any other project. Our friends also believed God could provide but would only do so through those who had knowledge of a project. They therefore took a pragmatic view and urged us to write round all the assemblies in Britain mentioning the prospect of developing an Arabic Christian Literature Centre in Beirut. In addition to outlining its functions they also suggested a request be made for financial support. On this point of an open request for financial aid we strongly disagreed. It went directly against our conviction that to the Lord alone we looked for aid. Furthermore, provision of funds in answer to prayer would, in our judgment, be one of the ways in which the Lord would confirm the project being in line with His will. Finally we agreed to Noel Allen's suggestion that a number of leading brethren be asked to sign a letter detailing the matters we had discussed and he would ensure its distribution to as many assemblies as possible. He further proposed acting as secretary and treasurer for any project which might result, providing we would undertake responsibility for its development. In due course a letter was prepared and before the end of the year, it was distributed under the title of 'Christian Literature for Arab Lands'. Time alone would tell if it would generate any interest. Even if not we prayed the Lord would, in His own way, enable us to rise to the challenge and turn vision into reality.

CHAPTER 22

The Vision Unfolds

(1960)

I will lead them in paths they have not known
(Isaiah 46:16).

With the holiday consigned to the realm of memory we faced the busy autumn months and as the weeks flew by plans for returning to Lebanon occupied our thoughts. George Kelsey's efficient oversight of the Nile Mission Press had ensured excellent progress and he felt he should now concentrate on his ministry in Jordan. Most of the items prepared before we left for furlough were now in print but, as George had more in the pipeline, it was essential we return without too much delay. Distribution had likewise increased, sometimes in ways we had not anticipated. One of these involved an Arab Christian who, having obtained permission to enter every prison in Lebanon for the purpose of holding meetings, extended his spoken ministry by the use of the printed page. With his help many Gospel portions and scores of tracts reached those who, probably, would never dream of darkening the doors of a church. Thus we had no doubt that our return would give little opportunity for idleness, especially if the vision of developing a literature centre became a reality. Appointments made for the rest of 1959 precluded our returning until the New Year but provisional arrangements were in hand for returning by rail and sea sometime in February.

The good-byes said, all that remained was for us to get ourselves down to Dover and, finally, the train from Calais; then on through the night to arrive midmorning, somewhat dishevelled and tired, to a cloud covered, sombre looking Venice. The following day we boarded the *Ausonia*. Steerage definitely applied to our cabin for it was not only some decks down but, judging by the noise, seemed to be next to the churning screw! However, only nights would be spent down there and as the temperature rose most daylight time would be spent on deck. With nothing on the menu suitable for a fifteen month old the first evening meal presented a problem for Ruth. However an obliging steward provided the solution by producing vegetable soup which, being delicious, became her favourite dish for the whole of the journey.

Late in the afternoon the *Ausonia* slipped from her berth and, slowly nosing her way across the outer lagoon, headed south for the Adriatic and her first port of call, Brindisi. Through the night the cabin's gentle creak conjured up pictures of a choppy sea and an initial stagger on rising confirmed the impression. It only needed a few minutes to corroborate the loss of both appetite and sea legs, the result being neither of us felt any desire to face the upper decks! However with Andrew and Ruth becoming increasingly active, and the claustrophobic atmosphere of our stuffy, windowless cabin being almost unendurable, fresh air beckoned and we staggered aloft. Gleams of sunshine through broken clouds greeted us whilst the nature of the Italian coastline, together with the lessening sea, spoke of harbour ahead. By the time the ship glided across Brindisi's calmer waters appetites were renewed and spirits in fine fettle. Our sea legs were never really tested again. The waters of the Mediterranean remained relatively quiet until, on encountering the confluence of the Nile and the sea, the inevitable long, smooth, roll began.

A major event took place in Ruth's life on that voyage - she took her first unaided steps on the *Ausonia's* sun deck. For a while she had been happily relying on her push chair as a walking support, manoeuvring it here and there, much to the danger of unsuspecting shins. But then came the moment when something caught her inquisitive gaze and, letting go of the handles to investigate, she walked. From then on it became imperative to keep an even closer watch as she tottered around in her new found freedom, which took her to companionways beckoning up or down, and to places where a wee figure could slip between rails into the open sea. If we had been given the choice, a safer place than a ship's deck would have been selected for her first unsupported steps! By the time the boat berthed in Alexandria, she had clocked up some hundreds of yards, and her gait had become relatively steady.

News of our journey must have preceded us for we were met by an Egyptian Christian who, for many years, had been full time in the Lord's service. He invited us home and, later in the day, he regaled us with an account of his former years and, in so doing, gave a vivid insight into the problems and dangers of witnessing to Muslims. He had spent a few years in the United States where his name 'Mikhail' had been anglicized to Mitchell, a change which caused many to believe that, in spite of a swarthy complexion, he was European. After studying at a theological college he returned to Egypt and later developed an itinerant ministry amongst the assemblies of brethren. For an extensive period the house boat community on the Nile and riverside villages were his parish and there were times when, being in difficult situations, his foreign sounding name stood him in good stead.

However, on one occasion, he needed far more protection than any human name could give. Having spent a few days visiting house boats he decided to move on to a village for the night. A small house, somewhat isolated, was made available to him. Some Muslims had listened attentively and discussed the Christian message without rancour. On the other hand a few were incensed and considered it would be meritorious to murder the infidel while he slept. With night well advanced a small party set out to accomplish the deed and, creeping silently, made their way to the house. Suddenly the startling appearance of a figure in brilliant white, standing at the door, froze them in their tracks. Boldness evaporated, one broke to run and the others followed at his heels. Back in the safety of the village they discussed the sight and, possibly urged on by others, came to the conclusion it had been a mere trick of light. Back they went, but superstitious fear drove them to avoid the front and approach from the rear. All went according to plan until within a few feet of the door they saw the figure again barring their path! The ground burned beneath their feet as they took the road back to the village! In the morning Mr. Mitchell left for home completely unaware of the night's proceedings. Many years later, while chatting to a tradesman in

Alexandria he learnt of the miraculous way in which the angel of the Lord had preserved him. The shopkeeper suddenly broke the thread of the conversation by asking, "Were you ever in such and such a village at such and such a time?" Mr. Mitchell confirmed he had been and only then did he learn how wonderfully the Lord had saved his life. Surely the day of miracles has not passed.

By evening we were back on board and as darkness fell the *Ausonia*, moderating her speed to reach Beirut by breakfast time, headed north across the muddied conflux of the Nile estuary. Disembarkation created the inevitable crush, rush and bustle. Those with a modicum of cabin luggage were soon on their way, especially if they were on a wink and a nod acquaintance with the customs' officers. Others with trunks in the hold, and that included us, were delayed until net loads of luggage, and other sundry goods, were swung ashore, and then endured further delay until one's porter managed to secure the attention of an official usually, it seemed, an intimate acquaintance. A cynic may have assumed the perfunctory manner in which questions were asked, and the speedy affixing of clearance labels to individual items, indicated the porter's extortionate fee would be shared. Others, of a more generous and unsuspicious disposition, would simply admire, and be impressed by, the welcoming friendly attitude of the Lebanese Customs' staff.

Being at that juncture homeless in Beirut we were grateful when the girls' school provided us with temporary accommodation. There was ample room for the four of us in one of their spacious bedrooms. The garden provided space for Andrew to work off his energy. Ruth, having taken her first steps on the rolling deck of a ship, had a problem coping with solid land. Her staggering progress continued and, as this coincided with sore gums and signs of the ability to chew, she suffered many bumps from the one and discomfort from the other. However she usually managed to come through each day with more smiles than tears.

Obtaining our own accommodation had now to take priority. First we needed to locate a Simsar; the indispensable go-between when transacting any business deal in the Middle East. The Simsar would be aware of places to rent (usually by relatives or close friends!) and his mediation between owner and prospective tenant prevented loss of face on either side. An impossibly high rent could be rejected, or a hopelessly low offer turned down, without either party being offended. The Simsar, with one eye on not losing a customer and the other on obtaining the highest commission possible for himself, did his best to bring the two parties to an amicable agreement. Our first Simsar, rather an unsavoury looking fellow, showed us a few flats in an area and condition similar to himself. Not surprisingly our search ended with our still being flatless. We were more successful on our second foray and before the end of the day, footsore and weary, we returned to the school triumphant. The search had stretched as far as the lighthouse area of Ras Beirut where we had negotiated a deal for an empty three bedroom flat. The customary procedure of rent in advance had to be observed, fortunately for us only three months at a time.

Our new home lay on the seaward side of two blocks of four storey flats. These were situated some two hundred yards down, or should one say up, a partially completed cul de sac which rose steeply from the main coast road. The whole area was still under development with a few large apartment blocks on the opposite side of the street to ours, whilst open, rough, uncultivated land surrounded the other three sides. The lie of the land meant our flat was one floor up at the front and ground level at the back. Two bedrooms fronted the cul de sac and were separated by the third and a hallway from the kitchen and dining area. The latter led on to a tiled semi circular patio from which a magnificent view across the waste land down to the shore, and over a vast expanse of sea westward, invited one to relax and meditate. The glory of the sunsets seen from that patio remain one of life's pleasant memories. Two steps led down to a patch of ground, surrounded by cement block walls, which could hardly be described as a garden, though it did provide a little extra space in which Andrew and Ruth could amuse themselves. The flat was excellently placed as far as the English speaking Ras Beirut church was concerned. There we experienced the joy of burgeoning friendships and many months of delightful fellowship, all without losing contact with the Arabic speaking church on the other side of town.

Within a couple of weeks of moving to Ras Beirut the pace became hectic. A backlog of publishing work, either to be prepared or seen through the press, remained in the Nile Mission Press office but through Tewfiq Khoury's efficient and speedy proof-reading this soon vanished. My main responsibility at that time comprised supervising the running of the office, finding suitable material for publishing, arranging, if need be, for its translation, organising the Publication Committee's programme, negotiating terms with local printers, and making visits to the press to ensure work proceeded according to schedule. Marjorie spent more time at home but her input in searching out, and checking, material which might be suitable for publishing was invaluable.

So we had the pleasure of seeing the work of the Nile Mission Press expand. At the same time we prayed for the Lord's help in developing the wider literature ministry envisaged during our time at home. It did not take us long to realise that vision could not come to fruition as long as we were fully responsible for the NMP. The Committee in London had promised that, if the need arose, they would send their own accredited worker, so I now wrote emphasising that time had now arrived. The letter must have been filed, and forgotten, for no reply came and we simply pressed on coping as best we could. But consideration of ways and means of opening a Christian bookshop, which could also be a centre for the Emmaus Bible Correspondence Courses, was constantly before us. The Courses continued to be processed and dispatched with Marjorie's help but it was axiomatic this work could not grow without extra assistance and facilities. We were burdened with a sense of urgency; and the consciousness that the vision of a wider ministry would dim and become a mere dream unless positive steps were taken. The first step soon became obvious; the need for a review of all that would be involved in implementing the project. We were in the dark concerning the area in which a Christian bookshop could best be located, the amount of finance needed for renting of premises, the laws affecting such a project, the best sources of supplies and their cost, plus a number of other matters all of which revealed how naive we were to consider such a plan.

But we believed that when the Lord gives a vision He will provide the means for its accomplishment, the ability to cope with it and the wisdom to fulfill it. We were also convinced when a life is yielded to the Lord's service He can, and will, make good use of one's previous training. So it transpired in this case: our earlier days in clerical situations, especially Marjorie's, provided a foundation for business administration. Our objectives were clear. The spread of the Gospel and Biblical teaching by means of literature and Bible Courses, the production of suitable material and the opening of a centre through which personal contacts could be made. Such a project called for careful accounting and good management. A haphazard approach to any work done for the Lord is never glorifying to Him and can, by its very imperfections, even bring dishonour on His Name. Only the best of which we are capable is good enough and if, in the consciousness of our own deficiencies we commit our service to Him, the Lord is able to supply all that we lack to enable it to be effectively accomplished. In retrospect we are aware that without the Lord's overruling and timely help, the vision during those days in the Isle of Wight would have faded and vanished.

Visions to be transformed into reality call for action. Our first move was to share the plans with three Lebanese who readily joined us in considering ways and means for its fulfillment. The task of finding suitable premises became our responsibility and a frustrating one it proved to be. Lock up shops abounded but most of the areas were not suitable. In those which were, the key money, required in advance and usually about £1,000 sterling, lay away beyond our present means. We had just about reached the point of concluding the project would have to be temporarily shelved when, as so often happens when facing an apparently insurmountable barrier, the Lord opened the way.

In June our attention had been drawn to a vacant double fronted shop in one of the main thoroughfares in Ras Beirut. Being on the corner of a busy cross roads, and within a few minutes' walk of the American University with its considerable multi-racial student body, its position could hardly be bettered. Moreover we were assured the proprietor, Miss Selma Nasr, would be sympathetic to our aims. So to this lady we went and placed before her our plans which, initially, received a very enthusiastic and encouraging response. Then the nitty gritty details of the business side of the matter came to the fore. The key money, being fixed at 10,000 Lebanese liras (about £1,200) and the annual rent at 6,000 (approximately £720), soon took off the gloss. With barely £1,000 in the literature fund we decided it would not be possible to go ahead. But during the next few weeks our thoughts constantly returned to that shop. We decided some positive action needed to be taken. We agreed it would be wonderful if Miss Nasr allowed us to rent the place without the payment of the key money: so we should go and ask her! The very audacity of making such an approach caused us to shy away from doing so. However the feeling I should go pressed so strongly I agreed to do so, providing one of the Lebanese brethren, Adib Daghfal, would go with me. I was soon on my way to Adib's lodgings only to discover him preparing to leave. Immediately I assumed my visit was inopportune but his opening words proved otherwise. He too had been convinced we should take some action about Miss Nasr's shop, and was on the point of coming to me to suggest we should ask her if the key money would be remitted.

Encouraged by our mutual feelings we made tracks for Miss Nasr's home. I cannot say she seemed pleased to see us, though we were certainly not kept at the door. Her welcome appeared cool and remote and I concluded there would be a negative result from our visit. But within minutes of being seated, and without any preamble, she almost knocked us off our seats by saying, "Oh, if you want my premises for a Christian bookshop you can have them without key money!" Inwardly I gave a hearty 'hallelujah and thank you Lord'; outwardly both Adib and I expressed grateful appreciation for her generosity. Her decision was no emotional burst of enthusiasm because of the plans we had shared with her. She told how, over a number of weeks, various people had sought to rent, and of her objections to their proposed use. Only the previous evening she had refused a trader, dealing in merchandise which went against her Christian principles. The fact he was able to make a generous cash offer of both key money and rent, had not influenced her. Then, in conclusion, she revealed how for over a year she believed the Lord had been urging her to have the premises used for some form of Christian service. After reflecting more fully on our proposals she became convinced the premises had been kept vacant specially for this project. Our interview then turned to the matter of the rent. To aid us with this Miss Nasr suggested dividing off one section of the double front, resulting in her having another small shop to rent. We would then have an L-shaped portion, plus a narrow back room for storage which, we felt at the time, would be adequate for our purposes. If we agreed this proposal the rent would be reduced by a third to 4,000 Lebanese liras. No wonder we went home rejoicing!

The next two hectic months were devoted to preparations for opening in September. Marjorie undertook the ordering of books and sundries from overseas. Arabic stock was available locally at the NMP whilst the Lebanon Bible Society could supply us with Scriptures in various languages. Dividing walls to separate the two shops had to be built; bookcases, storage cupboards, display stands and window fittings planned and made. A suitable lighting system needed to be installed and, in every area, we were operating in unfamiliar territory. No wonder we prayed for wisdom. There were a few unexpected setbacks. The first came when a buildings' inspector spotted the dividing walls were being built and demanded the builder produce his permit. Only when we were contacted by a distraught workman, plaintively complaining all his tools had been confiscated, did we know of this situation! As all the alterations were internal the inspector had gone beyond his powers, perhaps because he thought he saw an opportunity to obtain a little supplement to his salary. Finding he had to deal with influential locals, not merely an insignificant workman and a couple of foreigners, he rapidly returned the tools and work proceeded. The next delay arose from the kindness of an Arab friend who offered to help by erecting a set of bookshelves. Hearing he had finished the work I popped in to examine the results. Three planks were attached with plenty evidence of faith but little material support to the newly built dividing wall. Putting the matter to the test, in response to a little pressure, the structure promptly collapsed leaving significant holes in the wall. The comment that we had decided to alter the arrangements and have a free standing case in that spot, satisfied the DIY enthusiast! Gradually most of the problems were overcome and we had hopes of opening early in September.

When that time came, the three Lebanese friends had joined us to form an executive committee. First we had to register the work with the Government. We were anxious for it be recognised as a Lebanese ministry and not a foreign missionary Society, so we insisted it be registered in the name of the nationals with ourselves as helpers. We knew the unstable character of the region, and there could well be circumstances which would compel the expulsion of foreigners resulting in the cessation of the work and, maybe, sequestration of its assets. We had personal experience of the loss of possessions on having to leave Jordan, and the experience of the Nile Mission Press in Egypt served as a warning. That work had been officially registered in Egypt shortly after the commencement of the twentieth century, but it was still a foreign mission. At the time of the Suez crisis, the Press and all its property, together with any liquid assets, was sequestrated and the missionaries expelled. We had no idea how the work we were commencing would grow, but as a Lebanese Society, be it large or small, its activities and its assets would remain intact even if all foreigner workers had to leave.

But registration called for two things, firstly a name and secondly a sympathetic and hopefully efficient solicitor to see the matter through. Many hours were spent over a suitable name, ending in the choice of *'The Manarah Society'* (The Lighthouse). Bearing in mind the Hebrew name for the six branched candlestick of the tabernacle, there was a faint risk the name might seem to have a Jewish flavour. But, with the Beirut lighthouse only a short distance from the shop we felt it was appropriate. One friend complained the lighthouse could indicate the Watchtower Society, but we thought that possibility would be mitigated by the sign over the shop - an old fashioned oil lamp.

The second step was to find a lawyer. David Tleel had contacts with a Miss Qarih and, on his recommendation, the affairs of the Manarah Society were placed in her hands. A small, energetic, and somewhat forceful lady, Miss Qarih did her utmost to push through the registration. But the wheels of Government move slowly. There were investigations, reports, questions and more questions, with still no sign of being completed by the opening date. One of her comments sheds revealing light on Middle East thought. Having been informed of an impending visit to her office by two inspectors, and hoping to obtain a quick and favourable decision, she suggested to David matters might be expedited by a monetary gift. His rather indignant reply that he eschewed bribery, brought an even more indignant reply from her, to the effect that she abhorred bribery and the suggested gift would merely be thanks in advance for 'recognition of services rendered'. Had she said 'in hope of services' it would have been more logical! However, the comment gave us a new view of what we would still call bribery. We hoped for an opening date in September, in spite of the procrastination of the officials, then the lawyer pointed out that we need not delay. She had completed our responsibility by presenting all the necessary information and documentation to the appropriate Government Department. Now, in her view, as there had been no negative response we should assume all was well and go ahead! It is a good thing we did for, if I remember correctly, five years were to elapse, before everything was finally sealed and settled.

Forming a small committee to oversee the development of the project had not been difficult. The Lord had wonderfully opened the way for obtaining suitable, well placed, premises, the generous giving of individuals and assemblies in Britain ensured sufficient funds for an advance on the rent and purchase of equipment and stock. But one problem still remained, how could the place be staffed? To be effective it needed to be open daily at regular hours - we envisaged operating a lending library, and selling Christian literature. There was also the matter of language. In Lebanon much could be accomplished in English and French, but it was important there be someone knowledgeable in Arabic available regularly. Marjorie was already busy at home handling administrative work; ordering material, keeping accounts and various records; coping with household responsibilities including two active young children, as well as involvement with the Bible Correspondence Courses. My responsibilities still included the directing of the Nile Mission Press, and involvement in the growing ministry of the Ras Beirut church, so had only limited time for assisting in the bookstore.

Help however lay to hand. Adib Daghfil offered to help on a part time basis and an Australian missionary, who had already been involved in a literature ministry, was free to assist for some hours each week. Also for the next few years we had good assistance from young Christian men who then went on to more lucrative employment. Memories of their valued help and friendship, as well as some of the problems they created, are woven into the pattern of the Manarah Society's history. Without them the work would have been less effective, we would have missed the stimulus of their fellowship, and been spared some hours of anxiety over their problems. Help also came periodically through other missionaries and for the next fifteen years, before civic strife caused a temporary closure, the shop remained open on a regular weekly schedule.

With the commencement of this work the expression 'full time service' became impregnated with added meaning, the years 1960-65 being some of the busiest in our lives. The bookstore, the Nile Mission Press literature ministry, the Emmaus Bible Correspondence Courses, the Ras Beirut church, an interest in the Arab assembly in Ashrafiyeh, visitation and entertaining filled our days. Alongside was an attempt to maintain a normal home life in which the children had their rightful share of attention, could feel secure being loved, and know their affairs were of vital interest to us. Perhaps it is not surprising the pressure, especially of the next three years, took their toll emotionally, physically and spiritually. Marjorie particularly felt the emotional strain, especially during the first few months in 1961. Some time later both of us passed through a period of spiritual darkness, a time when we had to strive hard to maintain any semblance of fellowship with the Lord. It was simply a case of holding on to the belief that somehow we were doing His will, even though we felt like giving up. In retrospect we know it was not our grimly holding on which brought us through the dark period but the Lord holding us, and carrying us through, until we had a renewed experience of His love and care. Then through His grace, His joy flooded our lives afresh. Such experiences were allowed not only to strengthen our faith but also to enable us to sympathise with and be a help to others on their Christian pathway. Through the bookshop we were to come into contact with many who were passing through spiritual crises and, though their stories cannot be fully told, a glimpse of the way the work developed may show some of the opportunities which were created.

CHAPTER 23

Developing the Vision

(1960 - 61)

To Him who is able to do exceedingly abundantly above all we ask...be glory (Eph. 3:20).

The new Manarah bookshop opened early in October. It was a stimulating experience to discover so many Lebanese and expatriates were interested in it, especially as they represented a cross section of Beirut's evangelical churches. Many who embraced the same firm belief in the inerrancy of the Bible, but differed concerning church order and practice, found personal barriers falling as they met and talked on what could be termed neutral ground. In due course not only Protestants but Greek Orthodox and Catholic priests came seeking evangelistic material, particularly booklets published by the Scripture Gift Mission.

We soon realised we had not envisaged the range of materials required to meet all the special needs. The basic range was obvious: Bibles, New Testaments, commentaries, study helps, theological and doctrinal beliefs, biographies etc. But also workers amongst children required lesson material, printed and visual, as well as prizes for the end of a school year. Those of musical bent anticipated finding a variety of hymn books and recordings, especially of hymns old and new. Others required Christian fiction for themselves, or books suitable as presents for their unconverted friends. Still others looked for a selection of wall plaques or sundry small items to adorn a wall or shelf, whilst requests for appropriate gifts for special occasions became increasingly frequent.

Marjorie, being responsible for all the ordering from overseas, found her workload steadily increasing. Many were the hours spent poring over catalogues whilst, being aware of limited finances, she juggled between the types and numbers of books to be ordered, and the necessity of leaving enough funds for local supplies. Then records, both of stock in hand and that anticipated, had to be updated and the account books completed. As most of this had to be done at home our already cramped flat had to yield some work space. So the hallway lost its status as a playroom and became an office. Marjorie's contribution, though to a great extent unseen, was vital to the effectiveness of our literature ministry and, with much of it having to be done in the evening after the children were in bed, leisure time was minimal. But the resulting benefits were obvious. Before the end of the year the window, shelves and racks of a bright and attractive shop' were filled with a comprehensive range of material which would have done credit to an old established business.

Whilst both of us were busy with the founding of the Manarah's ministry, and giving time to the activities of the Ras Beirut church, I was still responsible for overseeing the publishing programme of the Nile Mission Press. Consequently time was at a premium and there was little to spare for leisure with the children. Nile Mission Press management and publishing committees always met in the daytime but recording their minutes became an evening chore. With such varied matters calling for attention they inevitably began to spill over into the weekends. As one or the other of us had to take a share in manning the bookshop Saturdays became as busy as any other weekday. Sundays, with active participation in morning and evening services, provided a change but little rest and, as a consequence, we reached the danger point of carrying a seven day workload. I well remember visitors from Britain warning us of the spiritual and physical dangers of neglecting the Biblical principle of a Sabbath rest.

Sometime in June we realised Marjorie's squeamishness could be more than a sustained bout of indigestion, and a visit to Dr. Manoukian at the Christian Medical Centre might confirm an interesting possibility. It did: we could look forward to an increase in the family some time in January and we confidently anticipated happy results. As 1961 dawned we realised afresh how much we owed to the goodness of the Lord, not least for His care over our two children. We did have one very anxious time with Andrew. He was no longer his usual bright self and his temperature went away up. A visit to the Christian Medical Centre resulted in him receiving an injection of penicillin which, to my inexperienced eye, seemed excessive. He was soon in bed and quickly fell into what appeared to be a deep sleep. Thankfully we relaxed but only to be disturbed with him crying out in distress. He did not recognise us and showed signs of horror and screamed when one of us bent down to comfort him. Gradually he sank back to sleep. Twice more this occurred and we realised Andrew was slipping in and out of a coma. Late Sunday afternoon seemed an unlikely time to obtain help but I managed to contact the doctor who prescribed an antihistamine. A few hours later the traumatic though brief episode was over.

With three weeks of January gone, late one evening Marjorie realised she should be making tracks to the hospital. Lebanon was still enjoying a period of peace so, unlike the night of Ruth's arrival, there were no road blocks to negotiate, no trigger happy soldiers patrolling the streets and nothing to worry about except Marjorie and the anticipated arrival. It seemed the little one was very reluctant to enter this hard world and many hours passed before Marjorie, in a hazy atmosphere of sheer exhaustion, heard Dr. Manoukian murmur, "Ten little fingers and ten little toes." Philip Mark had arrived. The doctor's remarks to Marjorie were important. In the fourth month of pregnancy very good friends had paid us a visit; their recent firstborn was malformed in both hands and feet. In view of her age, Marjorie had lived under the shadow of the thought that her babe might also be deformed and the news of perfect hands and feet was sheer bliss.

Life, with a baby in the home, became more hectic, especially as the NMP literature ministry made increasing calls upon our time. Finance had arrived making it possible to progress with their publishing programme. Billy Graham's *Peace With God* and *World Aflame* had been approved and translated, whilst the daily Scripture readings entitled *Daily Light* was already at one of the local presses. Tewfiq Khoury laboured long over *Daily Light*, checking and rechecking every reference with the result that, as far as we were ever able to ascertain, the text was free from error. Other projects in hand included a reprint of *Christ In All the Scriptures* for which, due to the generosity of their students, a Christian University in America had forwarded funds. Tewfiq's faithful service became a key factor in the Nile Mission Press being re-established as an effective ministry. The content and accuracy of many a manuscript was enhanced by his careful reviewing and editing.

But now I was having a conflict of loyalties. There was still no sign of the Nile Mission Press sending anyone to replace me and its developing ministry made my commitment to their interests essential. But the increasing Manarah ministry, supported by the assemblies who had commended us, obviously had a major claim on our time and it was becoming difficult to give both ministries the attention they deserved. A few weeks later I heard a replacement was on the way. In due course Hugh Thomas, an ex army officer and former missionary with the Red Sea Mission Team, arrived and soon willingly took full control of the NMP's activities. My only regret was that for some reason Tewfiq had to leave. It was an unhappy situation, and for him a very difficult one as he now had a young family to support. But the NMP's loss became the North Africa Mission's gain. For the next twenty five years or so he headed a very effective and extensive radio ministry to Arabs, based in the South of France.

The next three months saw a significant development in the Emmaus Bible Correspondence Courses. The range was increased by three courses one of which was specially written with Muslims in view. These were all translations from English but, with careful editing, proved suitable for the Arab world. During this same period came our first involvement with the production of material in Arabic for the Scripture Gift Mission. They proposed having a new edition of the Gospel of Luke typeset in Beirut with the final, fully corrected proof copies sent to Britain for printing and distribution. The original Gospel portions, both of the SGM and the Bible Society, were too large to fit comfortably into a shirt pocket. Consequently many a Muslim, having accepted a Gospel, found it difficult to conceal it from his compatriots who could well object to its possession, never mind it being read. So we suggested a slightly smaller size and, as soon as this was accepted, placed the contract with the printers. It proved to be an onerous task as the firm was still setting type by hand and mistakes were frequent. Even after they introduced linotype three, or even four, proofs were needed seeing as in correcting one mistake the operator could introduce two more! During the next few years we had the privilege of assisting the SGM in reissuing a few of their publications in Arabic, as well as increasing the number of titles available. It was a worthwhile addition to our workload and one never regretted, especially as many of those publications are still in circulation in many parts of the Arabic speaking world.

By the end of July it was time to pause and review the progress of the bookshop ministry during the past ten months. A consideration of the various contacts made confirmed the value of every part of our ministry. The unusual nature of a shop displaying a whole window full of Christian literature with, usually an open Bible as a centre piece, was enough to draw the curious inside whilst casual passers by who simply saw books, would drift in searching for secular material. In both cases there were opportunities for friendly discussions, some of which turned to the deeper and more important things of life. It was amazing how many were prepared to linger and, in some cases, talk freely of their concerns, hopes and fears, thus opening the way for discussing the spiritual solution to their problems. In the early days we attempted to keep a record of the various situations encountered but, when they became more numerous, this well intentioned practice fell by the wayside. We sought to pray, as often as we could, for those who had shared their concerns with us, trusting that through the spoken and the written word they would be led to place their faith in the Lord Jesus and experience the joy and peace which He alone can give.

But although those early records are lost it is possible to recall the Christian teachers who purchased evangelical literature as graduation gifts for their students, many of whom were Muslim; the two Catholic Priests who desired booklets for distribution during their visits to the local prison; the Maronite lady from a remote village in the mountains who wanted her daughter to learn what the Bible really says; the Muslim from Indonesia who, fascinated by the sight of the New Testament in the window, came in to chat and left taking Scriptures with him; the two belligerent Lebanese Muslim youths who began with arguing but left peacefully; the South

African business man, successful but dissatisfied, who unburdened his heart and, we trust, was helped by the counsel given; the two Iraqi Christians delighted and encouraged by finding Christian fellowship; a visitor from Damascus needing evangelistic material for distribution in Syria; and a United Nation's soldier from Gaza who told of his distribution of Bible correspondence courses there.

Many and varied were the contacts and, though we rejoiced in knowing the message of the Gospel was being spread far and wide through the efforts of those who visited us, we were not often privileged to have the encouragement of hearing of the results which followed. On occasion this did take place, though it might be some time after the contact was first made. In the early days an English lady, married to a Lebanese verging on alcoholism, desperately lonely and homesick, came to browse around simply because she had been told there were English folk at the shop. A few years later I heard that same lady, when giving her testimony of how she and her husband had been converted, conclude her story with the comment that the first kind words she received in Beirut were in the Manarah bookstore. A simple friendly conversation often opens the way for the reception of the Gospel.

But encouragement came also from the lending library. Most days Miss Betts had visits from students who, faced with some theological question, would seek her counsel as well as study the books provided. The library also became a haven for more than one senior student who, unable to read the Bible at home, could do so there without any hindrance, and at the same time enjoy a brief time of Christian fellowship. Not all students were scrupulously honest and from time to time books disappeared though, due to the number available, sometimes without detection. On at least one occasion this led to happy results. A lady came to purchase a Bible as a gift for a Muslim who had recently made an open confession of his faith in the Lord Jesus Christ. A few days later, this man appeared in the shop and, laying on the counter a fairly hefty tome, surprised us by saying he had stolen it nearly a year before. Now, being a Christian, he wanted to confess and pay for it. The book he had no intention of returning not only opened his eyes to the message of the Gospel but led to him taking the first step towards faith in Christ.

The Manarah Bookshop

During the hot and humid summer of 1961 our main concern was how to keep Manarah's various activities operational. During June the exodus from Beirut to the mountains commenced, and by August half the population seemed to have vanished. Buses and cars brought a multitude of commuters to the city in the morning; mid afternoon saw the roads choked by the frantic rush to cooler heights, whilst the less fortunate endured the city's sticky humidity and stifling heat. Our children found it almost impossible to sleep and tossing and turning only added to their discomfort. For us disturbed nights increased the strain on nerves already taut from work filled days and the pressure of living on a very slim budget. However every need continued to be met and constantly we were learning it is not the measure of our faith which counts but the fact of the Lord's faithfulness. Our responsibility was to trust and that summer, as we saw the children's lack of energy and need of change that trust was strongly tested.

The thought of a holiday in the hills, however brief, was alluring, but it seemed it would have to remain a dream. But then in July our concern for the children increased as the three of them suffered from some form of skin infection. Calamine lotion gave some relief to the boys but, in spite of using the remedies prescribed by the doctors, Ruth's skin problem persisted. Possibly stimulated by an unexpected gift we decided at the end of July a break was essential. We remembered our previous visit to Ain Zahalta and were delighted to discover the Christian guest house had one large room available for the two weeks we had in mind. It was sheer delight as the bus faced the Damascus road and, climbed away from the environs of Beirut, steadily, though laboriously, winding its way up and around the various hill towns. Finally the mountain range with Ain Zahalta nestling at its foot came into view. The evening was cool, our reception warm, the large airy room allotted to us a delight, the first night one of unbroken slumber; our holiday had really begun. Within a few days the children recovered their usual bounce, prickly heat and rash vanished, boils disappeared without trace and we were invigorated. There and then we decided that we would attempt to escape from Beirut's heat for a brief period each year.

The fortnight seemed to pass in a flash and we were again on the bus travelling back to the heat, noise and dust of Beirut. Activity at the shop being minimal one wondered at times if it was worth while being open. But one never knew when the apparently casual visitor would be one with a deep spiritual need, or a Christian worker urgently requiring material to assist them in their ministry. Such was the American lady visiting from Saudi Arabia who encouraged and challenged us by her personal testimony. She had been converted in 1949 at a Billy Graham campaign in Los Angeles and a year later moved with her husband, who had no interest in spiritual matters, to an oil company's station in the Arabian desert. There, being concerned for the children of other expatriates, and without any help or encouragement, she commenced a Christian work amongst them. Now, ten years later, she was back in Arabia and on this brief visit to Beirut found, to her delight, the Manarah store had an ample supply of material which would enable her to continue the good work. Some months later, requests were received from Saudi Arabia for a wide range of Sunday School material: in all probability due to that lady finding the bookstore open on a sultry August day.

We had much to encourage both as regards the literature ministry and the activities of the Ras Beirut assembly. Whilst maintaining contact with the Arab assembly in Ashrafiya we found ourselves becoming more involved with this English speaking one. The American pattern of Sunday School for all ages was followed with every class being well attended. My main responsibility was the Senior Bible Class and with a goodly number of adults present these were challenging and profitable times. With its freedom for all members to participate in discussion, it provided a very helpful depth of study. The leader's comments were open to challenge so learning became a two way process.

Over the years the assembly kept a visitors' book and during the next few years more than one thousand names were recorded. A quick glance revealed families and individuals from various nationalities, people from Pakistan, Ethiopia, Sudan, Lebanon, South Africa as well as Armenians, Americans, Germans and British. Only a coming day will reveal how much spiritual fruit resulted from that fellowship in Beirut.

CHAPTER 24

The Vision Expands

(1962 - 63)

Oh, taste and see that the Lord is good; Blessed is the man who trusts in Him! (Psalm 34:8)

'God is dishonoured, and His integrity insulted, if you doubt His existence or the veracity of His word.' 'Genuine believers never doubt the reality of their salvation nor lack the assurance of the constant presence of Christ.' Statements like these have distressed many Christians. They feel they are the only believers ever assailed by doubts, are afraid to discuss these fears with others who appear to be firmly rooted in their faith, and as a result their distress is increased and prolonged.

During a period which might have merited the term 'the dark night of the soul', I had no doubt concerning God's existence, but only the feeling He was no longer accessible and therefore what was the point in praying? I was convinced that genuine disciples of Jesus Christ had a mission to the world and could expect to see the Holy Spirit touching and changing lives. Without seeing more of that, how could I be sure my efforts were under God's direction and not merely an attempt to justify being included on a missionary prayer list? Furthermore, I knew there were those who, looking alone to God, had all their material needs abundantly met, so what was lacking in my faith that we were often near the end of our resources? My inner turmoil increased because my responsibilities in preaching and leading Bible studies meant the spectre of hypocrisy loomed every time I spoke. At the same time, if I were to share my problems with anyone else, I was literally afraid of ruining their faith by confessing to the weakness of my own. There are times when the Lord has to teach us our utter dependence upon Him by bringing us right down to the depths. At such times He in His love and mercy, takes us on through the darkness to the place of restoration and joy, to discover, with tremendous gratitude, He has never left us alone. Throughout the vicious onslaughts of the Evil One, His right hand has led, His mighty arm has upheld, His grace has enfolded.

Throughout those weeks, unable to share my thoughts and feelings with anyone, even my desire for Christian fellowship began to wane. The daily busy routine continued unabated. Early evenings were spent in the pleasant occupation of reading and playing with the children, revelling in the all too short period of their childhood. Later hours were occupied with administrative details or attempts to prepare for a forthcoming sermon. But church attendance had become a joyless duty, Bible studies and prayer meetings cold and formal. In short, I had entered a spiritual wilderness from which only the Lord could deliver me, and He did. One evening I decided to miss the weekly Bible study and lingered at home until it became almost too late to attend. But an inner compulsion to attend increased until, reluctantly, I made my way to the meeting room. Having arrived I waited at the door not wishing to intrude on what I thought was a time of prayer. Then suddenly I realised a portion from Joel 2 was being read and certain phrases penetrated loud and clear to where I stood. *'Fear not, be glad and rejoice; for the Lord will do great things ..... be not afraid';.... 'Be glad and rejoice in the Lord your God for He has given you the former rain and will cause to come down the latter rain';..... 'The floors shall be full of wheat.'* Then the reader's voice rose to a note of jubilation as he read, *'I will restore to you the years the locusts have eaten'..... 'and ye will be satisfied and praise the name of the Lord your God that hath dealt wondrously with you';.... 'and ye shall know that I am the Lord your God and none else':... 'my people shall never be ashamed.'* As I stood gripped especially by the last words, it was as if God Himself had spoken directly to me. I breathed a quiet 'thank you Lord' and found the burden lifted, the darkness dispelled. Faith renewed, and the joy, mentioned by the Apostle Peter as being 'inexpressible', flooded my being.

Through His word the Lord had made Himself real to me and in so doing, had prepared me to help others passing through similar times of spiritual gloom, or even despair. Some months later a very gifted and godly missionary friend asked if I would discuss his own special problem. He was obviously distressed and his opening comments implied I might not understand his situation and might be judgmental in my attitude. His problem was almost identical to mine. I could only share my experience with him and refer him to the same passage of Scripture which had spoken so clearly to my own heart. As we talked and read and prayed, the Lord spoke to him and, with faith renewed and joy in his heart, he returned to his sphere of service which, through various and traumatic vicissitudes, has continued to the present day.

With a renewed sense of the presence of the Lord my life took on a new aura. The joy in service returned and in our next news letter to friends at home it was possible to write enthusiastically about the opportunities for missionary endeavour and the need for new workers. We could not foretell how He would open doors for the spread of the Gospel, but evidences were constantly before us. Visitors from the Gulf States, and even much further afield, obtained literature to take to areas we would never see; missionaries holidaying in Lebanon ordered supplies for use in hospitals in Gaza and Kuwait; mail requests came from a worker in Dubai for material to aid him in his work amongst Indians and his many Muslim contacts. One of the most unusual contacts occurred when a heavy cold and bronchial asthma had kept me housebound for days. Towards the end of the week Marjorie found it impossible to continue in my place in the shop and we agreed the shop would have shut on the Saturday. It seemed a wise decision but I felt profoundly uneasy wondering if there might just be someone who needed to be contacted that afternoon. Finally, pressured by my thoughts, I decided to go and, somewhat shakily, made my way to the bottom of the road where, fortunately, I soon found transport. It was a cold, unpleasant day, and the streets were virtually traffic free and void of pedestrians. As I opened up the premises it was hard to resist the thought that I was foolishly wasting my time. The first person through the door was a close friend so at least I had company for a while. Then a heavily cloaked Arab, after a few indecisive moments, located the Arabic material and began to browse through the titles. I decided to wait a while before approaching him but, just as I was about to voice a greeting, he spun round and, in a rather harsh voice, asked if we had a copy of the holy book.

Inside Manarah Bookshop

I didn't think to ask him if he meant the Koran but immediately answered in the affirmative and produced a well bound Bible, mentioning of course, exactly what it was. He appeared to be content, his only query being 'Would it tell him about the prophets?' I had no hesitation in telling him it did and mentioned a few names, quite unintentionally including Isaac. That really brought him to life and quickly and loudly he exclaimed, 'Ishmael for us Muslims, Ishmael not Isaac!' I hastened to assure him Ishmael's name was there and then waited to see his response. All he did was to ask the price and looking at his somewhat rough garb, I wondered if I should give it to him or sell it at a reduced price. However, when I mentioned the normal price, he drew from under his cloak one of the biggest wads of money I have ever seen! Without more ado he placed the price on the counter, reverently picked up his now wrapped possession and, placing it under his cloak, made for the door. Having been struck by his unfamiliar accent I politely enquired concerning his homeland. His reply gave me another surprise. He said he came from Mecca and, furthermore, he desired to compare the Bible with the Koran. As he left I had no doubt why I had been led to be in the shop that afternoon. It was also evident why Marjorie had been prevented from going back. Had she been there on her own it is very doubtful if a Muslim from Mecca would have even darkened the door of the premises. To know that someone from the holiest city of Islam wanted to discover the message of the Scriptures was a stimulus to faith and prayer - Mecca was not completely closed to the power of the Gospel of Christ.

The first few months of 1963 brought some spiritual blessing. Two who had been attending the English speaking assembly desired to be baptised as a public confession of their new found faith. Their so doing gave the churches with which we were associated an opportunity to manifest their unity. Of the three fellowships, Armenian, Arabic and English speaking, only the first had a baptistry and, as the season precluded making use of the sea, they readily placed their facilities at our disposal. A goodly number came from each assembly so the hall was filled to capacity. The singing in three languages may not have been the most harmonious on earth, but no doubt heaven understood it all. If we were delighted because unity prevailed where language could have caused division, how much more pleasure must have been brought to our Father in heaven. One of the many vital lessons we learnt in the Middle East was that Christian fellowship can cross boundaries of language, culture and religious denominationalism. One also learnt the danger of contextualising the Gospel in an attempt to make it more acceptable to those of other faiths. The uniqueness of Jesus Christ is nullified when His deity is denied, and His teachings are destroyed when attempts are made to interweave them with beliefs and practices of other faiths.

I had the clearest evidence of the result of combining the characteristics of different systems of religion from a man who, one day, casually wandered into the bookstore, Finding a place to sit he deposited his tarboosh on the floor and settled down as if he intended a lengthy visit. He was a slightly built, fresh faced man of some thirty years of age whose garments and head covering declared him to be a Druze, possibly one holding the status of a religious leader. Like many of his class he supported himself by some trade, his being weaving and knitting for which, he informed me, he needed both a new machine and, preferably, a new environment in which to operate it. Could I help in both cases? I explained why the Manarah Society existed, and made plain that, whilst we desired to exercise Christian virtues, we were not in a position to supply knitting or weaving machines. As regards a new venue, to him a home in Britain, we were completely powerless to help. Moreover, the fact that he might become a Christian, as he seemed to suggest, would, I assured him, carry no weight with the British Government. Our conversation, which included an explanation of what it means to be a Christian, ended on a cordial note. Later when he heard we were planning a visit home he suggested I could temporarily adopt him and take him as my son! Over the years we received a variety of requests covering finance, clothing, intercession with British officials, visas, provision of wives etc. but this was the first time anyone had thought we could oblige by adding him to our family. In time he who hoped to be our adopted son came to see us no more. One cannot help but wonder whether the seeds of our many discussions and his perusals of the Scripture, bore any spiritual fruit. Only eternity will tell.

The first week of September commenced a period when, due to the lack of personnel, we found it difficult to cope with all that lay to hand. We were therefore grateful when a friend asked if we could use in the shop the services of an Arab Christian. Actually we could do better than that, he would also be an ideal person to handle the Bible Course lessons. Our need for personnel coincided with his need for support and so, in the goodness of the Lord, there was benefit all round. Jaleel Hanna was not the liveliest of persons but he was a lovely, patient worker and, whilst marking test papers, could staff the shop during the slackest period of the day. With his help the Bible Course ministry progressed and within a short time new contacts were averaging just over 100 a month from countries as far apart as Iraq and Morocco. Especially encouraging were the number of letters from Syria, a country which in recent years had taken positive steps to close down Christian missionary work.

This period also included increased activity at the Ras Beirut church, progress in the children's education and an increase in our circle of friends. During the summer the number attending the meetings had decreased, but the situation changed rapidly as people returned from the hills and students from their long vacation. Within a few weeks a hunt began for larger premises and, within a month, a flat situated towards the end of Ras Beirut's main thoroughfare had been rented. It was ideal but there was a snag; the rent was far beyond the fellowship's means. Nothing daunted, an offer was made and, after further negotiations, a figure two fifths below the asking price brought it down to the amount first offered. These premises sufficed for just over a year when another move was required. Similar facilities were rented in a more suitable location within a few yards of the Manarah Society's bookshop. This was of mutual benefit for a small room, extra to the church's needs, could be used as an office for the Bible Correspondence Courses. For our family, Ras Beirut assembly provided some of the happiest Christian fellowship we have been privileged to enjoy.

Our children also benefitted educationally from a new school. For some years Mrs. Bullen and her daughter had been responsible for an independent, fee paying, school in Egypt, concentrating on preparing students for British 'O' and 'A' levels. The Suez Crisis of 1956 forced them to leave and they moved to Lebanon. Having obtained the Government's permission, they rented premises in an Eastern suburb of Beirut and opened Manor House School. English was the main language and classes ranged from kindergarten to 'O' level, with the prospect of including 'A' level if necessary. We hoped our three would stay within the home environment until at least their 'O' levels so it seemed wise to enroll them there. Thus both Andrew and Ruth were registered with Mrs. Bullen and daily caught the noisy, overcrowded school bus, usually seen off by Mark at the bottom of the road.

CHAPTER 25

New Ventures

(1964 - 65)

His compassions fail not. They are new every morning. Great is Your faithfulness (Lam. 3:22,23).

From the time the Manarah Society had been established we fostered the hope that other full time workers would be led to join us. We were deeply indebted to the Society's advisory committee for their wise counsel and encouragement. Without them we would have made many more mistakes and, when the going became tough their support helped to see us through. Nevertheless the expanding work was calling for a more active contribution and we were thankful when, during the last few months of 1963, we received a letter. Frank and Rena Lennox wrote from Aurora, Illinois, suggesting the possibility of their being involved in the Society's work. Their interest in a literature ministry stemmed from being involved with 'Send the Light' (the forerunner of Operation Mobilisation) in Mexico. They mentioned having been students at the Moody Bible Institute, their family consisted of two young children and, whilst they were not sure where the Lord would have them serve, they would be interested in coming to Lebanon. About the same time another similar letter arrived from a couple in Glasgow. Pleased and encouraged to have such enquiries, we promptly wrote to both, simply giving details of the nature of the Manarah ministry and the principles governing our lives and work. Anxious though we were for help we did not consider we should try and persuade anyone to launch out into full time service. As our own leading in the 1940s had been crystal clear we were anxious this should be the case for others.

We heard no more from Glasgow. But Frank and Rena wrote by return of post saying they were fully in accord with our way of living and prepared to step out in faith looking to the Lord for all their provision. All they wanted to know was whether there would definitely be a sphere of ministry for them with Manarah, and what would be the monthly minimum needed to cover the cost of living in Lebanon. We wrote giving the financial information, but pointed out that the important question was not, 'Would there be a place for them in Manarah?' but rather, 'Were they absolutely sure the Lord wanted them in Lebanon?' They replied that not only were they sure the Lord wanted them in Lebanon, but had booked their passage and would be with us in March. Late in that month we welcomed them off the boat after what had been a rough and tedious voyage.

Initial impressions, as they came down the gangplank loaded with hand luggage, precariously leading Ellen and carrying Ann, were certainly favourable. By the time we had seen them through Customs, noticed how they endured a nerve chilling taxi ride, and observed their response to the welcoming group at the church, we were assured there would be good days of fellowship ahead. Frank and Rena fitted in very well and we had every reason to be thankful for their close cooperation in the Manarah Society's ministry. They were pleased we had found accommodation for them but did not find it easy to settle into the small and rather dark flat. After finding a place more suitable for their needs they settled down to a period of language study and also took a practical interest in the workings of the Manarah Society. The Bible Correspondence Course ministry appealed to them most and, eventually, they took complete responsibility for it. Their friendship and collaboration over the years is gratefully remembered.

About the same time as the Lennoxes arrived, the Manarah Committee made the important decision to expand their own publishing programme. The need for a wider range of Christian material in Arabic had been a concern to us all and when Miss Nasr, the shop's landlady and now a member of the Committee, offered to cover the cost of a Christian novel, it appeared to be the opportune time to do so. In those days there was a dearth of original writers in Arabic and most of the literature had to be translated from English. During the next few years, Manarah produced four Christian novels, simple commentaries on the Pentateuch, Dr. Ironside's expositions of Mark and Romans, an edition of Mrs. Cowan's 'Streams in the Desert', plus two new items for the Correspondence Course work, 'A summary of the Bible' and 'Lessons from Philippians'. Also a series of five booklets written especially for Muslims was issued in fellowship with the Lebanon Evangelical Mission.

The Lord provided in various ways to finance this publishing work. Miss Nasr generously contributed towards the items she herself proposed, whilst in the early days sundry gifts, usually unexpected, covered the cost of others. Later generous gifts earmarked for publishing came from the Laing Trust in Britain. The decision to go ahead with a project involved taking a step in faith, and the provision made for it testified to the validity of the promise, 'My God shall supply all your need according to His riches in glory by Christ Jesus.'

The Lord supplied our own need early in 1964 in an unusual way. For some weeks family expenditure had been heavier than usual and by mid February our funds could only be described as low. By the end of the month the purse was virtually empty and the cupboard nearly bare. A trip to town to check the post office box only drew a blank and Sunday loomed as a day of fasting. Late in the Saturday afternoon we decided to make a brief visit to friends but it extended to a couple of hours. The children were enjoying themselves and it seemed a pity to curtail their activities. We chatted with the adults until dusk fell and we strolled home to find that in our absence something had been slipped under the door. That something turned out to be two hundred Lebanese pounds, equivalent at that time to £20. We could hardly believe our eyes but there was no doubting the reality of those notes, nor the fact that with the local shop still open Sunday would not be a fast day after all. We never knew who brought them but we knew who had directed them. Our Heavenly Father had again supplied our needs. Those Lebanese pounds were just enough to bridge the gap until a gift from Clumber arrived. That gift covered a doctor's bill and medicine. On 5th March Andrew went down with measles and predictably nine days later Ruth followed suit, the very next day, Mark. A year before it had been chicken pox. Then on 13th April, Mark developed mumps, followed by Andrew two weeks later with a more severe dose. We waited for Ruth to follow, but she seemed to be impervious to mumps.

Summer was again encouraging thoughts of cool nights in the hills, when we received a letter offering us accommodation in even cooler realms. The assemblies in Essex had recently opened a home for missionaries on furlough and were offering it to us for the summer. However we concluded we could not leave the Manarah Society's ministries without adequate arrangements for their continuance, nor neglect our commitments to the ongoing work of the church. Neither could we go on furlough without spending some time with our home assembly; a matter which required consultation with them. So, the offer had to be refused, but we mentioned the possibility of a visit to Britain the following year. In the meantime we accepted the offer of a couple of rooms in the grounds of the LEM property in Shemlan, little realising our summer stay would be a prelude to moving to the area for a year. We took advantage of an opportunity to rent a house in Ainab, near Shemlan, and planned to move at the end of the summer season, having good reasons for vacating our apartment in Beirut. At the end of August we moved to Ainab. The reasons which made our move desirable included Marjorie being faced with a rat, overflowing toilet drains, the prospect of a water logged bedroom, then infestation by cockroaches.

We discovered that Ainab had one big drawback, the paucity of public transport. However this was overcome by arrangements with our neighbours who were also in fellowship at the Ras Beirut church. Their children were at the same school as ours and for the daily journey to town we shared their vehicle. The advantages of being more mobile were brought home to us by the comments of a Christian couple from Aberdeen. The Cordiners were touring in the Levant and, having missed contacting us at the shop, decided to visit us at home. During the evening comments were made about our isolation and, in view of their links with Ford Motors in Aberdeen, it was not surprising they anticipated we would have a car. As they spoke enthusiastically about certain models, and which one would be most suitable for our situation, we could only listen politely and agree.

Had we been in possession of extra funds they would not have been used for a car but for a special literature project. For a long time we had been aware of the need for an Arabic edition of well illustrated Christian literature for young children but hardly knew what steps to take. Then a casual comment that something similar to the Ladybird series would be ideal prompted an enquiry to the publishers. They had no plans for such a project, but they could supply paper complete with the coloured pictures and blank spaces to overprint in Arabic. A sheet containing thirty two pictures and their corresponding blank pages was enclosed and we then realised the book of sixty four pages was printed on one sheet. The prospect was exciting; beautiful pictures just waiting for the Arabic script and permission already granted by the publishers to print. The minimum number of sheets we could purchase would be 3,000 and would be sent immediately on receipt of our payment. We prayed and decided to go ahead. Within a few weeks the paper was on its way, and only then did I have a horrible thought, the money might have been wasted! Lying awake, thinking how good it would be to have such books available for Arab children, I suddenly remembered we had all missed a vital point. The pictures on the sheets were arranged for European languages but Arabic books opened the reverse way! Unless the sheets could be folded differently the project was doomed.

Something had to be done about the arrangement of the pictures, and done quickly. The next day we folded and refolded the sheet in every conceivable pattern. Finally, deciding to place the problem with the experts, we passed it to the manager of the printing press. His delight at the prospect of a print-run of 3,000 books diminished on hearing the order depended upon him getting the paper folded the right way! Two days later came the good news - he had solved the problem. Before Christmas the book 'Little Lord Jesus' was in circulation and this success became the prelude to Arabic versions of six more of the Ladybird series, all of which were also printed in Armenian. Later one more title was published by a missionary friend. We had anticipated more but, when the English publishers were taken over by a larger organisation, the agreement finished. However something new had been introduced in Arabic Christian literature which met a definite need.

During the early 1965 our thoughts were being more and more directed towards the possibility of furlough, especially as we had received confirmation that the Missionary Home in Romford had been reserved for us as from July. As a result we checked with the elders of Clumber Hall the possibility of our obtaining further temporary accommodation in Nottingham. As usual they were most co-operative. One member had recently sold his butcher's business and offered the use of the accommodation over the shop, others offered a miscellany of items to make it inhabitable, whilst the top room was to be divided to make it suitable for the children's bedrooms.Thus with housing arrangements in hand we could concentrate on praying for guidance as to the date of leaving and the method and route of travel. The availability of the home in Romford governed the date. The route was settled by a gift from Marjorie's father. This was designated for a holiday, so we decided to include Italy in our itinerary. Swiss missionary friends had often urged us to savour the delights of their land and spend a few days in Beatenberg. The fact that the rail route from Naples to the Channel ports passed within a few miles of Interlaken, the nearest town to Beatenberg, encouraged us to respond to their suggestion. Then we discovered that the direct route from Naples ran northwards through Rome and Florence, towns we would enjoy visiting. By mid-afternoon on 24th June we were waving good-bye to friends from the deck of the MV *Esperia* and, just as the sun in a blaze of glory tipped the horizon, the haze shrouded mountains of Lebanon gradually slipped from view. Naples via Alexandria plus a host of new experiences now lay before us.

The journey home came up to expectations and the warmth of our welcome in Romford could not have been bettered. We were soon deposited at Hebron, 260 Pettits Lane North, Rise Park. Hebron turned out to be a modern, detached, chalet type house, complete with garage and small garden, situated on a wide road bordered by typical suburban homes. It was convenient for local transport into Romford whilst shops supplying most general needs were within a five minutes walk. Management and maintenance of the home was the responsibility of a small committee and the only cost to the missionaries was the normal expenses of running a home. It was a wonderful provision, especially for families like ourselves who had neither a home in Britain nor relatives able to provide long term accommodation. For us it was another confirmation that if we were prepared to trust Him, the Lord would provide.

Within a short period, life settled into a semblance of routine. Most weeks one or the other of us would be participating in a missionary conference or speaking at meetings, large and small, near and far. Our schedule seemed to make the weeks fly by and, almost before we were aware of it, September arrived and it was time for Andrew and Ruth to share the new experience of attending school in England. Making new friends, and settling in to a new educational system was not easy, though there were no signs of any abiding traumatic effects. The three of them soon became very familiar with the area and began to experience one of the joys they had never known in Lebanon, the freedom to run down to the local precincts and, like normal British children, spend precious moments viewing sweet shops and decide on how to spend their weekly pocket money.

In the first week of 1966 we moved to Nottingham to occupy the flat provided by our local assembly. By this time our personal possessions exceeded the capacity of the few suitcases brought from Lebanon and that of the car's small boot. So Marjorie, with Andrew and Mark, took to the rail while Ruth kept me company on the road. The flat was in an old building in which the shop and ground-floor premises were still devoted to a butcher's business. The front door opened onto the street and the only recreational area was a tiny back yard devoid of any vegetation. Within a few days Marjorie and I were feeling at home and enjoying opportunities of renewing fellowship with our friends at Clumber Hall. For the children the situation was more difficult. There was lack of space for play and, for Andrew and Ruth the problem was adjusting to schools still held in old and rather gloomy premises little different from those of our own childhood.

Being in Nottingham opened the door for many engagements in the Midlands and the northern parts of Britain. It was good to find such an interest in the Lord's work in the lands of the Middle East though much of it was engendered by people's concern for Israel rather than the Arabs. This meant that before accepting an invitation we had to make clear we had no link with that part of the Levant. People in Britain found it difficult to accept that there was no freedom of movement between the Arab world and Israel. No matter how much we proclaimed our ignorance of missionary work in that land some still anticipated a report on the situation there. Fortunately we had gleaned from friends in Cyprus some details about Israel and, stressing my information was second hand, I would spend a few minutes on the subject. Then it would be a pleasure to turn to our own sphere and share the latest news from Beirut. According to this the needs of the literature ministry were being met. Our colleagues reported that the project of publishing four more titles in the Ladybird series was well under way, and paper for another title had been ordered. They spoke of an increasing distribution of the Bible Correspondence Courses, and that many letters telling of definite spiritual blessing had been received. The only disturbing note was a hint that a slight problem in connection with the shop was resulting in it not being as busy as might be expected.

All this news set us thinking about returning and by April we were considering the matter more fully. The complete absence of funds earmarked for travel made us wonder if the Lord was speaking to us through this and, strange as it may seem, even telling us not to return. Such thoughts made me reflect more fully upon our future. I was now approaching my fiftieth birthday. If during the next few years circumstances in the Middle East compelled us to return home what chance would I have then of getting employment? It might be possible in 1966 but very unlikely a few years hence. Then the children had to be considered, not only with regard to education but also in the matter of citizenship and the whole of their future. Educational standards at Mrs. Bullen's in Beirut were reasonable but would they continue to be so? Would the children grow up feeling they were neither British nor Lebanese? Moreover, would there ever be suitable prospects of employment for them in the Middle East? These queries began to dominate our view of the future, as did the realisation that the decisions we made would affect the whole direction of their lives. For them the people they would meet, the experiences they would have, the nature of their secular employment and the spiritual influences which would affect their lives, all depended on the decision we would make. It was a burden too big to be borne on our own, so we simply took it to the Lord asking Him to clarify His will for us all.

As we waited on the Lord we felt emboldened to lay out a 'fleece'. Being afraid of allowing our desires and emotions to sway us one way or the other, we believed it right to seek positive guidance. We had nothing saved towards our passages back to Beirut, nor did we know where it would come from, so we asked the Lord that if it was His will we return, please would He enable us to save enough to do so. The provision of the passage money would be our guide and, as far as we could see, there would have to be an emphasis on saving during the coming months for that to be accomplished. But the Lord has His own ways of springing surprises and He did not keep us waiting long. One evening an elder from our assembly came to visit. There was nothing unusual about that, but there was about the purpose of his visit. He had called to ask when we anticipated returning overseas! No way could we tell him it depended on our financial situation; we could only speak the truth and say we trusted it would not be too far in the future. However his next question was how much would it cost to travel to Beirut. After a few moments of reflection we gave an estimate. Then he stated the elders had already decided to meet the entire cost of our passage! The money would be ready whenever required; all we needed to do was to mention the date. In view of our prayer we could not doubt it being the Lord's will for us to return.

The months spent in Nottingham enjoying the fellowship of our friends at Clumber Hall were very pleasant. By mid June we were buying larger cases to contain our accumulated luggage, and making preliminary arrangements through a local shipping agent to have the bulk forwarded to Venice to await our arrival. But before leaving Nottingham we had another unexpected item to ship back. We were now in a position to obtain a new car. We remembered the Cordiners and their comments when visiting us in Ainaab. So we wrote and in response received a telegram asking us to phone them immediately. Apparently they had in stock a Ford Anglia Estate car, colour white which they considered would be best for a hot climate and, more importantly and somewhat surprisingly, equipped for right hand driving. With certain details settled I was on my way to Aberdeen to pick it up. The vehicle was excellent and provided us with thousands of miles of enjoyable motoring.

We now had to decide who would go to Venice by train and who by car. The vehicle was invaluable for conveying our luggage but no way could we squeeze five in. I was uneasy at the thought of Marjorie and the children travelling on their own but there appeared to be no alternative. Then Florence Betts, whose help we appreciated in Beirut, was visiting England and she was staying with us the week before we returned to Lebanon. During that week we discovered she was prepared to drive to Venice on her own, and three days before we were due to travel she took the heavily loaded Anglia to catch the boat. Space between the luggage and the roof of the car was, to say the least, scanty, and we wondered how she would cope as it was her intention to park in campsites and sleep in the car. She found that by moving items onto the front seats there was just room for her to get a good night's rest.

Final news from Beirut arrived very late the night before we left. Arthur Trebble, with whom we had stayed in Baghdad, was now retired and living in England. Being extremely interested in the work in Beirut he had gone out for a few weeks to help in the bookstore. He wrote to say that, if at all possible, he wanted to give us a report on the work which he thought was running into difficulties. Arthur's train was badly delayed and midnight was almost upon us when he rang our doorbell. His lengthy report took us into the early hours. As usually happens at such times we were over tired and this, plus the news from Beirut meant we hardly slept. Next day the excitement of travel kept us alert and by relaxing on the overnight journey from Paris to Venice, we arrived refreshed; but only to be greeted by a cold, cloud covered city.

CHAPTER 26

Troublesome Years

(1966 - 1968)

The Lord, He is their strength in time of trouble (Psalm 37:39).

A brighter welcome awaited us in Beirut. It was early morning when Lebanon's mountain dominated coastline came into view. By the time we had finished breakfast the *Ausonia* was moving slowly to her berth and a group of welcoming friends could now be seen. There was no doubting the warmth of our reception, though it was slightly marred by the knowledge that during our absence personality clashes had caused hurt to some of our friends. There were bridges to mend and, whilst endeavouring to ensure our own relationships were not allowed to suffer through other people's disagreements, we sought to help the situation.

Our first responsibility was to locate accommodation and after three days a flat had been rented in the village of Hadeth on the southern outskirts of the town. The ground floor flat, in a completely new and not yet finished block, had much to commend it. The situation was pleasant, partially because the area was still mainly undeveloped. Being on the slope of a hill there were on one side views towards Beirut; on the other the steep tree covered slope provided an extensive area for recreation. Getting back into some form of routine was a varied experience. For the children there was the readjustment to the local system of teaching whilst we immersed ourselves in the Manarah's various activities. As soon as the children were off to school I would be on my way to town and Marjorie at her desk handling accounts, completing stock records, reordering supplies or coping with any correspondence relative to the bookshop. Within a short time activity in the bookshop increased and a number of folk, who had said they would not darken its doors again, began to visit once more. The increased business, occasioned in part by the forthcoming Christmas season, highlighted the need for more staff and a young Palestinian joined on a part time basis. It was a joy to have Shukri Habibi willing to help in the store especially in view of his previous antagonism to evangelical Christianity. His family, refugees from Palestine, were keen Christians whom we had known well in Amman when Shukri was hardly a teenager. The family's financial position was very precarious, especially at one time when Shukri's father lost his job because as a Christian he would not lie concerning a certain incident. The person who dismissed him was an Englishman and, because the English in Shukri's opinion were also responsible for the loss of Palestine and consequently for his family's plight, he had no love for any of that nation. Moreover his antipathy to Christianity, and especially evangelicals, was fostered by having embraced Communism and its atheistic teaching while studying at a college in Damascus. However he had a vital conversion experience and the erstwhile enemy became both friend and colleague.

Gradually the outreach of the Manarah was increasing and a review of one particular day indicated its geographical extent. During the morning Frank, helped by a missionary from the Lebanon Evangelical Mission, packaged copies of a children's Christian paper in Arabic to be sent to addresses all over the Arab world. In the afternoon there was a series of customers, amongst them a Swedish lady who bought a quantity of Christian literature for distribution in Beirut amongst Muslims and Maronites. This lady was followed by a Danish seaman who, spending a few hours in port came, as he said 'upon the store by chance' (not an unusual comment). His purchase was only a Christian record but there was a long personal conversation on spiritual matters and who can tell what effect this had on his life. A few minutes later two rather nervous looking Lebanese gentlemen, who for some reason seemed to be ill at ease in a Christian bookstore, came to enquire about olive wood bound Bibles to be sent to the United States. The pleasure of supplying their needs was increased by the ice being broken to the extent that one of them was happy to chat about himself. Then at the end of the day came the completion of invoices for the third shipment of parcels sent to seventeen students in Indonesia.

In spite of feeling encouraged by all this activity I had an uneasy feeling that matters were going ahead too smoothly and in some way we would be facing difficulties in the near future. It has often been said that when Christian work is progressing with signs of blessing, Satanic opposition soon makes its presence known. This came in the form of two shop inspectors who demanded to see my work permit. I quite confidently showed them my residence permit card and pointed out that for missionary work no work permit was required. However they insisted that because they had seen me accept money in exchange for a book I had been engaged in an activity outside a missionary's vocation. That, they declared, consisted only of preaching in a church, and forthwith presented me with a notice indicating I would be reported to the appropriate authorities. The Society's lawyer kept check on developments and soon discovered there would be a court case. It seems the inspectors had embroidered their report by declaring the Manarah was not all it claimed to be, stating that apart from Bibles and books, it provided many other items.

In spite of the threat of a court case, which our lawyer anticipated would result in nothing more than a warning, there was every reason to be content with the way things were going. In addition to the satisfactory state of affairs in the shop the number attending Ras Beirut church continued to increase with, at times, as many as twelve nationalities represented in the Sunday morning services. The Bible Correspondence Courses under the direction of Frank Lennox continued to reach out to an ever widening area, there was the prospect of increased production in Arabic Christian literature and on the domestic front all was well.

In fact it proved to be a brief calm before a storm, a lull before the onset of a military enterprise which changed the boundaries between the Arab states and Israel. It brought disaster and death to many, created a fresh wave of Palestinian refugees, disordered the lives of numerous individuals and, in the ultimate, changed dramatically life's direction for others. It was never clear whether Arab military intelligence knew of the possibility of war but it came as a shock to the general populace. Early in June Israeli forces launched a surprise attack on three fronts and pushed Egypt out of Sinai, forced Jordan from the West Bank and drove Syria from the Golan heights. No moves were initiated against Lebanon though Israel made threatening noises and many feared an invasion in the south.

Immediately the Arab propaganda machine swung into action with constant radio broadcasts containing vitriolic accusations against the United States for their suspected support of Israel's territorial aims. As the Arab situation worsened another scapegoat had to be found and the broadcasts began to include rumours of Britain supplying military hardware and the preposterous claim that her air force had been in action on the enemy's behalf. For a couple of days these events made no difference to our routine but the situation changed overnight when the Americans decided to evacuate their nationals. Our first intimation of this was at 2.30 am. when an insistent banging on our front door dragged us reluctantly out of sleep. There was Frank Lennox looking for transport, both for himself and another missionary family, in order to be at the airport in time for evacuation shortly after dawn. Within minutes we were on our way round the outskirts of town to pick up another missionary family and then to the airport. The whole of Beirut had been placed under curfew and, due to the fear of air raids, car lights had to be dimmed so it was not the most enjoyable of rides. Every minute I was wondering if some trigger happy patrol would make its presence felt and, after my passengers had disembarked, wasted no time making for home.

Andrew, Ruth and Mark had been vaguely aware of the disturbance during the night but showed little curiosity or interest when they heard some of our American friends had left the country. However, it was a different matter when at school they discovered a number of their contemporaries were missing and people were talking about war. Mark especially felt his little world had been shattered when his bosom friend failed to appear. It was difficult for them to comprehend what was happening, neither could they understand why, if so many of their friends had left the country, they should not go too. We explained the situation and at the same time we pointed out that if we had to stay we could trust the Lord

Jesus to keep us safe. During our family evening prayers we asked the Lord for guidance and a sense of His peace, and with Mark as usual preceding the others, they went to bed apparently unconcerned about events. But Mark who normally was asleep in minutes was still wide awake at 10pm, so I asked why he couldn't sleep. His reply highlighted the deep effect a few comments can have on the mind of a child. The night visit of Frank, and the disappearance of so many children, had raised the spectre of a flight by night and he was afraid. He said, 'Daddy, if you have to go in the night you won't forget me will you?' After snuggling him in my arms for a few moments I made him a promise; if we had to leave during the night we would ensure he was woken up first. Within a few minutes he was asleep and had provided a lovely example of faith in action. A promise had been made by those he trusted and that was sufficient; he was resting on a word which he believed would not be broken.

As the conflict intensified, and the possibility of Lebanon being drawn into the fray increased, there was nothing we could do but wait further developments. These were not long delayed for within six days the Israeli forces had obtained all their objectives. The whole of Jerusalem and the West Bank of the Jordan; the Golan Heights from which Syria had been shelling Jewish settlements, the Sinai peninsula, where Egypt threatened her southern border and, I believe, a vital oil pipe line from the Gulf of Aqaba, were now in Jewish hands. Overwhelming air superiority and skillful use of military hardware had ensured Israel's victory, but it was a victory at the price of displacing many thousand more Palestinians, a legacy of bitterness and hatred which continues to demand a price till the present day, and the destabilizing of Lebanon politically and economically.

The brief war had a profound effect upon our activities. Frank and Rena's departure disrupted the Bible Correspondence Course ministry, the anti-western feeling made it advisable for us not to be too prominent in the affairs of the bookstore, and the evacuation of many expatriates deprived the Ras Beirut church of a large segment of its congregation and the help of some of its more able servants. The situation affected our daily programme and concern for the welfare of the children caused us to make a complete change to our summer schedule. All schools closed with no prospect of re-opening for four months and we realised it would be wise, at least for the children's sake, to arrange a short holiday away from the area of tension. So we made a promise. As soon as possible after the conflict ceased we would drive along the coast into Syria and relax for a couple of weeks at one of its beach resorts. But we discovered roads into Syria were barred to nationals whose countries had been accused of assisting Israel's war effort. This left us with a choice of going somewhere by air or sea and, fixing on Cyprus as a possibility, we contacted friends in Nicosia about accommodation. But Cyprus was in the throes of internal turmoil with riots against the British and to go there could be out of the frying pan into the fire. The solution to the problem came from two directions. The friends whom I had ferried during the night to the airport, had been evacuated to Greece and in a letter describing the tranquil atmosphere suggested we should take a break and visit. Two or three days later we heard from missionary friends in India, who had planned to visit us, that they were now flying to Greece and, giving us details of their hotel, asked if we could meet them in Athens. This resulted in a visit to Greece the memories of which would fill many a page.

With the summer season drawing to a close Beirut reverted to its normal noisy, bustling self. The place hardly ever seemed to sleep. Following the morning rush hours the markets, shops and commercial quarters were a hive of activity, whilst after the evening's snarled up, traffic congested, ride home, the city resounded with the activity of a vibrant nightlife. The temperature and humidity remained high, draining energy during the day and preventing sleep at night. Heat had always been one of Marjorie's problems and shortly after returning from Greece recurrent headaches made her life very unpleasant. A trip into the hills would sometimes give relief and one of these led to a change of address. Chouit sprawled along a ledge with the mountains rising steeply behind and the land in front falling away in a series of terraces to sea level some 2,000 feet below. Spurs of the mountains both north and south reached out towards the sea hindering extensive views of the coastline and narrowing one's perspective to Beirut and its environs, often haze-shrouded by day and glistening with a plethora of lights by night. We moved into the most spacious flat we were privileged to rent in all our service overseas. Marjorie's heath improved and we all benefitted from the cooler climate. The flats faced west with balconies providing a splendid vista across the sea to the horizon, one often enriched by glorious sunsets. According to the season it would be either clear and bright, or laden with sullen clouds heavy with rain and, at times, resounding with thunderstorms enlivened by vivid flashes of lightening blinding in their intensity.

As 1967 drew towards its close we could recall many evidences of God's goodness during this momentous year. There had been definite progress in connection with the literature ministry. More Arabic publications had come on to the market, including two more titles in the Ladybird series. In spite of certain difficulties the distribution of Bible Correspondence Courses had been maintained and sales of Christian literature increased. The ongoing testimony of Ras Beirut church also gave us much joy. At this time our involvement in Ras Beirut precluded any participation in the Arab assembly at Ashrafiyeh, but we rejoiced in knowing of that meeting's valuable service and continued growth. Also there was progress in connection with my Court case when, to our lawyer's surprise the verdict was a fine, a month in jail and then deportation from the country! The proceedings were all in Arabic and with the witnesses having their backs to me, and my lack of knowledge of any legal terms, there was no way I could discern what they said. However, as a prison sentence was involved we were allowed to appeal which our lawyer immediately did. After that it was simply a question of waiting.

But there was a happier ending to the year. On 15th December the Lennoxes returned from the United States. Immediately on returning, Frank renewed control of the Bible Correspondence Courses and so relieved us of some of the pressures. Evenings were rarely free. Normally the children had homework to finish before playtime and bed. We might be busy catching up with correspondence, attending the midweek meetings or occupied in study. There were administrative matters relating to the bookshop, the entertaining of visitors or, on occasion, being entertained. These were very active, encouraging, happy, and satisfying months. The shop was busy and our partnership in the recently formed Christian Arabic Literature League (CALL for short), meant publishing made more rapid progress. Books which had been in the pipe line for some time were produced, three of the Arabic Bible Courses were reprinted, and arrangements were being made for the translation of some of the books written by Watchman Nee. At the same time there was a move away from reliance on translated material as national believers tried their hand at authorship. In fact two of the recent publications had been from the pens of local believers, one of them being our good friend Samuel Shahid whose writing skills have been further developed over the years.

But with all this activity we realised there was a danger that family affairs could be neglected to the detriment of our relationship with the children. Missionaries' children have more than their fair share of problems. In addition to those normal in the maturing experience of every child they can feel disadvantaged in comparison to their peers, especially those from more affluent expatriate families. Their missionary parents proclaim that the One whom they serve is a faithful God who will supply for every need, yet sometimes they cannot understand why their friends possess more of this world's goods, or enjoy more of its luxuries, than they do. Consequently, unless time is taken to elucidate the vital difference between want and need, the young people are faced with the problem of deciding whether God has failed in His promises or their parents are deceiving them. Furthermore quite a number of missionary children feel their parents are so busy for God they seem to have no time for them. As a result there is not only the possibility of estrangement within the family but antagonism towards God whom, they believe, demands the total affection of their parents at their expense.

So we now decided, if at all possible, to set aside the whole of Saturday for the family. Often this simply meant being on hand ready to share in their amusements, or waiting to welcome them home after outdoor activities. Others times it would be a trip to the beach or an outing into the hills. The car enabled us to have a good measure of freedom and the low cost of petrol ensured the longest day out being accomplished at minimum cost. Armed with a detailed guide and a well packed picnic box we would visit some of the remotest archeological and historical sites in Lebanon and, in so doing, explored areas rarely visited by the average tourist. Whilst widening our own horizons we were sharing in the children's pleasures, strengthening family ties and laying the foundations for the loving, strong relationships which, in spite of being scattered, bind the family together today.

But one anxious thought tended to obtrude upon our minds. The appeal against my court conviction had been made late in December and we were mystified at the absence of a date for a retrial. The lawyer seemed to take the attitude of 'let sleeping dogs lie', and believing she knew best we left the matter there. Only towards the end of summer did the reason for the delay and the serious problems it could have caused become known. A phone call from our lawyer warned me not to leave the country as there was a warrant out for my arrest! Curious to know the reason I called at her office and found her fuming about the situation. She had queried the matter and found herself being criticised for not notifying the authorities that her client had fled the country. In no uncertain terms she told them I was still in the country and laid great stress on the fact that her client was an honourable person and would not dream of doing anything so underhand. It transpired a summons had been sent to our old address in Hadath and with there being no reply, the official simply jumped to a conclusion without making any enquiries. Now, Miss Qareh warned, I was on the black list and no matter which border post I tried to cross I would be immediately apprehended.

At this time Manarah bookshop faced a completely unexpected situation which, initially, had all the appearance of a major disaster. Autumn's sporadic heavy showers, the certain harbingers of the long awaited early rains, had come hard on the heels of the hot and humid summer months. Heavy clouds massed upon the horizon then drew steadily nearer until shrouding the mountain peaks they spilt their contents over the thirsty land. Brief spells of sunshine punctuated the early days but these soon gave way to constant gloom and downpours of varying intensity. Within minutes, gutters would overflow and as rushing waters swept over inadequate and partially blocked drains, sloping streets took on the appearance of rivers. On the 14th November, the rain which had fallen steadily since the early hours gradually increased to torrential tropical proportions as a violent thunder storm struck the coast and, in the snugness of the CALL office, I congratulated myself on being cocooned from its effects. But then the phone rang shattering my complacency. An anxious Elias declared the shop was being flooded and what was he to do about it. Knowing the situation of the shop, and having a mental picture of Abd Al Azis Street, I could not visualise how water rushing down its long incline could be a danger to the shop and assumed Elias was getting excited about a trickle penetrating the front door. I suggested that he and Rafiq mop up and find something to hold back any further flow. A few minutes later a far more urgent call beseeched me to get to the shop as the waters were rising. Resignedly I exchanged the snugness of the office for the rain sodden streets and went to investigate. There I found Marjorie, who having preceded me by a few minutes, had taken action.

The L-shaped shop had two levels with steps leading down to the larger lower display area and the first glimpse Marjorie had was of dirty evil smelling water swirling round beginning to spill over the top step. Elias and Rafiq, minus socks and shoes and with trousers turned up above their knees, were wading in this filthy mess seeking to rescue stock as the water inched higher. Marjorie promptly took charge and phoned the Fire Department for pumps and left it to them to notify the Municipal Offices. From Elias she learned the whole of the lower floor had flooded to a depth of two feet or more. Somewhere down the street the main sewers were blocked and, unfortunately, the nearest outlet for the main sewer had been the drain in the Manarah bookstore. The boys had absolutely no time to rescue more than a portion of the Bibles, books, Sunday School material, Manarah writing pads, children's literature and colouring books. As a first estimate we believed the damage would be in the region of £1,200, including some damage to equipment. Some idea of the amount involved can be assessed by realising this was when a hard bound book cost about a pound! Most of the special stock for the Christmas trade had been affected and, of course it was now almost too late to bring in more. So, apart from the amount of material damaged we anticipated our ministry would be curailed. By the time I arrived the rain had stopped and the flow into the upper level was stayed; one dreads to think of what the situation would have been like if it hadn't.

Three quarters of an hour later the fire brigade came with a small mobile pump. It coughed into life and commenced spewing the vile smelling liquid into the street, but with a fresh downpour in progress pumping seemed a forlorn task. Fortunately the men persisted and, due to a slight easing of the rain, the level never lipped over the top of the steps. Then two municipal workmen arrived, viewed the scene and promptly drifted out again. I followed them, only to be told they had come without any tools and one would have to fetch some! Frankly I think it was more likely they had no desire to work in the rain, and who could blame them in such a downpour?

By this time a small crowd had gathered outside, among them three or four members of Operation Mobilisation. Marjorie then did a little mobilising of her own and enlisting their help began a salvage operation. Cartons were filled and carried to the church building across the road to get the contents sorted. I remained in the shop salvaging all I could and sending carton after carton across until there was nothing worth sending, while the work of sorting went on apace. We were wondering what we would do if the firemen decided to call it a day, but suddenly the water fell dramatically. The shop's drains began to gurgle, and then a final whoosh confirmed the delayed tools had arrived and been put to good effect. The sight of the residue of sodden paper, dirt, slime, smell, combined with the general chaos throughout the place, was discouraging to say the least but, as Marjorie had already commented, 'it was not the time for tears'. In fact the united effort to rectify the problem transformed the situation. Late in the afternoon a willing group of friends, Lebanese, American, Australian, English, armed with bottles of disinfectant, a multitude of cleaning cloths and scrubbers, plus gallons of water, worked late into the evening until all was fresh and clean. At the same time a group of ladies continued sorting through the damaged stock, dividing the good from the not so bad and discarding the worthless. The result was that on the following morning we were able to rearrange the furniture, bring back saleable material, replenish the shelves and just after noon be open again for business. Except for a rather overpowering smell of pine disinfectant and Dettol the shop was as visitable as it ever had been.

For all who were closely linked with Manarah this was a definite test of faith and, at the same time, a reminder that any work done with a desire to honour God and exalt the Lord Jesus is bound to raise Satanic opposition. It is fatuous to speak about God's love, goodness and mercy and at the same time ignore the fact there will be an opposing power creating situations which demand an expression of those attributes. No matter what form of Christian service is undertaken to manifest the attributes of a God of love, it is bound at some time to rouse the ire of God's adversary. We had no doubt that in the present experience we were at the receiving end of some of that ire. As we separated, Frank quoted the words of Romans 8, 'We know all things work together for good to them that love God' and, during the cleaning up process someone picked up a sodden card which read, 'In all these things we are more than conquerors.' Whilst we could not see it at the time we were able to rest in that promise.

The next few days brought ample evidence that literature we had discarded as unsaleable found its way into many hands. Ruined stock, some of it not too filthy but still beyond the normal 'shop soiled' description, was dumped on an adjacent empty space to be removed by the rubbish department. As the day progressed the clouds rolled back, the sun shone and gradually dried the literature and before long curiosity drew a few of the passers-by to examine the dump. Examination turned to searching and gradually the pile decreased as lesser soiled material disappeared to unknown destinations. Books in Arabic and English, books for adults and children, Scripture portions, evangelistic material, Christian stories, even notepaper with Scripture texts, all went we knew not where. But shortly afterwards we knew the destination of some of the items. Rafiq, passing through one of the main shopping areas in town saw, to his amazement, part of our damaged stock spread out for sale. His excitement, which we could share, stemmed from the fact that a seeming disaster had resulted in a wider distribution of the Word of God. One could only trust that those books and pamphlets would become as seed sown in good ground bringing a blessing to many lives.

Within a few days Marjorie was able to place orders for the replenishing of the shelves. Unfortunately one of these orders landed the Agent who saw our goods through Customs and Excise in jail. The situation centred around a shipment from the United States. Firms who had direct dealings with Israel were blacklisted by the Arab countries and any piece of printed matter which acknowledged the existence of Israel, could bring down the wrath of certain officials. I had faced this twice at the Customs' section of the Post Office; once over an invoice from the Bible Lands' Society which bore a sketch of Israel's borders, and another when a well meaning individual sent us a beautifully detailed National Geographic map of the whole land. This time a Customs' official pounced on a consignment of records with the legend 'pressed by RCA Victor' - a blacklisted firm, arrested the clearing Agent on a charge of dealing with the enemy and impounded all the records. This was an occasion when it was good that the Manarah Society was registered as Lebanese. Two members of the Committee dealt with the matter and it ended with them making an apology, the Agent being released, and Manarah paying a fine.

Two months into the new year my court case was heard. I had to wait outside until our solicitor came with the verdict which would decide whether I went home or to prison prior to deportation. Mary Qareh came out smiling. Not only had the sentence been revoked but the appeal judges ruled there was no case to answer which meant the record was wiped clean. Whilst I was waiting Marjorie was praying at home for a favourable result and, before I returned, she was sure she knew it. Being early in March the latter rains were pending and, sitting in our study in Chouit, she looked out over a sullen cloud laden scene. Beirut lay sombre in a grey haze and the sea stretched flat and dull to merge into the dark line of the horizon - a depressing scene altogether. Then, suddenly, the clouds parted, the glory of the sun shone through, brilliant shafts of light illuminated the scene and Marjorie felt that there in the centre was God Himself saying, 'Be of good cheer, all is well.'

CHAPTER 27

Further Changes and Travels

(1969 - 70)

My thoughts are not your thoughts, nor are your ways My ways says the Lord (Isaiah 55:9).

About this time we were faced with making another vital decision concerning the children's future. Their school curriculum was geared to the British system and the expatriate staff were equipped for this. But, when the Government restricted the issue of work permits, more local staff had to be employed and standards tended to fall. It became obvious that if the children were to have higher education this would have to be in England. Andrew was now fourteen and already behind in some subjects relative to British standards. So we shared our concern with him and his response was pragmatic. 'Well,' he said, 'if it is going to be for my own good I had better go.' We never knew how much it cost him to say that, neither did he know our ache at the thought of his going!

Deciding where Andrew should go was to an extent dictated by our previous contacts with the principal of Scarisbrick Hall School near Southport. However this had to be matched with the ability to pay boarding and tuition fees, a matter which became the subject of much prayer. We were advised to seek a grant from a local Education Committee and we forwarded an application to Ipswich. This resulted in a partial grant, the balance met by our contribution plus an unexpected annual gift from a friend who had an interest in our children's education.

As the summer months slipped by, consideration had to be given to Andrew's journey to England. Finally, believing it would be good for Andrew to see something of Europe, we decided he and I should travel by car, commencing the road journey at Athens. Friends made the excellent suggestion that expenses could be reduced by using camp sites and one of them offered us his (very!) small tent. Ruth and Mark viewed our arrangements with mixed feelings but were consoled by the promise of a family visit to England the following year. This turned to delight when, unexpectedly, provision was made for them to have a holiday in Cyprus within a few weeks. In all our planning we were very conscious of our need of the Lord's guidance and provision.

Andrew and I left Beirut towards the middle of August on a Greek ship which had seen much better days. In addition to being dirty and rusty, it appeared to have developed a permanent list and strangely enough this gave the impression that we sailed in a crab-like fashion. I am sure this must have been sheer imagination but the list was real enough and could have been disturbing to any nervous passenger. Finally, after calling at Alexandria and giving us a stomach turning ride to Famagusta, it berthed at Piraeus's crowded port from where we commenced a journey which would take us through Greece, Yugoslavia, Austria, Germany, Belgium and France before a wave tossed hovercraft deposited us at Dover.

In the lobby of Scarisbrick Hall our united travels ended. Those last few minutes of saying good-bye and watching Andrew walk confidently away, turn a corner and disappear, have always remained etched in my mind. Fresh experiences, new relationships and other voices would soon mould Andrew's career. How did he feel as he turned to give that last wave before facing a whole new world from which there was no easy escape? I wondered if he had mixed emotions similar to mine when in 1939 I left home for the first time to join the armed forces. Now in 1969 I again had my own feelings to contend with.

On leaving Scarisbrick I commenced a hectic few weeks of meetings scattered around the country, interspersed with brief visits to Ipswich where there was always welcome news from the family in Beirut. But the good news of the family's refreshing holiday in Cyprus and their safe return to Chouit was soon overshadowed by disturbing events. Before the end of October, political storm clouds loomed again in the Middle East; particularly over Lebanon as the country moved into a further time of crisis. War seemed imminent as external enemies threatened and internal factions defied the Security forces. Growing unrest in the refugee camps and propaganda from alien sources helped to inflame an already volatile situation and Government forces were hard pressed in their endeavours to ensure a measure of peace. Would the situation be such that the family would be on their way to England instead of me returning after Andrew's first half term? The comment made to us in 1946, that living in the Middle East was like living on top of a volcano, again seemed true though a few more years passed before the threatening rumblings ended in explosion.

As the time approached for my return to Beirut I became increasingly concerned about the payment of the school fees. There had been no communication from the Education Department in Ipswich nor any invoice from the school so I had no idea if the first term's fees had been paid. I decided to check with the authorities and in due course found myself facing a lady who, with commendable speed, checked the relevant file, and assured me the fees would be paid and then dropped her bombshell. She informed me our application had been reviewed resulting in our contribution being increased! Unintentionally I must have shown some disquiet for after a moment's reflection she mentioned the situation might be affected by the cost of living in Beirut. She then asked if I considered this to be higher or lower than in Britain. I said this was hardly a question for me to answer as I could well be influenced by wrong motives, and that a satisfactory answer could be obtained from a reliable source such as the British Embassy. There was then nothing more for me to do but make a note of the increased contribution and take my leave praying that provision would be made for the proposed increase in expenditure.

Half term arrived and Andrew's brief holiday with its hurried round of family visits flew by, and all too soon we were on our way back to Southport and a longer separation. By 2.30 pm I was on the M6 facing South with a comfortable seven hours in hand to reach Dover for the crossing to Ostend. Apart from a long delay due to a broken fan belt all went well and I made the port in time to board the 21.30 sailing. Darkness still reigned as the ferry nosed into Ostend and, after apathetic looking officials had casually waved the line of cars through Customs and Immigration, the long, straight road to Brussels lay ahead. That evening, the German Customs Post hove in view. Even as I slowed to stop, guards, maybe edgy because of a Middle East number plate, applied a braking device which gave a hefty thump somewhere under the chassis. Only after a year and many hundreds of miles of travel, did I discover the device had cracked a steel ball joint linking the gear box assembly to the drive shaft. Being blissfully ignorant at the time of such damage, and the possibility of some vital part of the drive system coming adrift, I pressed on cheerfully in the gathering dusk.

At Venice my journey's final lap began. A quick tour round the boat confirmed that war clouds still overshadowed the Middle East. The normal crowds of first class tourists were absent and about thirty travellers graced the tourist class, most of whom were of Middle Eastern origin. After leaving Venice there were no interesting ports of call and time passed on leaden feet. Judging by various comments others shared the same experience and most passengers seemed to find the final two hours after sighting Beirut lighthouse were the longest of all. The family's enthusiastic greetings, plus the welcome from local friends paved the way for a delightful homecoming, but one note of sadness remained, Andrew was sorely missed.

Catching up on family news, one prime item was information Marjorie had received from Ipswich. A letter from the Education authorities contained the simple statement that, due to the cost of living in Lebanon, they would be meeting the full cost of Andrew's tuition and boarding fees. Without our seeking to engineer it, ample provision had been made for a special need. On our part we could only express thanks to the Lord for this further evidence of His overruling. In addition to this, with local education standards declining we realised it would be beneficial for Ruth to commence middle school in England before her twelfth birthday. So we contacted the principal of Clarendon School for Girls, near Prestatyn, North Wales and, in due course, a place for the Autumn term was granted. Again we had good reason for being thankful as arrangements were made for the fees to be paid.

These arrangements for schooling were intertwined with the daily activities of the Manarah Society and the local church. Whatever free time I had was given to the literature efforts of the Christian

Arabic Literature League and, as a result, I missed some of the very interesting contacts made when Beirut became a stopover on the hippie route from Europe to more exotic lands. A number of these travellers found their way to the shop and a warm welcome from Elias and Rafiq. Many were bound for India and beyond where they believed their desperate search for spiritual satisfaction would be satiated by the gods of Hinduism and Buddhism. Frank, in addition to providing some material help, pointed a number of these wayfarers to the Lord Jesus. He counted it a privilege to speak to them of the only One who could meet their deepest spiritual needs, and grant true joy and abiding peace.

But it was not only hippies who found a friendly welcome. Living in the hotel opposite the shop were three young Westerners who, after visiting the shop for some months made an open confession of their faith in the Lord Jesus and declared, in New Testament parlance, they had been 'born again'. None of us was sure what led them to this decision, but there was no doubting the joy they found in their new spiritual experience nor their desire to give witness to it. The unusual thing about them was that they were all dancers under contract to one of Beirut's night clubs. Far from home and fearful of being stranded they felt they had no option but to continue with the contracts they had recently made. Our responsibility was to encourage them to continue in the faith, and in this respect the warmhearted friendliness of Elias and Rafiq proved a tremendous help; perhaps never more so than on the day when Tom, another drifter from America, hooked on drugs, lonely and miserable, wandered in seeking companionship.

Like dozens of others Tom got as far as Beirut and landed in the same hotel as Gary and his friends. His curiosity, aroused by their interest in the bookstore across the road, caused him to follow and the scene was set for a tremendous spiritual struggle. Tom was challenged by a group of young people who were rejoicing in a drug free source of peace and contentment. They spent hours sharing with him their personal experiences and the joy they had found in yielding their lives to the control of Christ. Tom was not convinced, but the warmth of the friendliness, and the absence of any sense of rejection, was sufficient to draw him back again and again. Frank and Rena took a great interest in him and the bonds of nationality, plus their open hearted hospitality and practical help, softened his attitudes and made him more receptive to the spiritual solution to his problems. But the devil does not let his subjects go easily and, finally, Tom turned his back on the only One who could give him victory. My poignant memories of Tom include seeing him sitting, befuddled, bedraggled and despondent on the small wall adjacent to the Manarah shop, then utterly miserable, unkempt, furtive, coming into the shop desperately seeking - not for Christ but heroin: 'Where can I get it? I can't go on without it.'

As 1970 rolled on its way political tensions increased. Lebanese newspapers reported disturbances on the borders with Syria, and the possibility of civil unrest in Jordan where King Hussain's authority was being challenged. In Lebanon, sporadic clashes between militant Muslim and Christian factions increased and in the refugee camps there were more protests as hopes of regaining a homeland receded. The situation worsened when fanatics, nominally known as Christians but with little evidence of it, waylaid a lorry on the Damascus road and destroyed its entire load of Korans. This led to retaliation and many spoke of the possibility of civil war. Presidential elections were due later in the year and the various parties lost no time in challenging and decrying each other. The situation began to affect the schools whilst hotheads, desirous of making difficulties for the Government, would set fire to barricades of tyres on major roads. On more than one occasion when we heard of trouble brewing there had to be a hasty visit to Manor House to pick up the children and get them home before roads were closed. One day as we picked up Ruth and Mark we were asked to take three or four other children whose parents were unable to get to school. This entailed a roundabout journey and the first routes we tried were already blocked. Eventually a side road took us in the right direction only to land us at a barricade in the process of being ignited. We wasted no time in taking advantage of the one small space which was unlit.

The atmosphere was now tense. Syrian tanks could be seen trundling down the Damascus road towards Beirut, ostensibly in support of the Lebanese Government. Finally the uncertainty led to a shortening of the school year, and a premature start to the annual trek to cooler altitudes. For Ruth and Mark it meant the pleasure of two or three weeks' extra holiday before we commenced our planned furlough. By the beginning of June all arrangements concerning the Bookshop, Bible Courses, the Ras Beirut church, and our accommodation were in place and attention could be given to the final details for our departure. Having had a successful journey with Andrew mainly by road, and in view of the value the car would be on furlough, we decided to repeat the experience. On 10th June our old friend the *Ausonia* was scheduled to sail to Istanbul via Rhodes, and our white Ford Anglia graced its foredeck and we got a cabin somewhere near the engines as usual! The late afternoon saw us under way and early on the 12th, having passed through the Dardenelles, we glimpsed through the morning mists with their promise of a sweltering day, one of Christianity's most notable and controversial centres, ancient Byzantium.

We found Istanbul fascinating and the whole of our journey to England a memorable experience. It certainly gave us a glimpse into the culture of countries dominated by Communism, especially in Bulgaria which was reputed to be a nightmare for foreign motorists. Not only were the roads in poor condition but the police were notorious for their ability to find an excuse for imposing fines. Speed restrictions were very tight, often only 20 km per hour when passing through certain villages, and the police ready to pounce on an offender immediately on crossing the village boundary. From the reports we had heard it seemed hardly anyone could get through without a fine. That we did may have been due to the police having a day off. But the Customs' officials were not, though judging by the queue one might have thought they were. In due course two or three officials paraded round the car whilst another ran an inquisitive eye over the contents of the boot, fumbled through a case, and finally, taking a liking to a huge melon for our lunch, sequestrated it for himself. After the frustrating delays at Customs and Immigration we hoped for a speedy run to Sofia, a hope speedily scotched by the appalling state of the first few miles of road. As a result early evening found us well short of Sofia and the need to relax at a wayside motel. There we were allotted a large box of a room containing the minimum amount of furniture. But we were well content with our temporary accommodation. In any case, what else could one expect for the sum of £1 a head?

The atrocious state of the roads in the immediate vicinity of the Yugoslavian border had the effect of slowing us down for a number of miles. Then matters improved and with a well made road ahead we had every confidence of a quick run as far as Belgrade. No disturbing thoughts pervaded our minds, we could relax and enjoy a trouble free day. At least so we thought until, without any warning the temperature needle swung into the red and an ominous wisp of steam issued from under the bonnet. After topping up the radiator, I noticed the pump was giving a good imitation of a miniature fountain and realised we had an unexpected major problem on our hands. As we gathered round and I wondered how to solve the problem, it was ten year old Ruth who reminded us of the obvious way ahead. In a very positive tone of voice she asked, 'Shouldn't we pray about it?' We did and a child's faith soon received its reward. In less than three minutes a truck rumbled into view and the driver, with a display of gestures, asked what was wrong. His next gestures implied did we have a rope? I had invested two shillings and sixpence (23p) in one before we left Beirut and in spite of its seeming fragility, it took the strain. About three miles down the road our rescuer turned off the highway and there within a hundred yards both a garage and a motel came into view. There, after something like nine hours and the local manufacture of an essential part, we were roadworthy again. Our gratitude for the breakdown having occurred where we could obtain food and lodging for the night increased when we noted no garage or motel existed all the way to Belgrade. The rest of our journey took us to Koblenz, the valley of the Rhine, Cologne, a quick run to Calais, ferry to Dover and another warm welcome to the now familiar Rise Park Missionary Home.

CHAPTER 28

In the Valley of Decision

(1970 - 71)

I am the Lord... who leads you by the way you should go (Isaiah 48:17).

Throughout the 1960s our days had fallen into a fairly regular pattern with home life centered around the family, church responsibilities, and a daily routine governed by the varied activities linked to the Manarah Society. Now, except for not having Ruth with us, we anticipated a similar pattern would continue after our return from furlough. However, shortly after arriving in England we knew that for the sake of the children, adjustments would have to be made to our life style. At the commencement of the summer holidays, after six months at Scarisbrick, Andrew arrived at Pettits Lane, but for a few weeks the old happy relationships seemed to be at best muted and, on some days, almost non-existent. Maybe we had not realised how independent he would become and a return to family life would call for a period of adjustment. In miniature it was a repetition of my situation when returning from the Army to civilian life and possibly Andrew was just as unaware as I was that to others he could seem to be distant and reserved. The experience warned us that close family unity could be jeopardised by long periods of separation.

Ruth would soon be at Clarendon and we had to consider what effect boarding school would have on her, especially as she would be going two years younger than Andrew. But another factor gave cause for concern. Before leaving Lebanon, Mark had shown signs of nervous tension due to the changes affecting his young life. A close friend disappeared overnight and then, some months later, he found himself bereft of Andrew's companionship. He also had to leave his familiar surroundings and his one remaining bosom friend to visit unfamiliar England where he would also lose Ruth's support. It was enough to make a young and sensitive boy insecure and unsettled; how much became apparent when on hearing of our departure date he passionately asked us not to speak about it again. Now at Romford, his indications of insecurity plus our concern for Andrew and Ruth, caused us to reconsider seriously our plans for returning to the unsettled conditions in Lebanon.

We had no guidance from the Lord to forsake the ministry which He had committed to us. The question as to how we could best cater for all the needs of the family, and at the same time further the ministry of the Manarah Society, concerned us, and was resolved only when Marjorie reminded me of something I had said years before. She referred to the letter I had written from Abadan the night God had so clearly spoken concerning full time missionary service. Quite gently she reminded me of my words, 'I must go even though it means having to leave you behind.' Andrew and Ruth were at boarding school but needed a haven at holiday times; neither of us were really happy about taking Mark back to an increasingly unsettled country; the Lord had not told us to draw back from His work there. Therefore the only viable solution was for me to go whilst she made a home in England until Mark also went to boarding school. It was a challenging situation which drove us to prayer and the decision this must be the way ahead.

This decision led us to another problem very difficult to solve. Our tenure of the Missionary Home was for an allotted period - we needed other accommodation. This raised the question of where and how much would it cost? Renting furnished or unfurnished accommodation would be very expensive - should we try to purchase a small home? Money spent on rent was passing into oblivion, but money invested in a home through a mortgage at least meant a certain amount being retained. But two simple factors made the prospect of this very bleak. Where could we find a capital sum? and which financial institution would grant a mortgage to applicants who could only state their source of income was 'as the Lord provided'? In spite of this, we felt our responsibility was to commit these needs to Him. In various ways the matter of a capital sum was solved and we made enquiries for a mortgage. We were not surprised at the negative results, though hopes rose on our seeing an advertisement in a Christian magazine which seemed to indicate we could obtain the help we needed. A brief phone call shattered that hope. The financial advisor believed God could provide, and that in response to faith God did provide - but he was not willing to get us a mortgage!

One weekend away for meetings, my host and hostess were completely unknown to me but I immediately felt at home with them. My host plied me with questions concerning the past and our hopes for the future, leading me to raise the matter of a home in England and the problem of obtaining a mortgage. It came as a complete surprise when he asked if I would allow him to seek to solve our problem. Having shared so freely the basic details of our situation I felt I could not refuse his offer and, after answering further questions concerning our financial situation, the matter was left in his hands. Only later, after a mortgage had been arranged, did we discover he was a partner in one of London's leading firms of accountants.

Early in January 1971 we occupied our new home in Ipswich and on 28th February I was on my way to Lebanon alone. It was hard leaving Marjorie and Mark to cope on their own. My solitary journey took me first to Dover and then through Belgium, France and Italy to Venice to join the *Esperia* to Beirut, but it was not without interest and times of Christian fellowship on the way. A weekend with the Greens, missionaries in Metz, provided a glimpse of the difficulties they faced in an atheistically orientated France. Then a visit to the Hanleys in St. Etienne created the awareness of a mission field to Muslims in Europe and laid the foundations for cooperation in days to come; and a detour to Monte Carlo provided an insight into the work of Transworld Radio and its efficacy in reaching Muslim lands with the gospel.

From Venice the almost empty boat ploughed on through rough seas with little to relieve the dullness of the voyage but to read and write. On the morning of 9th March the now familiar harbour came in view and the *Esperia* eased to her berth. Few passengers meant a quick passage through Customs and a speedy delivery of the car, so I was in Rue Abd Al Aziz well before lunch. A welcome awaited there with Elias and Rafiq anxious to hear my comments on the refurbished store. Frank had invested in new bookshelves and better lighting which together with excellent displays ensured an attractive and welcoming store. Then the time arrived for the solitary trip back to Chouit where, in stark contrast to the early part of the day, an empty and echoing flat had no welcome to offer. Everywhere looked tidy, neat and clean, but the rooms held a multitude of memories and, for the first time since leaving England, I really felt the pain of loneliness.

With the reasons for maintaining the flat in Chouit no longer applicable I decided to seek a home nearer the book store. This was easier said than done, but a flat above the Lennoxes became available, and with my personal affairs under control attention could be given to the purpose of being in Beirut. There was a sense of satisfaction in the progress in each aspect of the work. The evangelistic aim of the bookstore through personal contacts and literature continued unabated. The objective of providing a wide range of Bible study aids and devotional material for the Christian community was also being fulfilled. The Bible Correspondence Course ministry, which had suffered a slight setback due to Egypt's censorship of Christian material, had again increased with a good response from a number of Arab countries. A new course on Galatians was being prepared and four others, the first of six which Frank had specially arranged for children, were already in use.

A review of the publishing to date also proved encouraging. The project of producing the Ladybird children's Bible series now covered the envisioned seven titles and 11,500 copies in Arabic and 2,500 in Armenian had been distributed. The simplified commentary on the Pentateuch had been published, and permission obtained for the Arabic edition of Dr. Ironside's commentary on the Gospel of Mark. At first the financial side of all the work was met by free will offerings from individuals and assemblies, and many a step had been taken in simple faith that provision would be made at the right time. Later there were gifts from the United States for specific publishing projects and, eventually, a generous annual donation from the JW Laing Trust in England to be divided between the bookshop, Bible courses and publishing. As the turnover in the bookshop increased, the gap between income and expenditure gradually decreased until, including the wages of national staff, it broke even. When one recalls the thousands of pounds required over the years for maintaining each aspect of the work, it is surely a testimony to the goodness and faithfulness of God that provision was made without any appeals for aid. Our own living expenses were, of course, completely separate from those of the work and it came as a complete, even devastating, surprise to be asked publicly in a conference in Britain how much we gained personally from the bookshop! I was grateful for the opportunity of publicly knocking on the head the rumour that we made a good living out of it - actually the opposite was true.

If we could have kept a record of all the interesting contacts made over the years it would have made stimulating reading. Occasionally there was encouragement, such as when two ladies from the Ajlaun Hospital in Jordan were enthusing over a certain booklet. It transpired one had purchased a copy and left it lying about in her room in the hospital. A young nurse found the booklet in the empty room and soon become so immersed in its contents that she lost all sense of time. The lady returned and asked why she was so interested. The girl came from a professing Christian home, so she added, 'You are a Christian aren't you?' To which the girl replied, 'I thought I was, but now I know I am not.' She realised for the first time what the name 'Christian' really meant and, in the words of Paul she became "a new creation" through faith in the Lord Jesus. That was not the end of the story - the girl had been so bright in her Christian testimony she had led ten others to faith in the Lord, some of whom had given witness to this in baptism.

At this time too a story from Marjorie made stimulating reading. Travelling on a train in England she commenced a conversation with a couple just returned from a visit to Cairo. They had been in touch with believers one of whom, a keen young man, stated he had become a Christian whilst in Irbid, Jordan, some fifteen years before. Further discussion revealed him to be a diffident youth whose profession of faith was received by the rest of the believers with a certain amount of reserve. For us this snippet of news arising from an apparently chance meeting with complete strangers, was a thrill and a reminder that if we faithfully sow the seed of the Word of God the results can be left with Him.

With the bookshop well established in Beirut we began to consider the possibility of extending to another area. My thoughts turned towards the bustling port town of Tripoli in the North but with no contacts there we hardly knew how to proceed. An exploratory trip by Rafiq revealed the very high cost of rents, so I decided nothing could be done at that time. But the way opened for an extension in another direction. A believer from the Arab assembly in Zahleh expressed a wish to display Christian books in his shop. Readily we took this as an indication that this town in the fertile Bekaa Valley should be our target. Zahleh was mainly Christian but, being the market town for the predominantly Muslim valley, it could provide a base for a Gospel witness to Islam as well. A small bookcase displaying a selection of Christian literature seemed a small step but it proved in due course to be one of vital importance.

During the first six months of 1971 Lebanon remained relatively quiet though unrest showed itself in public demonstrations and even violence. The assassination of a prominent journalist solved nothing; instead it laid the foundation for more hate and desire for revenge. Jordan also had problems. An uprising mainly of Palestinian refugees against King Hussain brought bloodshed to the capital and unrest throughout the land. The country verged on civil war. Our friends there, Roy and Dora Whitman, on a visit to Lebanon gave vivid accounts of the fighting near their home. On many occasions they experienced a deep consciousness of peace in the midst of danger and at the height of the troubles, neighbours would crowd into their home believing Roy and Dora had the special protection of God. Not surprisingly these times became impromptu meetings as they talked with and prayed for the people, comforting and encouraging them by readings from the Scriptures. Certain organisations in Lebanon tried to organise strikes in sympathy with their compatriots in Jordan but without success, for example attempting to keep all service cars off the road with the old trick of scattering quantities of nails across the main arteries leading into the City. But for once the police took prompt action and within days the practice ceased. In one way and another Lebanon seemed to be gradually slipping towards the tragedy of internal conflict; the only question was, when?

Before the end of the year another aspect of service came to our notice. In 1971 the Far East Broadcasting Association, transmitting from the Seychelles, contacted us mentioning that a programme based on one of the Emmaus Bible Courses had now been prepared and as it would end with an offer of a Bible Course, could we sponsor the weekly fifteen minute slot? If we could our address would be included for contact and follow up. For years we had hoped for an opportunity of some involvement with a radio ministry and now it seemed as if the Lord was telling us to go ahead. Interestingly, the first response from this broadcasting came not from the Middle East but from an Arab resident in France. This gave a clear indication of the extent of the coverage and, in view of later developments, may have been the means of sowing the thought of France being an alternative base for the Bible Course work.

By this time we believed that steps should be taken to develop the literature outreach in the Bekka Valley. We were grateful to our Lebanese friend in Zahleh for his willingness to display Christian literature in his shop, but knew this would only be a limited form of Christian testimony. Three main problems had to be faced: there had to be suitable premises in a good location, personnel to oversee the work, and the necessary finance. The first called for a reconnoitre of the town's main shopping area. Rafiq's initial visit drew a blank, but his next located premises in a row of newly built shops on the main road into town; not ideal but they were in a strategic position. Islamic influence prevailed in the Bekka Valley and, with many Muslims daily passing in and out of the town, we thought a good number of contacts could be made. Not surprisingly, especially as a towering pillar carrying a figure of the Virgin Mary stood on the opposite side of the road, the shop was owned by the Catholic Church but they made no objection to our renting it. Solving the problem of personnel proved more difficult and plans of opening by mid July seemed about to founder. However, shortly before the end of June we were introduced to a keen young man, a believer in Zahleh, free to commence work on the required date. With the bookshop in Beirut almost reaching the stage of breaking even, funds were liberated for Zahleh and thus the third problem melted away. With the new project commenced we could only wait and see if we had discerned the Lord's leading aright. Subsequent events proved we had and it is encouraging to know that, in spite of a number of almost inevitable problems, the place has borne a faithful witness to the Gospel up to the present time.

Rafiq in new Manarah bookshop

CHAPTER 29

Storm Clouds Gather

(1973 - 75)

Commit your works to the Lord and your thoughts will be established (Proverbs 16:3).

From January 1971 to May 1973 Marjorie stayed at home for the sake of the children. For me, 1973 seemed to be filled with the departure and arrival of colleagues, family and visitors! The first departure of the year was the Lennox family. Wishing to retain their beautifully situated flat at Souk El Gharb, they suggested we rent it on Marjorie's return. This we were happy to do, for then we could exchange the heat, humidity, noise and dust of the City for the peace and freshness of the hills. But before their departure Beirut had unwelcome visitors which one night rudely disturbed my sleep. In the dark hours, gunfire re-echoing round our enclosed cul-de-sac jerked me awake and curiosity drew me to the balcony doors. Another burst of gunfire very close, warned that curiosity should be replaced by discretion. As more shots, accompanied by shouting and turmoil, resounded round the flats, I listened to the noise of an engine racing and the comparatively subdued hum of a disturbed neighbourhood. Morning brought the needed enlightenment. Unknown to most in the area, an Arab organizer of certain raids against Israel, lived with some members of the Palestine Liberation Organisation in the block of flats adjacent to ours. An Israeli Commando Unit, after a reconnaissance by two of their number, made their way to our area, launched a raid against their target, and escaped uninjured. As was almost bound to happen in such a raid things went somewhat awry. The Commandos burst into the wrong flat wounding some innocent person before finding their real target and killing him, his wife and two other leading PLO members. The ones who had carried out the reconnaissance and arranged for the get away vehicle had first masqueraded as American tourists, so it was no wonder that Frank and I were warned to keep a low profile for a while.

The Lennox's departure just preceded an unexpected journey home for me. Our friends in England, Geoff and Gwyn Watkins, proposed fulfilling their often stated intention of visiting us in Lebanon. Having heard us speak of driving across Europe they had the idea of doing the same. They suggested that Marjorie should travel with them and generously offered to pay for the whole of her journey. The decision was made to travel by road to Venice then sea to Beirut. But Geoff and Gwyn had never driven on the Continent and felt the assistance of another driver would be invaluable; so could I spare the time to fly home and then accompany them? Their generosity would include me on their expense list and being able to arrange for the work to go on, I agreed.

Geoff and Gwyn's visit fulfilled their expectations, although during their visit they had a brush with a terrorist encampment. Rafiq had made his car available for sightseeing and often drove them around, on this occasion Tyre and Sidon being the points of interest. In Sidon a large building bearing the appearance of medieval origins attracted their attention for a visit. Rafiq had his doubts but, not wishing to go against the wishes of his guests, agreed. They were not far into the drive when rough looking, unsmiling men in semi military uniform surrounded them and Rafiq had a lot of explaining to do. Eventually he convinced them his friends were innocent tourists with no desire to pry into PLO's affairs. The rest of their time was incident free, apart from an occasional fear of heart attack due to Beirut's notorious traffic conditions! A current comment was that there are only good drivers in Lebanon - the others are dead! No wonder we never drove without prayer!

Now with Marjorie back, life for us took on a new sparkle but it coincided with a time when life had lost its sparkle for many Lebanese. The power struggle between Lebanon's main Christian political parties led to violent clashes; the antipathy of the increasing Muslim population to a Christian dominated land resulted in many more. Antagonism against Israel, with raids over the borders, led to further retaliation and by 1974 Israel began making pre-emptive strikes in the south against areas deemed to be sheltering terrorists. However, compared with the destruction and carnage of later years Beirut, and Lebanon as a whole, was still relatively peaceful. As spring gave way to summer our appreciation of the Lennox flat increased. A long, hot, tiring day in town would end with the steep climb up the winding Damascus road, with numerous horseshoe bends presenting alternating views of a diminishing Beirut and village studded slopes until we reached Souk Al Gharb some 2,500 feet above sea level. Behind the flat the land rose steeply whilst in front it fell away in a series of cultivated terraces before levelling to meet a sand-girt sea.

The arrival of Andrew, Ruth and Mark was a highlight - for them it was coming home and their initial excitement hardly knew any bounds. England was foreign territory as far as they were concerned, a place where some relatives lived and, for some mysterious reason, their parents felt they should be educated. Andrew, had sat his A levels and finished with Scarisbrick, and we agreed he should remain in Lebanon while plans for the future could be considered. He still needed to obtain a good grade in mathematics but we knew of no educational establishment in Beirut preparing students specifically for a British examination. The problem seemed insoluble but we took it to the Lord. The Lebanon Evangelical Mission at this time decided to organise a school for missionaries' children. The father of one of their own missionaries, Mr. J. Judson, a highly qualified mathematics' teacher, had recently retired and he accepted an invitation to run the school. He agreed to provide the tuition Andrew needed, and he received further help from a young physics teacher who gave freely of her time to advance him in this subject. Success resulted from these studies and opened the way to college and the desired degree.

Prayer for reinforcements to the work were also answered. Malcolm and Wadiah (Hannah) Coombes, after some years of preparation, felt the Lord had led them to join us in Beirut. The account of Malcolm's conversion and the various steps in both of their lives is a fascinating story in itself. Sufficient to say that early in the 1960s Malcolm, serving in the Navy, met an Arab Christian in an Arabian gulf port. Then on leave to Beirut he met Frank and ourselves. With his duty in the Navy completed Malcolm returned to Swansea and began to share with his Christian friends his interest in the Arab world. Believing if he was to be effective in that area he should have the support of a wife who shared the same concern, he made this one of his specific requests. Indeed, convinced he needed a wife already fluent in Arabic he prayed for the Lord to arrange it, in spite of his friends saying how unlikely would such a person be in Wales! But Hannah, born in Latakia, Syria, was just then applying to the Bible College in Swansea to fulfil her perceived need of Bible training. Step by step the Lord led these two servants of His, first to a deep desire to serve Him in the place of His choosing, then to marriage and finally to join us in Beirut. Originally, Malcolm had considered working in Aden and looked upon the move to Beirut as a step in that direction. So when they arrived early in September we appreciated their stay might be brief.

The Coombes soon swung into action. Within a few days they located a flat in Zahleh and were taking an active interest in the bookshop. Hannah's fluency in Arabic and Malcolm's zeal for the Gospel meant they were the ideal couple to take over the responsibility for the Bible Correspondence work. The number of letters received in response to the radio broadcasts was then comparatively small but the coverage wide, coming from Jordan, Iraq, Yemen, Egypt, Morocco and France. Requests for Bible Courses came from several prisoners in a town in South Lebanon. Under the Coombes' direction the Correspondence Course work expanded and, apart from a fairly lengthy break during the height of the civil war, this ministry has been one of their main concerns until the present day. Once the initial barrier of reserve had been broken down the small assembly in Zahleh also benefitted from their presence.

The new year opened with a brief spell of glorious weather but at the end of January this rapidly changed. Dark, heavily laden clouds rolled in from the west and torrential rain, often accompanied by brilliant flashes of lightning and peals of thunder echoed around the hills. Fierce winds swept the clouds along and as the rains increased so the temperature dropped and snow blanketed the crests of the mountains, gradually creeping lower and lower until it reached the coast - an event reckoned to occur about every ten years. At the end of January, Marjorie, for family reasons, left for England. Andrew and I did our best to entertain Mr. Stan Warren from Echoes of Service who had come to see us. There is no doubt he enjoyed the visit, although the snow blocked roads meant he could not reach Zaleh. Later he often referred to the first time he attended the Arab assembly in Ashrafiya. Outside was a badly damaged car belonging to one of the elders. Naturally I enquired how it had happened. It was a usual story. Just as Muneer slowed down outside the Hall, the car following was going too fast to stop. Mr. Warren asked, maybe somewhat facetiously, what he had said to the driver. The response almost left him speechless. Instead of creating a scene, Muneer had invited him to attend the meeting, and he came! A few days later our car had its the rear lights and a badge stolen outside the house. When he asked what my reaction would have been if I had caught them in the act, I had to confess I would possibly have been less forbearing than my Arab brother. Obviously I still had, and have, a long way to go in the matter of Christian grace.

During the first few weeks of 1974 activity in the bookshop decreased so that more time was available to concentrate on other aspects of the work. Publishing continued and we anticipated placing another booklet for the SGM, together with a children's book, with the printers by the beginning of February. The problems in the Middle East were mainly political and in Britain principally economic. Sterling had become unpopular in the local markets, and the pound (and the dollar) gradually slipped against other currencies including the Lebanese lira, resulting in gifts from the West falling in value by nearly 50%. Paradoxically prices in Lebanon began to rise. All this, however, was well known to the Lord and He provided accordingly.

Whilst we were coping with the situation in Lebanon Marjorie was putting into effect plans concerning our future home in England. Changes affecting the family meant it would be beneficial if we shared a home with my sister and a joint property was purchased in Church Stretton. With all the arrangements finalised Marjorie returned before the end of April and we anticipated eighteen months of service free from interruption. In the event my sister received a call to spend the next academic year in the primary department of the LEM school in Beirut. Consequently the base in England could only be maintained by our being there in September when she left. With the Lennoxes due in Beirut by the end of July and the Coombes well settled in Zahleh, we were able to arrange to be in England by the requisite date. Later we felt we could see God's over ruling in all these arrangements.

Before the sun rose on 22nd August we were on our way. With five passengers hemmed in by luggage, a boot with hardly an inch of space to spare, and four large cases on the roof, you could say the car was fully loaded. Thinking of some of the rough roads ahead and the lack of suspension I had some misgivings but these vanished as the miles rolled by without mishap. However, our headlights suddenly illuminated a vehicle with the end of a metal pole protruding from the rear, impaled on the safety barrier. It was a sobering sight especially at the commencement of a 3,000 mile journey through Syria, Turkey, Bulgaria, Yugoslavia, Austria, Germany and France. September 3rd saw us in Calais, by evening we were in Dover and a few hours later knocking on the door of our new home in Church Stretton, to return heartfelt thanks to the Lord for all His care.

Over the winter, news of increasing sectarian and political confrontations in Lebanon continued to reach us. By June the permit for our car to remain in England expired and it had to be returned to Lebanon. So with two friends, I had an opportunity to go and check the situation myself. An uneasy calm was then prevailing in Beirut and our movements around town were unhindered. There had been trouble in the area of Abd Al Aziz street forcing shops to close and some buildings had been damaged, but at Manarah the only sign of conflict was a dent in the metal shutter and a bullet hole through the clock. Occasional clashes in other parts of the country did not auger well for the future and the prospect of outright civil war could not be ignored. We could only trust and pray the situation would not cause a shutdown of the bookstore, but I felt we ought to take definite action to ensure the continuation of the Bible Correspondence Courses. This work had again been disrupted by long strikes in the postal services. It took only a brief visit to the main sorting office where many dozens of mail bags were piled from floor to ceiling, to convince me something had to be done. Contacts with many students in a number of countries had been lost and it seemed obvious the work would have to be located elsewhere less likely to be interrupted by civil strife.

Week after week the situation in Lebanon deteriorated. Bitter fighting spread across the country as violence supplanted dialogue over political and religious issues. Outside influences – socialist, communist, and Islam – inflamed the situation. Internal factors and dissension within both Islam and Christianity added a further militant factor. Sunni opposed Shiyah, and Maronites, Catholics, Orthodox and Protestants failed to agree. The effect on local believers was traumatic. Unable to enter into the political aspirations of their nominal Christian compatriots, whilst at the same time being regarded by the Muslims as part of the Christian enemy, they were caught between two fires. Some who were Palestinian in origin also faced the antagonism of many Lebanese against those who had come from that divided land. But the believers realised their need of each other and practical fellowship deepened.

The situation had a threefold effect on the work of Manarah. Shortage of paper supplies and the difficulties at the printers put any thought of publishing on hold. The shop opened intermittently because of the problem people had of getting into Beirut. The inability of the Post Office to maintain a regular postal service brought the Bible Correspondence Course work to an end. With regard to publishing and the shop, we felt happier times would again see them fully operative but the Bible Course ministry, or lack of it, caused concern. A long gap in communications could mean that all contacts would be lost and we were more fully convinced than ever that the work should be based elsewhere.

Before the end of October we believed the Lord had shown us where that should be. Back in the UK, we were able to attend the annual Missionary Convention at Central Hall, Westminster. As we sat with our thoughts tending to stray from Westminster Chapel to Lebanon we were suddenly arrested by the comments of a missionary from France. Brian Tatford, speaking of the tremendous spiritual need in that country, drew attention to the large numbers of Arab immigrants in France, and commented on the freedom that existed for reaching them with the Gospel. At the end of the day both Marjorie and I had the conviction that this could be where the Bible Course work should be situated.

The closing weeks of 1975 presented us with a problem and a challenge. The situation in Lebanon had worsened. A number of missionaries had left the country, some not intending to return. The Lennoxes and the Coombes had temporarily made their home in Jordan, in Ajlaun and Medaba respectively. Our excellent assistant, Rafiq Bustani, was to join another missionary enterprise working in the Arabian Gulf and we would be losing his help. The vital question for us was should we return to Beirut at this time or wait further developments? We wrote at the end of our December newsletter:

'In the centre of the circle
Of the will of God, we stand.
There can be no second causes,
All must come from His dear hand;
All is well, since 'tis my Father
Who my life has planned'

Being convinced no further guidance would be given until we were once again in the Middle East, we had no option but to go.

CHAPTER 30

Farewell to Lebanon

(1976 - 77)

In God is my salvation and my glory: the rock of my strength, and my refuge, is in God (Psalm 62:7).

For our return to Lebanon, a direct flight to Beirut was out of the question. We chose to fly to Damacus where Frank willingly agreed to meet us and then take us either to Amman or Beirut. We stayed at the Foreign Missions Club in London the night before our departure and there, much to our surprise, we met the Bruins family just arrived from Lebanon! We were delighted to meet Cor and Audrey again, but their presence in London did not auger well for the situation in Beirut. When they had been advised to leave, the situation had deteriorated to the point where it became impossible to reach the airport by road - they had to go by helicopter. Having shared our plans for the future, they offered us the use of their flat with its well stocked larder. We appreciated the offer but as the width of the city separated their flat from Ras Beirut, the possibility of our using it seemed remote.

The Syrian Airways flight was delayed and it was 4.30 am before we dipped towards Damascus airport. We didn't expect Frank at that early hour, but there he and Malcolm were waiting at the barrier bright and cheerful as usual. It gave a lift to our somewhat jaded spirits to see them and eventually we were ensconced in Frank's Volkswagen trying to decide which direction to go. We felt it would be wise to wait for the first news bulletin of the day at 6 am. The news of further outbreaks of fighting and the closure of roads made grim listening. No viable alternative remained but to turn eastward trusting to get visas at the Jordanian frontier, and hoping our friends at the Ajlaun hospital could cope with us for a few days, which they did.

We were grateful to find our car waiting for us at Ajlaun and one of our first visits was to Malcolm and Wadiah at their temporary lodgings in Medaba. From there we went to see friends in Amman and quite unexpectedly met a Canadian acquaintance who had recently left Beirut. On hearing of our need of accommodation there he immediately offered us the use of his flat, which was not far from the shop. He had already paid the rent for some months in advance and all we had to do was to take his keys, contact his landlord, and occupy the place. With news of a lull in the conflict in Lebanon, we decided to go and by the middle of February, three heavily laden cars set off, intending to stay in convoy all the way. At the Jordanian customs, an official took offense at Frank's reply to a question and ordered him to unload his vehicle completely. We were more or less waved through and so were the Coombes, but then Malcolm decided to stay and try to speak to the official in support of Frank - the result being an order to unload his vehicle as well. This meant that we were at the shop in Ras Beirut a couple of hours before Malcolm arrived.

Those two hours affected the rest of our time in Beirut. Having visited the shop we took the three minute walk to our proposed new abode, cheerful at having a flat so near. But as we approached the building our cheerfulness received a check. The long, gloomy looking, four storey building with its iron railings and latched gate seemed to repel us. The locked door to the block refused to respond to our key and, after much ringing, a woman as gloomy as the building grudgingly opened and demanded to know our business. Having our credentials and the keys we were allowed upstairs, on the way meeting the landlord whose demeanor was as unwelcoming as his wife's. This did not particularly worry me but an indefinable feeling of an evil presence did. I tried to shake off the impression as a figment of a tired mind but as I put the key in the lock Marjorie's comments indicated her feelings were the same.

The peculiar furnishings of the flat did nothing to lift our spirits; the large lounge was a replica of a Bedouin tent - dark walls and low ceiling engendered a feeling of claustrophobia, whilst the rest of the flat exuded drabness. But even the uninviting furnishing could not account for that inward sense of dread. Marjorie declared she could not live there even though it had seemed to be an ideal provision from the Lord! But could we turn our back on what appeared to be the Lord's providing? We decided to return to the shop to check if Malcolm had arrived, visit the grocery store and then, equipped with provisions return to take up residence. As we distanced ourselves from the building, the sense of dread decreased and by the time we reached Manarah had completely disappeared. We laughed at our foolish imaginations, did our shopping and with Malcolm for company, returned to the flat. As we climbed the flights of stairs the sense of dread recurred and deepened. Malcolm knew nothing about our feelings so when he suddenly burst out, 'You cannot live here, there is something wrong about this place!' it became obvious we needed clear guidance for our next step.

Down the stairs we went with exactly the same results as before and, as we considered the situation, our meeting with the Bruins in London came to mind. Was the Lord telling us not to be near the shop, or did the situation arise from the devil seeking to turn us aside? We decided to put the matter to the test. So we drove across town to the Bruins' flat and, the nearer we got to Ashrafiyah and the flat, the more we felt an inner calm. When an Egyptian brother, smiling broadly, opened the door and greeted us with words of welcome, no doubt remained as to where we should be living. He occupied a room on the ground floor adjacent to an 'exclusive' brethren's Meeting Room, whilst the first floor consisted of the Bruin's commodious, comfortably furnished, flat. There we were soon happily settled, even though a bullet hole through a window and an interior door, plus the balcony's splintered edge, were reminders of its exposed position.

Whilst we were at Ajlaun a consultation with one of the doctors revealed my need of an operation for hernia. Believing this would simply involve a road journey of a few hours and a brief period of rest we made a provisional appointment for 30th March. But for now we were back in Beirut and the conviction deepened that the Bible Correspondence Courses should be moved to a new base. We shared the thought of locating in France with our colleagues and, with their agreement, took the first step by contacting the Hanleys who were working amongst Arabic speaking people in the region of Carpentras. Malcolm and Wadiah, being confident they should continue with this aspect of the work, expressed their willingness to move there whilst Frank and Rena offered to stay in Lebanon and maintain the bookshops in Beirut and Zahleh. Marjorie and I would go ahead of the Coombes to locate a suitable venue and, in due course, assist in the development of a new base. In the event, the Lennoxes felt they had to return to the USA for the education of their children when we moved to France, and Adib, who shared in the opening of the work, felt it to be the Lord's will for him and his wife to assume responsibility for the Christian testimony of the shops.

Throughout the rest of February and well into March the situation in Beirut remained relatively calm in spite of news of sporadic fighting elsewhere. Moving from our new abode across the city to Ras Beirut presented no difficulty. In fact the area down town bustled with life and many a shattered building showed signs of being restored. The Bruin's flat, being barely ten minutes walk from the Ashrafiyah assembly Hall, enabled us to continue in fellowship there.

Being again at the centre of the Manarah's activities brought much pleasure, in spite of some of them being severely limited. We missed Rafiq's cheerful presence but his replacement, Joseph, was settling in well. The shop continued to be fairly busy though not all who came through the doors were friendly or in need of spiritual counsel. One day I found a worried assistant confronted by two well armed men. On entering I overheard him comment he had no authority to meet their request, so he directed their attention to me. Their weapons and semi military dress indicated they were members of some paramilitary organisation and it soon became apparent their request involved finance. In effect they were requesting funds under the pretext of protecting the building from terrorism - in reality a demand for protection money. It was a tricky situation, not least because a large bookshop in town had recently been burnt out after refusing to pay. My thoughts raced. We did not own the building and therefore were responsible for someone else's property; our national assistant might have to bear the brunt of any reaction arising from a refusal to pay; we were neutral as regards the conflict and, as Christians, had no desire to make any contribution towards violence. But whatever we said, nothing would convince these men that a refusal to contribute was not due to antagonism towards their cause. So, finding discussion valueless, I told Joseph to meet their demand -a demand, incidentally, so trifling it indicated that probably something had caused them to modify it. In any case we were relieved to watch them shoulder their automatic rifles and make for the door.

By the middle of March, Lebanon appeared to be returning to some normality and hopes of permanent peace were high. Government offices including the one which dealt with exit permits had been opening only sporadically. In two weeks' time we were due to travel to Ajlaun for my operation and then to France so, on hearing the office would be open for two hours, I went hoping to complete the formalities which would enable us to take the car out of the country. On returning with the requisite pieces of paper in hand I had a great sense of satisfaction. But within hours all hopes of peace were shattered. Shortly after midday a phone call brought news of the murder of a high ranking army officer and the possibility of violent repercussions. Malcolm had come from Zahleh for the day and, while discussing how this new situation might affect us, Joseph's father phoned. He advised his son to return home immediately and suggested we would be wise to do the same. Acting on this advice Malcolm left for Zahleh and I took Joseph home. On the way, shops were shutting, petrol stations locking their pumps and I noticed our petrol tank verged on empty. Fortunately, Joseph's father managed a station not far from our home, but as I drove onto the forecourt I saw the last pump being locked. However personal acquaintances counted for much at a time like this and in response to my plea the pump was unlocked again. At the same time I was warned not to delay getting home.

Arriving home I had hardly finished telling Marjorie about the situation when the phone rang. Our German friend, Walter Wassermann rang to warn us of the seriousness of the situation. He said some of his workers were leaving the country, and it would be necessary to leave within the hour to reach Damascus before the road closed. Immediately, and especially in view of the proposed journey to Ajlaun, we felt we should go. For such an emergency we had a suitcase already packed and only that morning I had obtained all the necessary documents for leaving the country. The car had been serviced a few days before and, almost at the last moment, petrol had been made available. Hurriedly we began to pack another case - and then simultaneously we stopped, looked at each other across the bed and in unison said, 'You know what we haven't done? Prayed!' In spite of years of trusting in the Lord, we could well be acting in panic and not under His guidance. So we knelt and asked the Lord what we should do. Deep peace came into that room as we unitedly felt the Lord was saying, 'Stay where you are.' We believed prayer had been answered and the safest place for us at that time was right where we were.

The rest of the day passed by peacefully but in the evening a Lebanese friend rang asking if we had any idea of what had happened to Malcolm seeing he had not arrived home by 5 pm. He himself had been delayed by numerous check points coming down the Damascus road and feared Malcolm might have run into trouble. By this time the lines to many parts of the country had been cut so we were unable to phone Zahleh and allay our fears. Many weeks were to slip by before we discovered what had happened to Malcolm and Wadiah; we could only trust all was well.

Within days of the assassination, Beirut divided into two main areas and it was impossible to reach the shop in Ras Beirut. Lebanon now plunged fully into a civil war which would drag on for a number of years. But apart from the periodic sound of shelling and rattle of machine guns, especially at night, our small area of the city could have been miles from the conflict. This was surprising, for Christian militias had headquarters not far from our building. Its effects were seen more in the shortage of some supplies rather than material damage, even though a few of the high rise flats were in the line of fire. Our Egyptian friend helped us tremendously with our shopping and standing in queues for long periods to get us bread. He feared that, as a foreigner, I might run into difficulties especially if there happened to be a mighty scramble when a load of bread arrived. We sincerely appreciated his concern even though at times it frustrated us. Apart from attending the Sunday and midweek meetings we were hardly out of the flat for days on end. The midweek prayer meeting, even on the noisiest of nights, was well attended. Even when conditions were at their worst, above fifty men and women were on their knees calmly speaking to the Lord. The faithfulness and devotion of the believers presented a constant challenge to our own faith. Many were out of employment, some had lost their homes, and not a few mourned a tragic death, but many were the testimonies one heard of a continuing reliance on the love and goodness of God.

With the cessation of the postal service we missed letters from home, but our main concern was our inability to communicate with the family and let them know all was well. No one could know how long the conflict would last and with the proposed date for my operation looming we felt we ought to make some attempt to be on our way, but how? To get to Damascus by road appeared to be impossible, there was no use thinking of flying as the dangers on the road to the airport were too great, any idea of going by sea and taking the car was baulked by the absence of shipping. We had to sit tight and wait for further guidance, then suddenly it came.

Information trickled through that a ferry service to Cyprus had been inaugurated from the Christian port of Juneih. We could drive to Rayfoun, leave the car with Adib and join the Lennox family going to Cyprus. Night after night the machine guns rattled, the occasional mortar bomb exploded, the answering wham of a gun helped to disturb sleep. Day by day hope that a cease-fire would be declared revived but all to no avail. The car had been serviced, all formalities completed for leaving the country and the petrol tank filled to the brim minutes before the pumps were finally locked, yet here we were hemmed in. But that ferry fostered hopes of a way out, if only we could be sure the thought was not merely the result of our impatience.

Sunday dawned and over breakfast we agreed to accept the often repeated invitation from our exclusive friends to fellowship with them in the breaking of bread. Within minutes of the start of the meeting concentration became difficult. Through one of the windows lay a lovely view across a wide valley to a mountain ridge and our former home in Chouit. Away to its right lay the Christian village of Araiya whilst slightly higher up and to the left nestled Abadiya occupied by the Druze. Suddenly bursts of smoke appeared in both those villages and, though distance muffled the sound of explosions, a gun battle had obviously erupted between the two. Shells and mortars were flying between them, arching over Chouit where, if like ourselves they had been prevented from leaving, resided the Wassermann family and their colleagues. It became difficult to draw one's eyes away from the scene and meditate but, thankfully, we managed to do so. One of the brethren began to read from Exodus 12 and the words, 'Go serve the Lord, as you have said,' arrested my attention and drove all thoughts of Chouit out of my mind. Was this the command to go? Back in the flat it did not surprise me when Marjorie quoted Exodus 12:31 and added, 'I think we are being told to go to Rayfoun.' The conviction deepened and within minutes we began packing the car. One or two of the brethren sought to dissuade us pointing out the dangers of a certain bridge which often came under sniper fire. But we believed it was right to go and the only hindrance might be the armed guard at the Christian check point outside Junieh. There we received a warm welcome, the barrier being thrown open with a cheery 'come on in'. As we climbed higher and higher, dense fog blanked out the sun and wrapped us in its embrace, so much so we overshot the entrance to Adib's property and had to retrace our steps. Just as we turned into his entrance the fog lifted and, to our further surprise, we faced a completely empty forecourt - the Lennox family had left for Cyprus the day before.

Adib confirmed a ferry of sorts was operating but a rumour existed that the militia were demanding it be cancelled. Many young men from Maronite and Orthodox families had left the area and the Christian militia, fearing a dearth of recruits, decided to block further emigration. Early Monday morning we were on our way to Junieh arriving at the crowded shipping office in time to hear a clerk declare no room remained on the boat. The news drew forth a chorus of disapproval but, in spite of the dissent, the clerk drew a sharp line across the passenger list. Being convinced the way had been opened for us to leave we couldn't turn away without making an attempt and, in reply to my request they take us, our names were added below the line and we were told to be back late in the afternoon. Then came the question of the fare. It had more than trebled from the time we first heard of it. Cheques would not be accepted, Banks were closed and the normal curbside money changers were conspicuous by their absence. Fortunately Adib and another friend were with us, and a diligent search through all our pockets produced the exact fare.

Later in the day, leaving our car in Adib's care hoping to be able to retrieve it later, we were driven down to Junieh and the commencement of a voyage we have no wish to repeat. At the quayside pandemonium reigned as a small tender took on passengers to ferry them to the boat. Armed militia scrutinised all who boarded, now and then hauling young men off in spite of vigorous resistance. Where strength failed money talked and a few young men came back, others more unfortunate were separated from their families. In spite of the chaos we got on the launch and within a few minutes were at the boat. There, like all the others who had been ferried for about three hundred yards, we were faced with another demand for cash - a demand enforced by the simple expedient of refusing to tie the tender to the ship until all had paid their due. Boarding the ferry meant climbing a short rope ladder, the only problem being the tender and ferry were never in harmony so a brief climb of two feet suddenly developed into six. The ferry proved, in fact, to be nothing more than a small cargo boat whose owner had found a simple way of turning a tragic situation into a money making opportunity. Conditions on board had been described as somewhat rough but that was a masterly understatement. Apart from the captain's tiny cabin no shelter existed on the deck, most of it now littered with cases, trunks and packets of all shapes and sizes. Sanitary conditions were nil except for one toilet off the captain's cozy little nook and that barred to all but his own favoured few. Benches, chairs or cushions were non-existent, and it was unthinkable that anything remotely connected with refreshments would be available. The raised edge around the open cargo hatch provided the only relief from standing and in due course even that was denied us.

As dusk fell, ominous looking clouds covered the horizon, and the crew - all three of them - came round urging all to go below where, according to them, 'a clean room, warm and dry, provided reasonable comfort for the night.' This delightfully comfortable room was a vast empty hold with a floor covered by a newly swept tarpaulin. Passengers could make the descent either by a series of iron steps welded to one of the upright stanchions or a fragile wooden ladder set at an angle of 30 degrees held in position by scraps of material once dignified by the name of rope. We chose the ladder, found a vacant spot near the side, used our coats for pillows and settled down for the night. Others gathered in groups spreading mats and laying out their evening meals, children played tag around the groups, jumping or tripping over recumbent forms, young people joined in song and chatter, until a slight swell caused many to recline. Then peace, more or less, reigned, the whole scene, dimly lit by three dull electric bulbs and a few oil lamps.

For the majority of the two hundred crammed into the hold, the wearisome hours crept by. About 3 am someone stirred setting off a chain reaction and the constant movement as one and another crept up to the deck, and the creakings of the rocking boat, negated any hope of sleep. Gradually the steady swish of water along the boat's side changed to bangs and thumps as wave after wave struck, rebounded and swirled round again. The steady roll increased accompanied by an irregular pitch and toss which soon placed most people on their backs again. Here we were in a dilapidated old craft with thin steel walls, carrying no lifeboats, rafts, jackets, fire extinguishers or any other safety device, bearing a human cargo whose only escape routes in an emergency were steel rungs and a flimsy wooden ladder. The ensuing panic if danger of any form struck added to one's wakefulness, until we remembered that 'underneath are the everlasting arms'.

Dawn came and with it news that the anticipated twelve hour journey would extend to fourteen. For many of the passengers distressing news increased the misery of the journey. Radios were plentiful and periodically news from Arab stations flooded in. It all made sombre listening, as news came of continued sectarian fighting; of Muslim and Communist victories; and of determined efforts to stamp out centres of Christian political influence. It all added to the distress of those who had left loved ones behind.

Finally the safety of Larnaca's harbour came in sight and immediately the atmosphere changed from despondency to joy. With the boat safely moored, passengers flocked to the gang plank looking, and possibly feeling, cheerful and content. For ourselves, the pleasure of being free from recent tensions was minimised by thoughts of the friends we had left behind. For them we could pray and at the same time look forward to meeting others already on the island. We knew a warm welcome would await us when we reached the office of the Middle East Christian Organisation some 45 miles away. The pleasure of meeting friends in Limassol increased when we discovered the Lennoxes were only a stone's throw away. Hearing they were due to fly to the United States that evening, tired and grubby as we were we hurried to enjoy their company before they set off on the next leg of their journey home.

Then came the greatest pleasure of the day, a telephone link with England and the joy of hearing the sound of familiar voices with their hearty 'Hi! Dad, Hi! Mum', followed by innumerable questions. We had been completely out of touch for six weeks and their joy and ours at renewed contact was tremendous. Then we had to make another important call. Our finances were low and expenses in Cyprus plus the forthcoming journey to Jordan called for replenishment. Were we to relax and wait for a miracle? Then we remembered the Lord does not work miracles if the way is open for a need to be met. Echoes of Service in Bath could well be holding gifts for us and so we contacted them. They quickly confirmed this to be the case and even before we booked in at a hotel for the night, we knew funds were on the way.

On 5th April, we flew to Damascus, and a few days later I was in the operating theatre of Ajlaun hospital listening to two doctors discussing how they were going to work on my hernia. But matters did not proceed according to plan. A few minutes after a spinal injection I must have gone into a state of shock. Try as I might I could not control the rapid shaking of my arms. For a few moments my rapidly numbing mind became vaguely conscious of anxious voices but then nothing more, until I felt my face being patted and heard the urgent voice of a Jordanian nurse pleading with brother Howell to come back! I was not sure where I had been but was certainly quite happy to be back! and happier still when the doctors pronounced all was well and the nurse wheeled me to the luxury of a private ward. There having all the time in the world to reflect on the situation I assumed I must have fainted. Marjorie had a different opinion founded on one of the doctor's comments that they thought they had lost me! Lost me they had not, and within the next few days enough strength returned to kindle thoughts of commencing the journey to France.

From the time we had said good-bye to Malcolm on his intended trip back to Zahleh we had been concerned for his welfare. We had no idea whether he got home safely nor where he and Wadiah with baby Matthew were now. Neither did we know what had happened to the Wassermann family and their colleagues. We knew only that on the day we left Ashrafiyeh, various missiles from two warring villages had been arching over their home. Three days into my convalescence our questions were answered by the appearance of Walter Wassermann himself. He had heard of our arrival and now came to share the tale of their own adventures. The day fighting broke out between the two villages they had planned to commence their journey to Germany whilst their co-workers would travel to Amman. Most of their luggage had been loaded the night before and all that remained was to pack two or three cases and leave. But that procedure received a sharp check when it became obvious the front door of their building had, for some unknown reason, become a sniper's target. Even a step outside the entrance hall drew fire and this, plus the increasing bombardment between the two villages, ruled out any hope of an immediate departure.

With no sign of the conflict diminishing the four missionaries decided to have another session of prayer. Much to Mr. Wassermann's surprise his wife prayed for what he considered to be an impossibility. Since dawn the day had been sunny and warm with hardly a fleck of cloud to be seen, but she simply asked the Lord to send fog so they could reach the cars and travel. I don't know if they all said amen to the prayer but, gradually, they became conscious of the barrage having ceased and in its place an eerie calm. Thick mist swirled round the windows; the time to leave had come. With the sound of the engines muffled by the fog, the two cars ventured out of the courtyard, turned right, nosed their way through Chouit until, to their dismay, through the fog they saw a barrier. Cautiously they approached and maneuvered round it, realising the dense mist had caused it to be left unmanned. With heightened confidence they increased their speed along the steeply rising road and, within a mile or so, brilliant sunshine and a cloudless sky replaced the murk below.

Before reaching Damascus their plans changed and, instead of turning north enroute to Germany, the Wassermanns accompanied their colleagues to Amman. How thankful we were they did. Not only were our anxieties on their behalf dissipated but, in due course, their help proved invaluable when we were faced with the problem of travelling to France. Also they had news of the Coombes. We were surprised to hear they were already in France. The day Malcolm left us in Beirut he had a slow but incident free drive until within a mile or so of home. There arms-wielding militia brought him to a halt. Their whole attitude indicated a high state of nervousness but this didn't trouble Malcolm, mainly because he thought the production of his passport would be sufficient for the way to be opened. Therefore it came as a surprise when almost hauling him out of the car, one of them demanded more evidence of identification. The situation then became more tense when another rifle toting individual expressed the opinion it would be best to shoot him on the spot. Happily the voice of the first prevailed and after making at least a pretence of inspecting the passport, he ordered Malcolm back into the car and told him to get going. He needed no second telling! That evening he and Wadiah decided the time had come to leave. Before dawn, with the car so heavily loaded its suspension was almost nil, and the bulging rear door tied down with rope, they set off for France and ended their trouble free journey in Carpentras. Within a few days, John and Ruth Hanley assisted them in locating an apartment in Orange, the town which was to become their home for many years.

CHAPTER 31

Welcome to France

(1976 -77)

The Lord shall preserve your going out and your coming in (Psalm 121:8).

Much as we enjoyed Ajlaun, the pine clad hills, the extensive views, the warm Christian fellowship and the luxury of being waited on while convalescing, we knew that work awaited us elsewhere. Flying to France we found would be more than we could afford. With the car we could reach our destination with a little in hand. The main question was how to recover our vehicle left at Rayfoun. The answer came within a few days - one of Walter Wassermann's colleagues would bring it through Syria into Jordan. While we waited we again visited Irbid which had grown almost out of recognition. Acres of houses and wide streets occupied what we had known as tilled fields or open unkempt, boulder strewn land. Our original home and meeting room, once fronted by an extensive area of open land, now lay hidden in some back street whilst a Baptist Church building openly displayed the Cross in this Muslim dominated town. We were thrilled to meet with the believers and to be welcomed by some whose Christian path commenced in our old home.

Pleasant though our surroundings were the days began to drag as we waited for news. Then came the afternoon when to our delight we saw our Peugeot, dirty and followed by a long trail of dust, come through the compound gates. The driver had a stirring tale to tell. They had been able to take remote mountain roads to reach Rayfoun but the road south had to pass through the outskirts of Beirut. It seemed almost miraculous that on that particular morning all was calm and they were unhindered until reaching the Green Line. This line, unmarked on the ground, separated the Christian and Muslim factions and to cross it indiscriminately could be dangerous. It seems on this morning a truce had been in operation but, just as they reached a crossing point the barriers were abruptly closed. The militia insisted the cars could not cross. Mr. Wassermann, anxious to reach the Carmel Mission's workers in the south, argued they could. With dire warnings of danger ahead, the guards raised the barriers and let the cars through moments before a missile landed near the spot where they had been waiting. Our friends heard the explosion but nothing more and continued on their way. With mission accomplished they resorted to remote roads to avoid many para-military check points in the Bekaah and gained the main road not far from the Syrian border. Our friend had much to tell of being guided and protected and we could certainly join with him in thanksgiving.

Nearly a month had passed in Ajlaun and, with my period of convalescence completed, it was time to move on. Our stay at the hospital had been longer than anticipated and this plus expenses in connection with recovering the car, had depleted our funds. These now consisted of just over £200 in various currencies. On 11th May, literally and metaphorically we commenced another stage on an unknown road. Some ten days later, after 2,500 miles, we arrived in Orange to be warmly welcomed by the Coombes. From there a short run brought us to journey's end and a warm welcome at the Hanley's home in Carpentras.

We turned to the pleasant occupation of opening the small pile of accumulated mail. Hungry for news from home we were not disappointed. Neither were we disappointed regarding the Lord's provision for our material needs. We had arrived in France with about £2. In our mail was a letter from Bath containing a cheque for £200! Once again we proved, 'My God shall supply all your needs according to His riches in glory.'

What was our next step to be? The original plan to arrive in advance of Malcolm and Wadiah and locate a base for the work, had been turned upside down. They were already in an area suitable for the work we had in mind. Having a list of students' names and addresses, along with a small supply of Bible Courses, they had already renewed contact with some of the students and were in no immediate need of help from us. Taking everything into account the best we could do for the next few weeks would be to go to Church Stretton for our young folk coming home for the summer break. In the event Ruth, Mark and ourselves spent the latter part of the summer holiday in Orange. The Coombes needed a break and the suggestion we occupy their flat provided an opportunity for Ruth and Mark to savour the atmosphere of France.

The move to France proved to be the commencement of the final period of our missionary service overseas. During the next three years there would be fairly frequent movement between France and England as well as a few changes in our French address. But at the end of 1976, in fellowship with the Hanleys and the Coombes, we prayed and planned for the development of an Arabic ministry in France. All of us were conscious of being on the threshold of a new and exciting development which would bring the Gospel to many who had never had the opportunity of hearing it before.

We rented accommodation on the second floor of a small block of flats a few minutes' walk from the Hanleys, without whose help we may well have floundered. John and Ruth had ploughed a lonely furrow for a number of years seeking mainly through personal contacts and literature distribution, to fulfill their missionary calling. With over three million Arabic speaking people in France, most of them from North Africa, they had a mission field on their doorstep. Visiting markets with literature already formed part of John's weekly programme and much more could be done in this respect. Many extremely interesting contacts were made, but afterwards individuals would melt away into the crowds around and further contact would be lost. John and Ruth were very conscious of the need for a centre in a main town where those contacted in the market could continue their enquiries about the Gospel.

Through Malcolm and Wadiah's use of the Bible Correspondence Courses, within a few weeks contact with students in six Arab countries had been renewed, confirming the possibility of the effective development of this ministry from France. Malcolm had also begun a weekly visit to one of the local markets, his stock being one small carton of books and his display area the top of the carton! From such small beginnings there developed larger and much more sophisticated displays in a number of markets in the region of Carpentras and Orange. But the work, whether personal contacts, market stalls or Bible Courses, could only operate effectively if a constant supply of suitable literature in Arabic was available. At that time, such did not exist in France. The need for a literature depot became obvious, not only for our own needs, but as a supply house for any other workers requiring Christian literature in Arabic.

During those early days I oscillated between John and Malcolm sometimes going with one to a market, or assisting with the Correspondence Courses. But the need for Arabic Bibles, books, tracts and lessons was paramount and the problem of how to meet it became a burning question. The only solution we could see would be for me to hire a small van and go to Beirut and bring supplies.

Market Bookstall

But where would one obtain a van? Would anyone share the journey? How much would it cost? Would the situation in Beirut be peaceful enough to make the project possible?

Gradually the answers to these questions came, the first being in response to a comment in one of our letters home. Two young men in Shrewsbury, having read of our hope of obtaining material from Beirut decided to act. The Hannay family had purchased an old ambulance. It would fill the purpose of caravan and load carrier and Paul and his friend Alan Peach, offered to join me for the journey to Beirut. At the beginning of April we decided to take the plunge and on the 25th, Paul and Alan reached Carpentras and we were on our way. It proved to be the trip of a lifetime as far as my two companions were concerned. Neither had been overseas before so every day, and almost every mile, became a new experience. Our diesel powered ex-ambulance was never intended for rapid transport. With a top speed of 50 mph, reduced often to 5 mph in mountainous country, we could roar past horses and carts and the occasional tractor, but more often than not we faced an empty road with a long queue of vehicles trailing behind. But it was all good experience and in due course our steady pace brought us through Italy and Yugoslavia to the borders of Turkey where our unusual approach could have had serious consequences.

The situation arose out of our having travelled for twenty four hours with only a few brief breaks. Actually sleeping in the van did not prove altogether comfortable! The three of us took turns to drive throughout the night though, being responsible for ensuring we were on the right route, my slumber could only be described as intermittent. About an hour before dawn I must have dropped off but wakened suddenly on hearing Alan shout at the top of his voice, 'Turkey here we come!' In the light of dawn I could see we were running down a long slope at our top speed towards a long bridge with armed guards at either end. Some hundred yards to the right a long building with a flag fluttering in the morning breeze, indicated the Greek immigration and customs post. To my dismay I realised our green military looking vehicle was fast approaching armed men who could well assume we had criminal reasons for charging out of Greece unofficially, and open fire. Alan had missed the turn to the border post and now, almost on top of the guards, it was too late to stop him. I think they were so surprised to see the speeding vehicle approaching that their reactions were numbed and, before they came to, we were half way across the bridge. By the time we reached the Turkish barrier at the other side I had got Alan to slow down and we made a dignified entry into Turkey as if we hadn't a care in the world. In fact I was wondering how we were going to get ourselves out of a very difficult situation. We had left Greece with all our documentation indicating we were still in that country. Our return journey had to be through Greece and I could just imagine the problem we would have when our passports showed we had never left!

There was nothing one could do except find a Turkish official and, hoping he had a reasonable command of English and maybe a sense of humour, explain the situation and seek permission to cross the bridge again. The person I saw proved quite helpful, ordered the guards to raise the barrier, and off we went to approach the Greek Customs Post from the wrong direction. To say the official there was angry is putting it mildly, but eventually he dealt with our documents and, bearing in mind we had to pass that way again, we made our profuse apologies and went our way.

In Lebanon the tensions which existed under the outward show of peace were obvious. Frequent check points, manned mainly by Syrian soldiers all the way from the border to Beirut caused delays, and many a suspicious look followed the progress of our rather unusual looking vehicle in its dark, and now very dirty, military green. Towns and villages bore scars of fierce battles, though in some areas of Tripoli, Jounieh and Beirut damage was slight, and bustling streets indicated an attempt to return to normal conditions. The down town area of Beirut, where shops, business premises and ancient markets were gutted or in ruins, was the most tragic sight. It was a relief to find the bookshop completely undamaged and functioning under the management of Ata. Later we found Zahleh to be free from conflict though the same could not be said of parts of the Bekkah valley. Paul in Zahleh, like Ata in Beirut, was maintaining an evangelical witness in spite of little encouragement from others. Both men could give accounts of the Lord's blessing on the Christian witness. Many Bibles, Scripture portions and books had gone out since the beginning of the truce.

Ata told of the joy of leading one of the Syrian peace keeping force to the Lord, whilst Paul had seen two young men professing faith in Jesus Christ as their personal Saviour. But sadly both Ata and Paul mentioned they would have to seek more remunerative employment, and we knew replacements would be difficult to find.

Meeting with Christians in Beirut who really loved the Lord, and hearing them tell of the wondrous works of God, brought us much joy. In view of the situation one might have expected an atmosphere of despondency amongst them. On the contrary there was a high note of optimism, a zeal for evangelism, a quiet confidence in the Lord, a consciousness of His power to protect and provide, and praise for every evidence of His goodness. One could appreciate the word 'miraculous' being used - one assembly elder told of threats to assassinate him simply because he was of Palestinian origin, and related how the Lord used unbelievers to deliver him. A young man testified how, having heard the Gospel, he believed and having been delivered from the power of drugs, he now zealously sought to serve the Lord. We also heard of how some two thousand rockets fell in one area but, in spite of the danger, meetings continued almost as usual. On the other hand there lingers the vivid memory of the despair, and even hate, expressed by others. 'How can we ever know the right way to God?' asked one desperately seeking to know the truth; a Catholic youth declared bitterly, 'Muslims hate the Christians and Christians the Muslims.'

It would have been easy to linger amongst so many friends but our object of collecting material for France had to be fulfilled and my companions had a dead-line for being back in England. A final visit to the shop in Ras Beirut led through the deserted centre of the town, past the once bustling commercial area and along the road to the University, for once strangely devoid of any sign of traffic. Calm appeared to prevail and it felt good to be alive on this sunny morning, but a sharp crack, the echo of a shot and a hole in the windscreen jerked us back into reality. Obviously our slow militarily looking vehicle had drawn someone's fire. How many bullets were fired we never knew. The one which holed, but failed to shatter, the toughened glass had been aimed at the driver but, if it had penetrated with force would, in our right-hand drive vehicle, have struck one of the passengers. We certainly had extra cause for thanksgiving that day.

The following day, with a good supply of literature loaded underneath the box like seats, and the enclosed space above the driver's cab filled, we headed for Syria and home. A number of friends warned us gloomily about the problems of getting the material through Syria, some going so far as to say we would never make it. For some time Syria had placed an embargo on the import of Christian literature and recently Customs had confiscated supplies of books and tracts. We had no desire to smuggle the literature but wisdom indicated it should not be too obvious. I had witnessed before the thoroughness of a Syrian search and felt it was more than likely they would poke under the lidded seats and open the door above the cab marked with a red cross. I decided to aim for a more remote crossing on the road to Homs. All went well until, having turned off the main route to take a minor road to the border, we hit, literally, our first problem. We had been weaving a way round numerous potholes and the journey had been slow but, with the side road looking smooth and undamaged, Paul considered it time for a turn of speed. He had just reached the maximum when a wide hole loomed ahead and within seconds we hit it and bounced out again with all four wheels clear of the ground. The van landed with its full weight on the right suspension, with the sound of breaking metal and then absolute silence. We clambered out to behold our transport forlornly sagging at the front but otherwise seemingly undamaged.

Since leaving the main road no traffic had passed us, no pedestrians had made their presence felt, no sign of habitation could be seen. But within minutes we were the cynosure of a small crowd of curious onlookers. We were achieving nothing by remaining there to be gaped at so deciding to check the van's mobility we climbed in, started up and then suddenly found our way blocked by a car speeding round the corner and stopping within inches of our radiator. From the driver came a torrent of questions mostly, as far as I could make out, concerning who we were, where had we come from, where were we going and finally, why had we parked by the roadside? We indicated the obvious reason why the van reclined by the edge of the road but he seemed unimpressed and, indicating we should follow him, began to reverse up the road. Only then did we discover humanity existed nearby. Round the corner lay the low buildings of the Lebanese border post and, at the further end of a long shed, those of Syria. The brief run from our unintended stop to the border convinced us that, providing we drove very slowly, all would be well and we spoke cheerfully of being in Homs long before nightfall.

We anticipated being cleared without delay through the Lebanese Customs before facing the more thorough checks of the Syrian officials. However our passports disappeared and when, after an hour, we made a polite complaint this brought only a grin and a comment they would be back soon. Hour after hour slipped by without any progress and only as daylight faded did the passports reappear and the barrier to the Custom's shed rise. A reasonably friendly official inspected our documents and, after making a brief survey of the interior of the van, indicated all was well and led me to the office to have the papers signed by his superior. Then to his surprise, and certainly mine, his chief said the van had to be completely emptied and a thorough search made through every item. He made a protest and added he knew all was well especially as, according to my passport, I was a Christian worker. It made no difference to the chief's decision. He stated we had acted suspiciously by stopping clear of the border and we were possibly involved in the smuggling of drugs. I now had no doubt that as we were waiting for our passports the telephone lines were humming as our names were checked at every border post in an attempt to confirm our smuggling connections. Fortunately I understood some of the comments, though my reaction from a Christian standpoint, was not so good. My patience had reached a low ebb and for a moment I snapped. He looked flabbergasted when he realised I understood what he had said, though whether he really understood my next few comments is another matter. I told him, somewhat forcibly, the reason for our enforced stop, and then asked what did he expect us to do in such circumstances? He signed the papers and said we could go which, with a warm expression of thanks, we readily did.

The next problem was the Syrians. I had noticed a very surly looking officer and hoped we would be spared facing him, but hope was not fulfilled! Before going into his office I told Paul and Alan they had better pray hard, and pray they did. Having obtained his signature I opened the back door of the van for his inspection but, quite brusquely, he indicated he did not want to look and walked off into the night. Almost bewildered by this turn of events we clambered in and, as I drove away, Alan let out a resounding 'Hallelujah!' but quickly suppressed a second when I told him to be quiet for we were not out of the woods yet - a minute later another barrier loomed ahead and two or three armed, torch waving soldiers brought us to a standstill. Then came the usual checking of passports and questions of what, why and where? followed by a cursory look inside. I wondered if they had been ordered to make the thorough check but, noting blankets and a bedroll, they assumed we were campers and waved us on into the darkness. Relieved once again we pressed on to Homs some 50 miles away, never daring to exceed 20 mph and wondering at almost every curve if the creaking suspension would finally give way and leave us well and truly immobilised.

The next day a friendly Syrian, staying in the 'no star' hotel in which we spent the rest of a very short night, gave directions to the industrial area and a blacksmith. Numerous bars of metal, varying in width and thickness, decorated the walls. As he got busy selecting and preparing the bars needed for our repair, another customer with an identical problem showed typical Middle Eastern curiosity in ourselves. His numerous questions concerning our nationality, occupations, destination and so forth, finally led to the subject of religion. I found it a pleasant if unusual experience to squat on a stool in the smithy's smoky atmosphere, sipping little cups of black coffee and, against the background of the furnace's roar and the clanging of hammer on steel, share with a Muslim the basics of the Christian faith. He proudly proclaimed his Muslim beliefs and hopes of paradise resulting from good works but, being completely ignorant of Christian doctrine, was prepared to listen and discuss without any rile or anger. He declared he had never seen a Bible, nor any portion of it, and happily accepted some items of Christian literature. I could only wonder if this was the second reason for the delay caused by the problem of the broken spring. Our long delay on the Lebanese side of the border had caused officials to be on duty much later than intended and the Syrian officer glad to get rid of us as quickly as possible. Now here in Homs was an unsought opportunity to speak of the Lord Jesus and His redemptive work to a man who, coming from a village 600 km away on the banks of the Euphrates, had never heard the substance of the Christian message. The delay and the expense of the broken spring had been a small price to pay for the opportunity of speaking to someone of the love of Christ.

The rest of the return journey to France could be described as a pleasant holiday trip - except for a Turkish Custom official mistaking my metal cased slide screen for an automatic gun; a broken fuel pipe near Antalya which, after Paul's DIY job lasted till we reached a garage; a defective starter which meant pushing the heavily loaded van whenever we wanted to start; and the complete failure of the fuel pipe miles from the nearest town. On 18th May, eleven days after leaving Beirut, we thankfully arrived in Carpentras. The whole journey covered 5,845 miles. It had been done at the average rate of 26.8 mph (a record for the slowness of travel?) at the total cost of £330. This included diesel fuel, oil, camp sites and hotels, repairs and motorway fees, but barely any food as supplies were taken from home. But the immediate need of Arabic literature for the work in France had been met and proved sufficient until bulk supplies could be shipped from Beirut. We deeply appreciated the sacrifice by Paul and Alan especially of precious holiday time. Their contribution in bringing the requisite literature from Beirut helped to give the Arabic ministry in France the impetus it needed. It is interesting to note that today Paul Hannay is a well travelled member of *Brass Tacks*.

CHAPTER 32

New Developments

(1978 - 81)

Show me Your ways, O Lord; teach me Your paths, lead me in Your truth and teach me (Psalm 25:4).

Gospel outreach in various markets now enabled us to contact many Arabs mainly from North Africa, though often from further afield. In groups of usually three or four, they wandered almost aimlessly around the stalls. For many the sight of literature in Arabic, some of it obviously referring to Allah, proved an irresistible draw. As they browsed or leafed through a booklet we could anticipate one of three reactions. The dawning knowledge that these books bore a Christian message could lead to a quick turning away accompanied by a muttered comment, maybe even a curse emphasised by a spit on the ground. The best we could do was to offer a tract which, if taken, could yet be read and in spite of initial antagonism, awaken an interest in the message of the Gospel. Or there might be a question, controversial in nature perhaps, but always providing an opening for discussion. This would usually lead to one of two conclusions: either an emphasis on the superiority of Islam and a disdainful heated rebuttal of all things Christian, or a preparedness to consider the claims of Jesus to be the Saviour of the world, with literature or even a New Testament bought. The third reaction would be a comment revealing someone already seeking for a deeper understanding of Jesus Christ and His redemptive work. The few who were really seeking soon showed this by their attitude and willingness for a calm discussion, followed by a desire to obtain a copy of the Christian Scriptures.

One morning in the town of Valence these situations followed in fairly swift succession. Compared to the regular traders we were late in arriving and this worked to our advantage. We were allocated a spot made vacant by the non-arrival of a regular. Being near the centre of the crowded, bustling market meant people passed by from every direction. The arrangement of our L shaped display had hardly begun before inquisitive hands were picking up and fingering through any item which caught the eye. The early interest subsided and then a small group of North Africans stopped to browse, gave unmistakable signs of disapproval, refused all offers of tracts, and sauntered away. Perhaps it was one of these who shortly after came back to give voice to his objections to the Christian faith. His loudly proclaimed opinions soon brought five or more men to the stall - the Bible has been corrupted, God could not have a son, Jesus was only a prophet and definitely never died. In his enthusiasm he spoke of Bible characters and events as if he had intimate knowledge of the Scriptures and, in reply to my question as to whether he had read them, gave a confident yes. By this time some twenty men had gathered and, as Sandy and Tim moved amongst them with booklets and tracts, their sullen rejection indicated we might have a problem on our hands. Any moment a question could be asked relative to the Koran or Muhammed, the answer to which could spark trouble. The time to close the discussion had obviously arrived. The question was how to do so? I believe that the Lord stepped in and took control. Waxing eloquent my interlocutor made certain false comments about one of the Old Testament characters who is also mentioned in the Koran, and firmly insisted he knew he was right. As his friends pressed closer to hear him reaffirm his case, I handed him a Bible and, courteously I hope, asked him to show me the passage to support what he said. In one way it was amusing to see his embarrassment as he thumbed through a few pages. He had possibly never held a Bible before and his agitated manner caused the assembled crowd to burst into laughter. A short and friendly chat ensued, whilst now, with their interest aroused, every man in the crowd readily received the tracts they had so recently refused.

Within a few minutes the men drifted away and after a while a solitary man edged out of the passing crowd. He wandered round the stall scrutinising titles, occasionally delving into the pages of a book until his obvious interest enabled one of us to open up a conversation. This led to a request for a copy of the Scriptures. Having selected and paid for his copy he requested it be wrapped. To our chagrin, we had to admit we had neither paper nor bag. Without more ado he replaced the Bible, took back his money, and disappeared. Ten minutes slipped by. We rebuked ourselves for the lost opportunity of supplying the Scriptures to one who obviously desired to read them. A zealous Muslim would not carry a Bible openly, especially with so many of his compatriots around. But suddenly our would be customer reappeared and once more asked for the Bible. This time he producing from his pocket a large newly purchased handkerchief in which he carefully wrapped his new, prized possession and without a further word went on his way.

We also became involved in the Bible Course ministry. When the Coombes went to South Wales for the birth of their second child, we took responsibility for this increasing outreach. Each day brought letters from various parts of the Arab world with requests for Courses, books, maybe an introduction to a Bible School, a hint that emigration to the USA would be appreciated, even requests for used stamps! Some letters indicated a genuine spiritual concern spiritually and, knowing an answer in fluent Arabic was best, such letters soon went to Swansea for Wadiah to deal with. By this time little Rhoda had come to grace their home, but Wadiah never grudged the time to make vital use of her native tongue. Occasionally letters arrived in French or English. One came from Ghana, written by a man who, judging by his use of the word Hadj, had been on the pilgrimage to Mecca. His initial greeting, 'My brethren in Islam' gave a wonderful opportunity to use the basic meaning of the word 'Islam'. We mentioned that according to the Bible, true surrender to God involved acceptance of the Lord Jesus as Saviour. He closed his letter with the comment that he 'hoped to hear good news from us soon', so we felt quite free to state we were presenting him with the best of news and trusted he would contact us again.

When Malcolm and Wadiah with their two children returned from Wales we came to England for matters related to Ruth's and Mark's education. Shortly before we left, John had located premises near the centre of Avignon suitable for a reading and counselling centre. It was a shop with a big display window and at least three rooms giving adequate accommodation, and close to an area popular with immigrants. When John phoned to tell us the contract had been signed, we felt that on our return this would be a work for us. At last, after more than two years of seeing the need for a Centre where Muslims could come for quiet study and conversation, the vision verged on realisation. The place needed a lot of repairs, alterations and decorating before it could be opened. John had already begun the work and anticipated it would be finished by the time of our return. This left just one segment of our vision to be fulfilled. For some time I had been convinced there were many believers in France and adjoining countries keen to reach Muslims with the Gospel, and a literature depot to supply their need of Arabic material would be invaluable. The missionary enterprise was expanding a step at a time and we prayerfully looked to the Lord to make the next phase possible. When there is a deep inner conviction that a particular step should be taken the hardest part is often having the patience to wait until the Lord makes it possible. Many of the Lord's servants will confess to having pressed forward impatiently with a plan which has faltered, or even failed, because it was not executed in His time. So we waited. At times we felt we were on the periphery of the work whilst our co-workers were immersed in theirs. Only much later did we realise that during the major part of 1980, just being there to listen, encourage and advise, had been a definite and vital part of our ministry for the Lord.

The vision of a depot to supply Arabic material to other workers in France and beyond had been more ours than our colleagues', understandably so with their respective spheres claiming so much of their time. But the problem remained of stimulating missionaries and national believers to take an interest in Muslims, and then turning that interest into practical outcomes. A solution came through our daughter Ruth being acquainted with believers in Vichy. From them she heard of an Evangelical Festival in the town of Nimes with various groups being offered space for displaying material relevant to their work. Display spaces were still available so she suggested that Al Manarah, the registered name for the

Bible Correspondence Course ministry, should apply for one, and we promptly took action.

The venue for the Festival was the ancient arena. All the display spaces were in the tunnels giving access to the seating accommodation. We were allocated a prime site adjacent to an entrance. A few days later Ruth Hanley was able to say, 'This must have been the most encouraging weekend you have had in France.' With believers coming from all over France it was a golden opportunity to introduce Arabic Scriptures and literature to many. The bookstand created much interest, expressed in comments such as, 'I have a burden for the Muslims but have had no idea where to get material in Arabic.' Many bought Scriptures and evangelical literature and quantities of tracts to pass on to Arab contacts. Hundreds of tracts and enrollment cards for the correspondence courses were handed out and certainly it made the name Al Manarah known more widely. It also confirmed the need for a literature depot.

At the Festival each of us had direct contact with Muslims. Coming into the ancient Roman arena merely out of curiosity they stopped to chat as soon as the Arabic books drew their attention. My first contact was a Muslim student from Baghdad and then each of us at different times met men from Tunis, Algeria and Morocco. My final contact, a nominal Christian from Lebanon, now truly converted, had a burden for the Muslims in his area of France. Interestingly, he first heard the Gospel from someone in the Arab assembly in Beirut. This encouraging weekend was supplemented by the arrival in Avignon of Robert and Janet Dann, with eleventh month old Becky, to add strength to the team.

But a cloud of uneasiness hung over Marjorie's health. She was unsettled, had little desire to go out, seemed depressed and clearly somewhat unhappy in France. I had an appointment at Mildmay Hospital in August and feeling Marjorie might be much happier in England, suggested she stayed there while I visited France from time to time. We prayed, but no clear direction came. It was then we learnt a further lesson about guidance. My reading had taken me to the verse 'the light shall shine upon thy ways' and I turned again to Job 22 to read the context. The words spoke to us as from the Lord Himself: *'You will make your prayer to Him'..... 'you will declare a thing and it will be established for you. So light will shine on your ways.'* (vv27-28). It seemed to us God was saying, 'You will make your prayer, it will be heard, wisdom will be given you to weigh up the circumstances. Make a decision and openly declare it. Then your way will be made plain.'

Shorly after this we received a completely unexpected letter. Miss Luff, owner of a Christian bookstore in Frinton, envisaged employing a new manager and wrote asking if we would be available to take over the post. We wondered if this was the light upon our way. In 1965 I had declared, 'It will be time to return to England when, without any asking or seeking on our part, a specific situation connected with a Christian ministry is offered to me', so this letter had to be considered seriously. First we assessed the effect our leaving would have on the Arabic work and we had to acknowledge that the Hanleys and the Coombes would not find their ministry hindered by our absence. In fact the Coombes, left to make their own decisions, would possibly widen theirs. There comes a time when senior workers need to move out of the way and let others develop their gifts. In any case new workers, the Danns, had just arrived and within a few weeks the Andersons would be back after their year of Arabic study in Tunis. The development of the literature depot appeared to be catered for already. Good supplies of material were available and listed; the accounts and any other paper work involved were all in order.

As to our personal circumstances, Marjorie was certainly not well, though we had no idea of the reason for this. The sign I had prayed for, years before, and resolutely held to ever since, had been given. These two facts indicated the time had come, reluctant though we both were to face it, to lay down the ministry overseas. We wrote to Miss Luff accepting her proposal and, believing firm decisions should be confirmed by making them known, notified our prayer partners, and the elders of our commending assembly in Nottingham. We believed the Lord would deal with our need of accommodation in England, and sure enough provision was at hand. The missionary home in Romford would be vacant when we arrived and could be ours for the next six months.

Back in the familiar home in Pettits Lane we began to plan for the days ahead. High on the agenda were my next visit to Mildmay

Hospital and a visit to Miss Luff. Her last letter contained a note of urgency so, within two days, we were on our way for an interview. The Christian bookstore occupied a prime site on one of the main streets and Miss Luff resided on the first floor of the premises. Though our reception was cordial, her manner appeared to be very hesitant due, I assumed, to her severe emphysema. Propped up on pillows, and at times finding speech difficult, it took her some little while to express her gratitude for our visit and to get down to its main purpose. We had hardly time to say how pleased we were to see her, and none to say we were looking forward to helping in the bookshop, before she dropped a bombshell. Since writing to us, her Committee had vetoed her decision to find a replacement manager. We appreciated this was an embarrassing situation for her, even as it was for us, especially as we had made it known fairly widely that our decision to leave France had its origin in a request to take over the bookshop in Frinton. We could only accept the situation and return to Romford feeling, at least momentarily, that the bottom had been knocked out of our world! Had we misunderstood the Lord's leading?

It has often been said that one can only be sure retrospectively of having been led. When the past is reviewed it is easy to say one is sure of having been led in certain circumstances. But it is possible, in faith, to say one is being led in a certain direction even though the result may be different from that anticipated. Every step of the path may be clear though the end is shrouded in mist. As we prayed over the unexpected turn of events, and reviewed the last few weeks, we still had the conviction that in a specific way the Lord had let us know when to return to England and we waited for events to confirm it. The first soon came. Neither of us had realised Marjorie was so near to a breakdown. In addition, being in England, we could provide a home when both Ruth and Mark ended their college years.

But how could we still be engaged in a spiritual ministry? We desired some form of service for the Lord which would somehow link with former years amongst Arabic speaking people, be they nominally Christian or Muslim. The significant increase of an Islamic influence in Britain spoke to us of a mission field on our doorstep. We knew of a number of agencies working amongst Muslims and if there existed a niche with one of them we would be happy to fill it. Tentative inquiries drew a blank and all we could do was to pray and wait patiently for the next steps to be made plain. In the meantime meetings and family visits plus entertaining visitors ensured the days did not drag. Then a visit in October to Mildmay Hospital confirmed there would be for me a few days of compulsory rest, then a prostate operation.

We were able to move from the Missionary home to our own near Colchester in Essex, but the problem remained of how we could be involved in reaching Muslims with the message of the Gospel of Christ. We had long been aware of the increasing Islamic influence in various parts of the country but had not realised its extent. Now as preaching engagements took us to many areas of the United Kingdom, the proliferation of Mosques, Hindu and Sikh temples confirmed that Britain had indeed become similar to a foreign mission field. The challenge to reach ethnic groups with the Gospel was evident; but how to do so was not. Only after visiting a number of assemblies, and discovering that many believers were unaware of the background of Islam and its teachings, did the way ahead become clear.

This lack of knowledge had what may be termed a knock-on effect. Being unaware of the Muslims' attitude towards the Bible and their false impressions concerning the person of Jesus Christ, many who made attempts at witnessing to them often received, much to their surprise, an antagonistic response. In addition, most of the evangelistic booklets and tracts they distributed were not relevant to those whose roots were deep in an alien culture and religion. We believed our ministry could address this situation. When speaking at meetings time could be spent in considering Islamic beliefs and practices, accompanied by offers of literature suitable for Muslim contacts. A literature depot providing Scriptures, books and tracts, mainly in Arabic, could be developed. Local churches could be encouraged to form prayer groups focusing on Islamic issues. The result of this was the establishment, in fellowship with Norman Murrary and Colin Williamson, of the Manarah Trust. We soon discovered that in some areas there was a keen interest in the Islamic question and, at almost every meeting, literature for distribution received a warm welcome. It was fascinating to hear of the contacts people made. Often these were in their professional practices, offices, schools, factories, or amongst neighbours, or when tracting from house to house. On the other hand it was at times disheartening to be faced with apathy and an attitude of indifference.

During the first few years of the Manarah Trust many meetings were addressed, hundreds of pieces of evangelical literature and Scripture portions distributed. We trusted our efforts would result in increased prayer for the spiritual needs both of Muslims and other religious minorities. I also realised that the majority of Muslims in Britain were from Pakistan, India, Iran, or Turkey, or were second generation Britishers for whom Arabic, other than that memorised for Koranic purposes, was a foreign language. This meant our range of literature was too circumscribed until a supply of Urdu from Lahore helped to address the balance. At the time we had no idea how the work would develop and could only trust that the Lord would raise up others to continue it if and when we had to lay it down. We need not have feared about having time on our hands in Britain!

Our colleagues in France meantime faced a new situation. Malcolm had received notice to vacate the accommodation used for the Bible Correspondence Courses, and was having a problem locating suitable alternative premises. His difficulty was compounded by the need to find space for both the Emmaus Courses and the literature depot which he and Robert Dann were now running. This became the focal point of many prayers. When the answer came it was far beyond the asking. The assembly in Orange had gradually outgrown its premises and, aware of their proposed move to a new venue, Malcolm offered to rent those. They were ideal both as regards size and location. Consisting of two large rooms, one of which had a display window facing the street, they provided ample space for the office, the stock and also room to relax. It was almost immediately behind the main Post Office, so it could not have been better placed for one who made frequent use of the postal services. The needed premises were now available, just in time to meet the increasing demand partially arising from the contacts made at the Festival at Nimes.

Ruth's school and college days ended in 1981, having obtained her BEd degree. Before her finals she had secured a year's teaching post in France and our next journey in that direction involved taking her and her belongings to St. Dizier. A year later another visit to France found Malcolm and Wadiah as busy as ever. Sandy and Elspeth Anderson were participating in the preparation of new material for Muslim outreach in French. But the Danns had moved on to Morocco and the Hanleys were also away, so I missed them on what proved to be the end of our direct involvement in the Arab work in the Middle East and France.

Danns, Hanleys, Howells, Coombes in France

CHAPTER 33

The Years Roll By

(1982 - 2000)

Jesus Christ is the same yesterday, today and for ever
(Hebrews 13:8).

1982 marked the end of an era. Almost forty years had rolled by since the call, 'How shall they hear?' had challenged us to surrender our lives to the Lord for His service in a foreign land. With the call came the conviction that such a surrender involved absolute trust in God for provision for each day, guidance for every step of the way, and protection in every hour of need. Then followed the further challenge of 'launch out into the deep' and we committed our future into the hands of Him who has promised 'I will never leave you nor forsake you.' Many like ourselves called to full time service are guided to work independent of any earthly control, completely dependent upon their heavenly Master in every respect. These memoirs were written out of a desire to bear witness to the faithfulness of the One who, centuries ago, said to His servant Moses, 'Behold I send an Angel before you to keep you in the way and bring you into the place which I have prepared.' If this record has proved that the living God is true to His promises, its writing will have been worth while.

A new era had now commenced. We were no longer missionaries on furlough with reports to give of activities in other lands, nor were we fully engaged in the Lord's service at home. Honesty causes me to confess that being very conscious of our new status as 'retired', I did wonder how our needs would be met. I had to remind myself of the confident statement made years before, when well meaning friends queried what provision we were making for old age: 'God does not die when we are sixty five!' At that time we were not being irresponsible or foolhardy concerning the future. The support we received came from freewill offerings, very often sacrificially given, and we thought it would be wrong to lay by for the future from such gifts intended for immediate use. Now as we actually faced the situation, our faith had its tests, just as much as it did many years before. The Christian, in every stage of the pilgrim way, truly lives by faith not by sight, and now after many more years we continue to rejoice in the faithfulness of our God.

During these many more years, guidance has come from circumstances rather than any direct word through the Scriptures. In the words of Job 22, we 'made our prayer to God' believing He would hear and, when certain decisions were made, 'the light shone on our way'. Those circumstances caused us first to move to Nottingham and then to Beeston Regis, a suburb of Sheringham, in Norfolk where we felt our roots were beginning to take hold.

But these years had other highlights, both in connection with the Manarah Trust and ourselves. With regard to the Trust, it was obvious this would cease to be effective unless arrangements were made for others to assume responsibility for its continuance. In answer to prayer, brethren in South Wales who also had close links with the Coombes, agreed to replace the original trustees and take over the running of the work. It was a relief to transfer everything into the hands of younger people and know they would do their utmost to ensure the aims of the Trust would be fulfilled, effective in reaching many from an Islamic background with the truths of the Gospel. It has been encouraging to hear some details of the outreach, and to know that not only Arabic speaking people but others from different ethnic backgrounds, are being reached with the good news of Jesus Christ.

Many of our American friends had invited us to visit them but we never thought this would be possible. However with Andrew, Ruth and family in Chicago the urge to make such a visit increased, and when they proposed turning the desire into reality we had no hesitation in acquiescing. Added to the pleasure of being with the family were the trips to visit long standing friends from the Middle East. The Lennoxes lived within an easy car ride from Andrew and Ruth, and a longer journey took us to become the guests of Costandi, Abu Ibrahim's youngest son, to see how the Lord had abundantly blessed one who, in his younger days in the midst of much poverty, had yielded his life to the Lordship of Christ. Another few hundred miles saw us in New York State being greeted by Samuel Shahid who, with his wife Ellen, gave us a renewed taste of Middle Eastern hospitality. It was a thrill to see one whose future had seemed to be very insecure, now successful and well accredited and using his gifts for the furtherance of the kingdom of God. Just knowing that by the grace of God we had been links in the chain which brought these to faith in Christ Jesus made the years spent in Irbid well worth while. Another special visit took us north to Canada to meet a couple in Toronto who took a keen interest in John and Ruth Hanley and, by extension, in ourselves and the

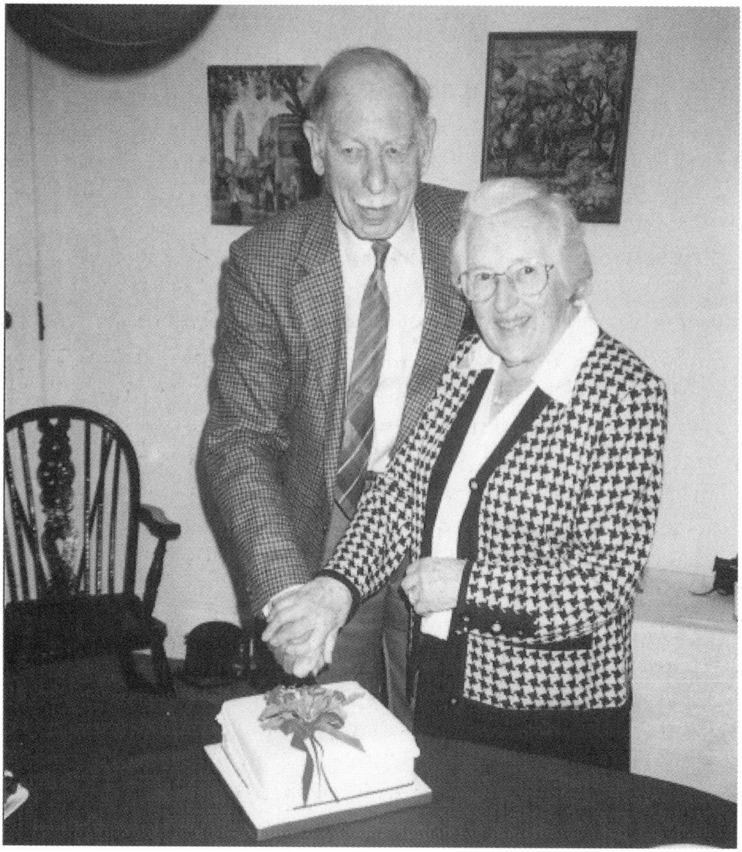

Coombes. Our arrival coincided with an annual missionary conference where, much to our surprise, we discovered the guest speakers included one of the Editors of *Echoes of Service*.

In 1990 we reached one of life's very special milestones, our Golden Wedding. With the family scattered there was little incentive to make it a time of celebration but there were enough greetings and tokens of affection to ensure we remembered the date. For the next four years we were kept well occupied, socially and spiritually, whilst a reasonably sized garden provided opportunities for our landscaping skills, such as they were, and ensured a fair amount of exercise. But, almost inevitably, the creeping effects of advancing years began to make the garden a burden rather than a pleasure. We also realised our distance from town and all its facilities made us very vulnerable if we could no longer use the car and wisdom dictated a move nearer to shops, post office and surgery. We did not find it an easy decision to make but, feeling driven to do so, made arrangement for the property to be valued prior to being placed on the market. A Monday morning had been fixed for the Estate Agent's visit. On Sunday an unexpected and unwelcome event confirmed it to be time to make a move.

Apart from periods of tiredness I had not been feeling particularly unwell. But when taking my morning bath I discovered certain movements lacked co-ordination. By the time I had dragged myself out of the bath, weaved my way to the kitchen, made the tea, discovered my left leg would not take my full weight, and the teacups rattled on the tray, I realised I was in trouble! Marjorie spared no time in getting me back to bed and seeking medical aid. When the doctor arrived it took but a brief examination to confirm our own diagnosis, a stroke. It appeared mild but the doctor warned the next forty eight hours could be critical and complete rest would be essential.

My initial reaction bordered on despair. There was so much I wanted to do, so many things left undone. During the previous months I had a fairly heavy schedule of meetings but now I wondered if I would ever be able to preach again. Then came the grim thought of possibly being immobile, of no longer being able to drive and, more importantly, of being a constant burden on Marjorie. Suddenly life seemed to have lost its joy, the future appeared desperately dark and, without realising it, I was nearly wallowing in self pity. But my Heavenly Father knew all about my feelings and in His own way catered for them. Propped up in bed I reached for my Bible but my temporarily useless left hand failed to grasp it. As I dragged it with my right it flopped open before me. There, Paul's inspired words to the Philippians almost seemed to stand out on the page, to bring the comfort, consolation and assurance I needed: 'Be anxious for nothing, but in everything by prayer and supplication, with thanksgiving, let your requests be made known to God; and the peace of God, which surpasses all understanding, will guard your hearts and minds through Christ Jesus.' It was light in the darkness and balm to my spirits, and an uplift for Marjorie as well. In His goodness God met our needs and, by His grace, over a period of time, I made a good measure of recovery.

There was now no doubt about having to move nearer town. But sixteen uncertain months passed before the sale went through, and we found a first floor, two bedroom flat in excellent condition, so much so it could be occupied immediately. We moved to Kerridge Court, Holt in December 1996, a complex of flats situated near the centre of the town. Shops, post office and surgery were now a mere five minutes' walk away, with the pleasure of a country park within a short car ride. We could not help but feel that the Lord had once more guided us to the place of His appointing.

We also are blessed with Christian fellowship and opportunities for Christian service. The assembly in Sheringham continues to be our spiritual home whilst my preaching engagements, though fewer than formerly, bring us in touch with other small assemblies, mainly in the Norfolk area. Our friends in Clumber Hall, Nottingham, still remember us and keep us informed of their activities, enabling us to feel we are still part of that assembly where we met, were baptized and married, and from which we were commended to the work which has occupied our lives.

The unknown road has had many a twist and turn, its hills and its valleys, but along it all there has been the guiding and sustaining hand of our Lord ever leading on to that which is surely known. His promise to those who trust and love Him is, 'Where I am there you shall be always', and so the end of the road will one day bring the joy of dwelling in the glory of His eternal presence. He, the Lord our God, has surely guided us every step of the way and with the Psalmist we can say,

'I will sing unto the Lord because He has dealt bountifully with me.'

As for God,
His way is perfect;
The word of the Lord is proven;
He is a shield
to all who trust in Him.

(Psalm 18:30)

The eternal God is your refuge,
and underneath are
the everlasting arms.

(Deuteronomy 33:27)

Surely goodness and mercy
shall follow me
all the days of my life,
and I will dwell in the
house of the Lord
forever.

(Psalm 23:6)

Appendix

Searching for Peace in the Middle East

Preamble

as from

Fifty years ago the comment was made that living in Palestine was like living on top of a volcano. Small eruptions constantly occurred and always rumblings of trouble. The main question was, 'When would the full force erupt?' Since then the State of Israel has been formed, and the world has become used to reading of acts of terrorism, brief but violent wars, massacres both of Jews and Muslims, civil unrest especially in Lebanon, and a horrendous refugee problem. The world's attention has been focussed on the war torn areas of the Middle East with its desperate need for peace. Many have wondered why it is so elusive whilst others have queried whether it can ever be achieved.

In dealing with this subject my aim is twofold: (1) to give the background to the unsettled conditions existing when the above comment was made, and (2) to bring together some of the facts of a very complex situation and in so doing highlight the problems facing would be peacemakers. It is not my intention to be critical of either side but to show, in conclusion, there is, at least for some, a way to peace.

1. **The Seed of the Problem**

The origins of the hostility between Arab and Jew have become obscured with time and many people today are asking the question, 'Why this seemingly endless conflict? Wherein is its origin, and what is the seed of the problem? Why do both Arab and Jew consider Palestine to be their homeland?'

The Jews have three main reasons, two of which are based on the Old Testament and the third on a fact of history.

(a) They firmly believe the land was promised to their forefather Abraham and his descendants through Isaac and Jacob. For them the promises in Genesis to these three patriarchs are clear. For example we read, The Lord appeared to Abraham and said, 'To your descendants I will give this land' (12:7); a promise reiterated later in13:15 and 15:18. In 26:1-3 the promise is to Isaac: The Lord appeared to him and said, 'Dwell in this land and I will be with you, and bless you, for to you and your descendants I give all these lands and I will perform the oath which I swore to Abraham your father.' Furthermore in 35:9-12: God appeared to Jacob ... and said to him.....'The land which I gave Abraham and Isaac I give to you, and to your descendants after you I give this land.' Also compare 28:13-14.

(b) There are the prophecies of return from exile, even from the four corners of the earth as recorded in such Scriptures as Isaiah 11:11-12; Ezekiel 36:21-22; Zechariah 8:7-8. To those Old Testament prophecies the Jews link the historical fact that they did return from captivity, and believe that in spite of a subsequent dispersion the promises to possess the land still obtain.

(c) The Jews have never had a national home other than in Palestine; they believe their roots are there. Since the dispersion in AD 70 they have been a minority, and often persecuted, group in the confines of other countries.

The above three factors are fostered by a constant hope. Every year at one of their religious feasts there is the repetition of the anticipatory words, 'Next year in Jerusalem.'

The Arabs also have every right to claim Abraham as their forefather and believe they have their promise through Ishmael though this is certainly not that which was reiterated to Isaac and Jacob. Their main claim to Palestine is founded on the basis of their occupation through many centuries. Furthermore by reason of its majority religion (Islam), and its culture, habits and language, they believe it to be logical that the area be linked both governmentally and economically with its Arab neighbours. Thus the problem - two peoples claiming the same small area of land which is, moreover, of vital interest to a third group, the Christians, who feel that because the roots of their faith lie there they too have a right to be interested in its future.

2. Development of the Problem

To understand how the problem developed, the attitude of the world to the Jews throughout the centuries needs to be noted. More often than not they were despised, humiliated, and frequently fiercely persecuted with so called Christian Europe, both East and West, being at times guilty. No wonder they longed for a home of their own and looked for a fulfillment of ancient prophecies. In 1881 there was a Jewish awakening and a realisation that such a home in Palestine would never materialise without active efforts on their part. In Russia, where Jews had been especially ill-treated, a group known as the 'Lovers of Zion' developed, who longed for liberation from their persecutors. Due to the severity of the pogroms, 500 young people, living in the Kharkov area and who were part of this group, issued a manifesto calling on Jews to set their hearts on a home in their ancient land. At that time Palestine was a small segment in the Ottoman Empire and the aim of the Kharkov group was to stir the Jews to plead with the Turkish authorities for the founding of a Jewish state in what they considered to be their own home land.

In 1896 Theodore Herzl, the founder of modern political Zionism, wrote a pamphlet declaring there could be no peace or safety for the Jews without the formation of a Jewish State. This became a rallying call and a year later the first Zionist Congress, held in Basle, voiced their demands for a national home in Palestine, preferably by land purchase not conflict.

About the same time the Arabs were growing restless under the Turkish yoke and feeling their way towards independence from the Ottoman Empire. They were also increasingly aware of Jewish hopes and aspirations and realised they would have to make their own claims known. In 1905 a Christian Arab (N. Azouri) living in Paris stated in the journal *Arab Independence*, "It is in the interests of Islam and the Arab nations to form an empire from the Tigris and the Euphrates to the Suez Isthmus and from the Mediterranean to the Arabian Sea." This provided an impetus to Arab aspirations and from then on Arab and Jew were obviously on a collision course.

The problem was further compounded by the fact that Turkey had no desire to give up any part of her Empire, and Germany, hoping to obtain domination over the land bridge from Turkey to Egypt, was willing to help her keep it. On the other hand, Britain and France had strong interests in the Middle East and were determined to guard them, whilst Russia also had her eyes on the area. Hence conflict loomed between the major powers and neither Arab nor Jew could realistically expect to obtain an independent state without help from one or the other. As a matter of fact as early as 1916 Britain and France (through the Sykes-Picot Agreement) were already carving up the Middle East between them.

3. **The Problem Crystallizes**

The confrontation between Arab and Jew took more definite shape in the first two decades of the twentieth century. By the time of the outbreak of World War I in 1914, there had been a certain amount of Jewish colonisation in Palestine, mainly due to land purchase, but the problem was to some degree still a war of words and ideals. That situation was to change in 1916. In her endeavours to protect the Suez Canal and Egypt and keep a foothold in the Middle East, Britain desperately needed the help of the Arabs. With the aid of Colonel Lawrence, and the persuasion of gold, she encouraged the Arabs of the Peninsula to revolt against Turkey. The prize was to be an Arab empire centred on Damascus under the control of the Hashemites who at that time were the predominant tribe in Arabia based at Mecca. The Arabs (and Lawrence) understood this empire was to include all the Arab countries of the Middle East which, for them, meant Palestine and Lebanon. This was in spite of the fact that Sir Henry MacMahon had written in 1915 to the Sheriff of Mecca mentioning that certain areas West of Damascus would be outside the limits demanded by the Arabs.

But Britain needed the help of the Jews as well as the Arabs. Jewish scientists had been a great help to Britain in developing explosives at a crucial time in the war, and naturally the Jews expected a reward. This was given in the form of a letter to Lord Rothschild in November 1917 stating, "His Majesty's Government view with favour the establishment in Palestine of a national home for the Jewish people... it being clearly understood that nothing shall be done which may prejudice the civil and religious rights of existing non-Jewish communities in Palestine." Thus the British, and to some degree her allies, through two irreconcilable and ambiguous promises, set the scene for inevitable conflict. Common sense should have indicated the impossibility of creating a national home in an already populated area without affecting the existing rights of the present inhabitants.

The problem having been created it fell to the League of Nations to find a way to solve it. This was attempted by placing the whole area under the control of Mandatories with Britain and France taking control of adjacent areas, Britain's responsibility being Iraq, Palestine and Transjordan.

4. **Seeking to Cope with the Problem**

In April 1920, Britain, with the authority of the League of Nations, undertook the Mandates, with Palestine becoming the immediate focal point for trouble. Then for the next 27 years she struggled to satisfy the aspirations of both Zionists and Arabs with barely a glimmer of hope that there would be success. The Arabs continued to demand an independent state and in 1929 and 1936 they fomented violent rebellions against the Government as they noted the increase in the Jewish population. This had increased from 10% in 1919 to 40% in 1937, and increased each year with 12,000 to 15,000 immigrants. In the same year, a Royal Commission (Peel Commission) acknowledged that Arab and Jewish interests could not be reconciled under the Mandate and the first suggestions were made for the partitioning of the land. Britain rejected the idea as being contrary to the terms of the Mandate and sought to pacify the Arabs by suggesting the restriction of immigrants. Needless to say this raised the ire of the Jews. By the time the second world war broke out they were demanding almost unlimited immigration. World War II raised the hopes of the Arabs and this was fostered by Hitler promising the Grand Mufti of Jerusalem Germany's help to liquidate Jewish hopes once he had won the war. Having that promise and believing in the invincibility of the Germans the Arabs were prepared to wait whilst the Jews realised their best hopes lay in an Allied victory. The problem seemed to be quiescent during the war but in 1946 it erupted again. The plight of the Jews in Europe turned their thoughts to Palestine and the Zionists clamoured again for unrestricted immigration. Thousands entered legally but many more illegally, aided by Zionist funds. These flowed freely, mainly from the United States where, it seems, little effort was made to assist Britain in her endeavours to maintain an equitable situation for both the contenders. Jewish terrorist groups also emerged and these, plus the retaliatory activities of the Arabs, made settled government almost impossible.

Faced with this insoluble situation Britain resigned the Mandate and responsibility for the well-being of Palestine passed in 1947 to the United Nations.

5. **Trying to Solve to the Problem**

Proposals for the future of Palestine included outright partition, a bi-national country or a Federal State. In November 1947 the United Nations voted by a majority of 33 to 13 in favour of the partition plan. The two thirds majority included the United States and Russia but not Britain. In due course, without reference to either the Arab or Jewish inhabitants, boundaries were drawn for both Arab and Jewish states whilst there was to be a special International Regime for the City of Jerusalem. The Jewish Agency accepted the partition plan as the 'indispensable minimum', no doubt on the principle that half a cake is better than none and you might get the whole later. The Arab Governments rejected the plan outright no doubt believing, as they were the majority in Palestine, they already had the whole cake and meant to keep it.

Those of us who lived in Jerusalem knew the plan would not be resolved without conflict. There was already Jewish terrorism and an Arab response. Britain, desperately trying to fulfill her responsibilities was caught in the middle and suffered most from the terrorists. By early 1947 Jerusalem began dividing of its own accord into two separate areas and each day saw a widening no-man's land across the city. It was obvious that as soon as the restraining hand of the British forces was removed the antagonists would be at each other's throats. In fact both sides seemed to be doing their utmost to get the British out so the war could proceed.

Early in 1948 Arab Governments were preparing to come to the aid of their Palestinian colleagues. In Palestine Jewish settlers were prepared for war and thousands waited outside the country to join them. On 14th May Britain finally withdrew all her troops and relinquished the Mandate. On the same date the Jews proclaimed the new State of Israel. Within hours the first Arab-Jewish war had begun, resulting in the new State of Israel occupying almost all the land apportioned to her under the partition plan. Forty six traumatic years have slipped by since then, during which there have been four major Israeli-Arab wars (1948, 1956, 1967, 1973); innumerable terrorist attacks, assassinations, a period of destabilization in Jordan and the virtual destruction of the former Christian state of Lebanon.

6. **The Problem Remains**

Peace is as elusive as ever in spite of all the diplomatic efforts and military campaigns leading to destruction and death. Why? It is not for want of trying. In 1948 the UN Mediator seeking a concrete plan for peace was assassinated. Shortly afterwards the Prime Minister of Lebanon on his way to Amman with peace proposals was likewise killed. Three years later the moderate and pragmatic King Abdullah of Jordan, who was reported to be in touch with the Jews, was shot down as he left a Mosque. Thus the message was plain: seek peace and be killed.

The Arabs went to war to regain lost territory and lost more, and each conflict resulted in a further flow of refugees, mainly Muslim, into Jordan and Lebanon. The United Nations provided relief for refugees but no hope for the future; and bitterness, resentment and hatred festered and grew amongst the thousands of displaced persons. The situation worsened to the extent of threatening hostilities between America and Russia as each armed and rearmed the opposing sides. It was the seriousness of this escalation of the conflict which seems to have at last driven the United Nations, under the insistence of Dr. Kissinger and with the consent of Russia, to arrange a peace conference in Geneva though Syria would not attend. To many it seemed that at long last a serious search for peace was being made. In spite of increasing tension in 1974 on the Syrian front, progress was made as under Anwar Sadat, Egypt agreed a peace treaty. Once again the peacemaker lost his life and hopes of peace were dashed as, with Muslim power in Lebanon increasing, militant elements presented a serious threat from the north which developed into further bloodshed.

But the search for peace has gone on, so much so that within recent months it seemed as if it lay within the grasp of the opposing factions. At long last a major obstacle was removed, the PLO and

Israel agreed to acknowledge each other, agreed to talk together, agreed to make a true endeavour to solve every outstanding problem and the world looked on with a sense of relief. Once again that relief was to be short lived. A zealot of Israel massacres Muslims, a Muslim backlash creates riots and, possibly, takes vengeance on Christians in Lebanon. In the light of all this it may well be asked, 'Is peace possible?'

7. **The Problem as it Stands Today**

Apart from the obvious intransigence of both sides, from the Jewish point of view they have an inalienable right to the whole of Palestine. The problems facing the Israeli Government are manifold:

· If they agree to a bi-national state they lose their sovereignty.

· To be within the confines of the borders allotted by the U.N. runs counter to all claims and hopes.

· To give up occupied lands means insufficient room for new immigrants.

· They have defied United Nations resolutions and allowed settlers to establish themselves on the West Bank.

· Those same settlers now refuse to obey the Government.

· To acknowledge the rights of the Palestinians is an economic nightmare as it means settling claims for expropriated lands.

· On the religious plane it means no hope of the re-occupying of the Temple area.

· Finally they know of no trustworthy representative of the Palestinians with whom they can negotiate.

In spite of the elections of January 1996, and the brave attempts to bring about a peaceful settlement, many Arabs still cannot trust Arafat fully and zealots on both sides are still prepared to foment trouble. On the Arab side the problems have also been compounded:

(a) On the religious level:

· Islam's pride has been wounded. They were assured by the Grand Mufti of Palestine that Allah was on their side and victory was assured. Furthermore, as Allah's chosen people they cannot accept defeat nor live contentedly as a minority group. Hence the rise of Islamic fundamentalism seeking to bring the faithful back to Allah's precepts that He might give them victory. (Hence, incidentally, the desire for the Islamisation of Lebanon: Allah will bless and reward His people for bringing the idolatrous Christians under subjection.)

· Jerusalem is the third most holy city for the Muslims and the Temple area its most prized possession which they can never tolerate coming into Jewish hands.

(b) On the social and economic level:

· Some 3 million people are claiming Palestinian status and seeking a home in that land.

· Thousands have been born and bred in refugee camps and from birth indoctrinated with hate of Israel. That hate cannot be negotiated away.

· Local agreements, e.g; such as made by Sadat and more recently Mubarak and Arafat are ruined by uncontrolled terrorists.

· Even as Palestinians have claims for compensation for land expropriated, the Jews have similar claims against Arab countries from which they were expelled.

· Finally, they claim to have also an inalienable right to Palestine.

Under these circumstances what hope is there of peace?

Humanly speaking, none! Only a miracle can achieve the seemingly impossible. That may seem hopelessly pessimistic but, as far as Christians who believe the Bible are concerned, there will be peace one day. In fact there are indications that many Muslims believe that the Bible in some way has an answer. It has been interesting to note that after every major set back, the Bible Society in Jordan and Lebanon has reported exceptional sales of the Bible in Arabic. Only recently in a predominantly Muslim town in North Jordan something like 3,000 copies of the New Testament were distributed in three months.

If the prophecies in the Bible are to be believed the day will come when the problem will finally be solved.

8. Problem finally Solved

The changing of swords into plowshares and spears into pruning hooks will take place, and the time when nation shall not lift up sword against nation will, in God's overruling, and in God's way, come. Isaiah 2:2-4 states: ✓

'Now it shall come to pass in the latter days that the mountain of the Lord's house shall be established on top of the mountains, and shall be exalted above the hills; and all nations shall flow to it.

Many people shall come and say, "Come, and let us go up to the mountain of the Lord, to the house of the God of Jacob: He will teach us His ways, and we shall walk in His paths." For out of Zion shall go forth the law, and the words of the Lord from Jerusalem. He shall judge between the nations, and rebuke many people; They shall beat their swords into plowshares, and their spears into pruning hooks; nation shall not lift up sword against nation, neither shall they learn war anymore.

This is repeated in Micah 4:1-3. Note also Luke 21:24 - a time will come when Jerusalem is not trodden down by the Gentiles. There will be a time when the Prince of Peace will truly reign (Isaiah 9:6-7).

But it is not only the nations who search for peace in the Middle East. Individuals are doing so all the time and finding the way whereby the gulf between Jew and Arab can be bridged. Christian Arabs, who have been dispossessed of home and land, pray sincerely for God to reveal to the Jews that their true peace lies in the recognition of Jesus as their Messiah. In the city of Jerusalem and elsewhere, groups of Jews and Arabs who have recognised Jesus as their Saviour and Lord, meet together for fellowship. The book *Blood Brothers* reveals in a poignant way one Arab's attempt to bridge the gap on the basis of the Sermon on the Mount. In these ways individuals are accomplishing what the United Nations and all the politicians are failing to do, uniting Jew and Arab in true brotherhood.

An outstanding example of this individual approach to peace is seen in the life of a Christian Arab from Nazareth. In his early teens the family were dispossessed of their property and fled to North Jordan. One of his uncles and also his father were killed, and he lived from day to day with hate burning in his heart and with the one desire to kill as many Jews as possible. In his late teens this hate filled young man came under deep spiritual conviction that his life was all wrong and there was a need to be reconciled to God. After days of spiritual struggle he finally trusted the Lord Jesus as his Saviour from sin's guilt and power with the result his life was radically changed. Some years later, and by now a full time Christian minister, he felt that all hate had gone and he now truly loved the Jews. The acid test came when leading a tour party in Israel he travelled by bus to Nazareth. Accompanying him was an Israeli guide who, as the bus drew near the town, casually mentioned that he had been the leader of the tank force which stormed into the place some years before killing many inhabitants. Like a flash the Christian remembered hiding behind a wall as the tanks came in, and again, in his mind, relived the moment when he saw his uncle shot down. The old burning hatred seemed to flame in his heart and for a few moments he sat and prayed, then, quietly turning to his companion told him of what had been his intention so many years before. The guide blanched and his face filled with fear until the Christian calmly said, 'But now I love you for Jesus' sake,' then went on to speak of what Jesus Christ meant to him. From then on, all hate truly disappeared and his great joy now when in Israel is to visit hospitals and spend time with wounded Israeli soldiers speaking to them of the Saviour who means so much to him. Blessed indeed are the peacemakers for they shall be called the sons of God (Matthew 5:9).

(Note: A detailed account of the Palestinian situation from 1882 to 1983 is contained in the *Israel - Arab Reader*, subitled 'A documentary history of the Middle East conflict' edited by Walter Laqueur & Barry Rubin, published by Pelican Books.)